Study Guide for

C Programming
A Modern Approach

Study Guide for

C Programming
A MODERN APPROACH

Manuel E. Bermudez

University of Florida

W. W. Norton & Company

New York   London

Copyright © 1998 by W. W. Norton & Company, Inc.

ISBN 0-393-96946-0 (pbk.)

W. W. Norton & Company, Inc., 500 Fifth Avenue, New York, N.Y. 10110
http://www.wwnorton.com

W. W. Norton & Company Ltd., 10 Coptic Street, London WC1A 1PU

1 2 3 4 5 6 7 8 9 0

CONTENTS

Preface

Dear Reader: Welcome! I hope this Study Guide will provide you with a wealth of opportunities to hone your programming skills in the C language. We will follow each chapter of K. N. King's book and supplement the material with a chapter summary, worked-out exercises, and plenty of programming projects for you to work on and enjoy. Programming in C is challenging, but fun!

How to Use This Study Guide

After reading a given chapter in the main text, you should first tackle some of the exercises at the end of that chapter, especially the straightforward ones.

Then read through the first two sections of the corresponding chapter in this Study Guide. They contain a chapter summary and some worked-out programming exercises that show you more on how it's done. All programs in the Solved Exercises sections appear in my World Wide Web Site: http://www.cise.ufl.edu/~manuel/. Or you may request them by e-mail from manuel@cise.ufl.edu. I suggest you compile and run each program, and experiment with them, making changes to see what happens.

By then, if you're taking a course, you'll be impatient to get your feet wet with the programming assignment your instructor has probably given you. Perhaps it's one of those in this Study Guide. The programming exercises generally consist of writing entire programs, or modifying earlier ones to add new features. Most programs should normally take between one and three hours to complete.

I assume you have some prior experience in programming in another language such as BASIC, Pascal, Fortran, or COBOL. If so, it shouldn't surprise you to learn that even professional computer programmers experience a large variation in their productivity. So don't be surprised if you spend much more time than you expected on some aspects of C programming and less on others. In particular, tracking down errors in C can be time-consuming and downright frustrating (defined as having no one to blame except yourself!). In C, it's easy to make subtle and difficult-to-catch errors, more so than in many other languages, including those mentioned above. To avoid as much of this as possible, please pay special attention to the warnings marked in the main text like this: ⚠. You'll be glad you did.

Enjoy learning C!

Acknowledgments

First of all, thanks to Kim King for writing such a great book. I wrote part of this Study Guide while on sabbatical leave from the University of Florida, and holding a Fulbright Scholar position at the University of Costa Rica. For that I am grateful to the J. William Fulbright Board, the Council for the International Exchange of Scholars in Washington D.C., and the University of Florida. While in Costa Rica, Manuel Cerdas and Humberto Hernández contributed many ideas that helped shape this Study Guide. Finally, there are always those special people that keep it all in perspective: my wife Ligia, and my partner and mentor Adrian Lewis.

M.E.B.
November 1997

1   Introducing C

1.1   Chapter Summary

Historically, the C language finds much of its ancestry in ALGOL 60. It was designed primarily for systems programming applications, especially for writing operating systems such as UNIX. Many people consider C to be both a high-level and a low-level language. It provides constructs for traditional high-level programming, such as iteration statements and subprograms. It also provides access to machine-level details through constructs such as bitwise operators.

Today, C is a mature language, with both ANSI and ISO standards having been established a few years ago. It is in widespread use, both in academia and in industry. Prior to the establishment of the standards, there was a *de facto* standard (now known as "Classic C") established in the book *The C Programming Language* by Brian Kernighan and Dennis Ritchie.

The main advantages of the C language are efficiency, portability, power, flexibility, the standard library, and its compatibility with UNIX. C does have drawbacks. Its main disadvantages are that C programs can be error-prone, difficult to understand, and difficult to modify.

So, you may ask, if C has so many problems, why is it so popular? The popular acceptance or rejection of a programming language is a complex issue. It involves not only the merits of the language, but also what happens to be fashionable at the moment in the programming community. One thing is clear: if you steer away from C's shortcomings and can learn to write robust, understandable, and maintainable C programs, you will benefit greatly from the advantages that C does have.

Here again, then, are the tips mentioned in Chapter 1 on how to use C effectively.

1. Avoid C's pitfalls, and don't rely on the compiler to detect problems in your code.
2. Use tools to improve your programs, especially `lint`.
3. Use existing code libraries, and whenever possible use the standard libraries. Many libraries are available commercially or in the public domain. Don't reinvent the wheel!
4. Adopt a set of coding conventions and stick to it.
5. Avoid "tricks" and code that is overly complex. Cute or clever solutions don't pay off in C. If it's efficiency you're after, C has plenty already. There's no need to resort to trickery to get things done efficiently.
6. Use Standard C. Use Standard C. Use Standard C. We can't say it enough.
7. Avoid nonportable features. Stick to the C Standard. Sometimes your C system will provide a convenient but nonstandard feature that will be very tempting to use. Resist the temptation and use that feature only if you must.

Finally, there's the question of C++. C++ is (almost) a superset of C, supporting object-oriented programming. I believe everyone should learn C before learning C++. In this Study Guide, as in the main text, I will encourage you to learn and practice good programming habits, which will pave the way for your future study of C++.

1.2   C and Other Languages

Well, we haven't really begun discussing the C language, have we? Rather than merely showing you some C programs, I thought it might be useful to perform a side-by-side comparison between C and some other languages. In the next three sections we'll compare C with Pascal, Fortran, and BASIC. Of course, you may skip a section if you're not familiar with that language. I certainly hope you're familiar with at least one of them!

1.2.1   C and Pascal

Below is a program written in C and in Pascal. The program reads one integer from the input, echo-prints it, squares it, and prints out the result.

C	Pascal
| ```
#include <stdio.h>
/*
  This program reads an
  integer, echo-prints it,
  squares it, and
  prints the result.
*/

main()
{
  int n;

  scanf("%d", &n);
  printf("  n: %5d\n", n);
  printf("nxn: %5d\n", n*n);
  return 0;
}
``` | ```
program square (input, output);
{
  This program reads an
  integer, echo-prints it,
  squares it, and
  prints the result.
}

var n:integer;
begin

  readln(n);
  writeln('  n: ', n:5);
  writeln('nxn: ', n*n:5);

end.
``` |

Here are some of the major differences and similarities between C and Pascal.

1. The syntax is somewhat different. Pascal programs begin with the keyword `program`, followed by the program's name and some optional additional information; C programs have no such thing. In Pascal, the main program is not a function or procedure: it is the `begin–end` block at the end of the program. In C, the main program is just another function, whose name must be `main`. The function in this case returns the value 0, which might be useful to the environment in which the program runs.

2. In C, the curious statement `#include <stdio.h>` is needed to invoke the ***standard library***, where the input/output functions `scanf` and `printf` reside. In Pascal, the I/O libraries (if any) are included automatically.

3. Input/output conventions are different. In C, a ***format string*** is used to specify printing in the `printf` statement. In the format string, `%5d` indicates that the value is to be printed as an integer, in five columns. The character sequence `\n` indicates a new-line character.

4. In Pascal, the declaration of global variable n cannot occur inside the body of the main program. In C, the declaration `int n;` can occur either inside or outside the main function, with different consequences, as we'll see later.

5. C is a terse language; Pascal is more verbose. Keywords in Pascal are generally longer—`integer` instead of `int`. Execution blocks are delimited by `begin` and `end` in Pascal, and by `{` and `}` in C.

6. Although the sample program doesn't illustrate it, C is both a high-level and a low-level programming language, allowing, for example, individual bit manipulation. Pascal was designed exclusively as a high-level language.

1.2.2 C and Fortran

Below is the program from Section 1.2.1, now shown in C and in Fortran. The program reads one integer from the input, echo-prints it, squares it, and prints out the result.

C	Fortran

<pre>#include <stdio.h>
/*
  This program reads an
  integer, echo-prints it,
  squares it, and
  prints the result.
*/
 	
main()
{
  int n;
 	
  scanf("%d", &n);
 	
  printf(" n: %5d\n", n);
 	
  printf("nxn: %5d\n", n*n);
 	
  return 0;
}</pre>
	<pre>C
	C This program reads an
	C integer, echo-prints it,
	C squares it, and
	C prints the result.
	C
	
	   INTEGER N, NS
	
	   READ(5, 10) N
	10 FORMAT (BN, I5)
	   NS=N*N
	   WRITE(6, 20) N
	20 FORMAT (' n: ',I5)
	   WRITE(6, 30) NS
	30 FORMAT ('nxn: ', I5)
	   STOP
	   END</pre>

Here are some of the major differences and similarities between C and Fortran.

1. A first major difference is the program format. The C language imposes essentially no format rules on the programmer, except for a few *lexical* rules that will be covered later. In Fortran, specific columns are set aside for specific purposes. A C in column 1 indicates that the rest of the line is a comment. In C, comments can appear almost anywhere. Columns 2–5 are for statement labels in Fortran, column 6 is for line continuations, and columns 72–80 are for an identification sequence. In C, labels can be placed in any column, and statements can cross line boundaries. Identification sequences are a historical remnant in Fortran: many a programmer is known to have watched in horror as his deck of 80-column Hollerith cards scattered across the floor. Identification sequences made it somewhat less painful to sort them out again.

2. Obviously, there are syntactical differences. Neither language requires a header. In Fortran, the main program is not a function or procedure: it is the collection of statements at the end of the program. In C, the main program can return a value (in this case zero).

3. The C input/output functions must be invoked explicitly using `#include <stdio.h>`. In Fortran, the I/O libraries (if any) are invoked automatically.

4. Input/output conventions are also different. In C, the `printf` statement requires a format string. In Fortran, the `WRITE` statement specifies the I/O device to use, and the label of the `FORMAT` statement. By (long-standing) convention, device 5 is a standard input device (such as a keyboard), and device 6 is an output device (such as a monitor).

5. In Fortran, declarations can be implicit; the program would have worked without the declaration `INTEGER N, NS`. In C, declarations are mandatory. The declaration `int n;` can occur either inside or outside the main function, with different consequences, as we'll see later.

6. Although the sample program doesn't show much of it, Fortran is a language originally designed for scientific applications and numeric computations. Its very name, FORmula TRANslation, indicates that it is primarily a vehicle for evaluating formulas. In contrast, C was designed as a language suitable for systems programming, which involves low-level programming as well as manipulation of numbers, characters, and symbols.

1.2.3   C and BASIC

Below is the program from Section 1.2.1, now shown in C and in BASIC. The program reads one integer from the input, echo-prints it, squares it, and prints out the result. Below these two programs we see some of the major differences and similarities between C and BASIC.

C	BASIC

`#include <stdio.h>`
`/*`
`  This program reads an`
`  integer, echo-prints it,`
`  squares it, and`
`  prints the result.`
`*/`
 	
`main()`
`{`
`  int n;`
 	
`  scanf("%d", &n);`
 	
`  printf("  n: %5d\n", n);`
`  printf("nxn: %5d\n", n*n);`
`  return 0;`
`}`
	
	`00010 REM This program reads an`
	`00020 REM integer, echo-prints it,`
	`00030 REM squares it, and`
	`00040 REM prints the result.`
	
	`00050 READ(5, 10) N`
	`00060 NS=N*N`
	`00070 PRINT "  n: ", N`
	`00080 PRINT "nxn: ", NS`
	
	`99999 END`

1. The first major difference between BASIC and C is that BASIC is generally implemented via an *interpreter*, while C is almost always implemented via a *compiler*. An interpreter processes each instruction in the program, first translating that instruction into machine language, then carrying out that instruction, and then moving on to the next instruction. In contrast, a C program usually goes through a three-part process. First, the compiler translates the entire program and creates an *object file*. Second, a *linker* (among other things) prepares the object file for execution. Finally, the program is executed.

2. Another major difference is in the environment in which programs are prepared and run. C programs are usually typed in using an editor, then compiled, linked, and executed. BASIC systems usually provide an environment in which one can type the program and run it directly.

3. There are differences in program format. In BASIC, every line has a number (the empty lines in the figure are there to allow a side-by-side comparison). These line numbers serve as statement labels.

4. Input/output libraries (if any) are invoked automatically in BASIC. In C, one must invoke the library explicitly using the statement `#include <stdio.h>`. I/O conventions are also different.

5. In BASIC, declarations are usually implicit. In C, declarations are mandatory.

6. Although there are subroutines in BASIC, the program itself cannot return a value. In C, `main` returns (in this case) zero.

1.3   Exercises

Since we haven't started discussing the C language yet, there's no point in having programming exercises, is there? Instead, the following questions provide food for thought.

1. What are some of the advantages and disadvantages of having a standard for a programming language?

2. Choose a language you are already familiar with. Is there an ANSI standard for it? An ISO standard? How long ago was the standard established? Was it the first standard for that language? If not, how did the language change between standards?

3. Choose a language you are already familiar with. What are some of the most desirable features of this language? What are some of its drawbacks? What are some of its pitfalls, especially those you have fallen into yourself?

4. In general, what makes programs difficult to read? Make a list of factors that affect readability of a program.

5. Determine which commands on your system (UNIX or DOS) accomplish each of the following: list the contents of the current directory, display the contents of a file on the screen, display the path to the current directory, change to another directory, copy the contents of one file into another, delete a file from the disk, and rename a file.

6. What is systems programming, and why is C suitable for it?

7. Learn how to use the C debugger on your system. If you have an integrated C system, a debugger probably comes with it.

8. Efficiency has been paramount in the historical development of the C language. With computers experiencing ever-increasing speeds, and ever-decreasing prices, is the efficiency of C likely to continue to be a major advantage in the future?

9. What are *your* reasons for wanting to learn C? Compare and contrast your reasons against C's advantages and disadvantages.

2 C Fundamentals

2.1 Chapter Summary

C programs have various components, such as *preprocessor directives*, *functions*, *variables*, *statements*, *comments*, and *identifiers*. An entirely typical first program is as follows:

```
#include <stdio.h>

main()
{
  printf("Hello!\n");
  return 0;
}
```

The first line makes available the standard input/output library, which contains the `printf` function. Every program must have a function named `main`, which contains a number of statements enclosed in braces (`{` and `}`). In this case, `main` has two statements: the `printf` statement, which prints a message string, and the `return` statement, discussed below. Inside the string, `\n` indicates the new-line character.

Programs must be preprocessed, compiled, and linked. The preprocessor handles directives, which begin with `#`. Then the compiler translates the program into machine language (producing an object file), and the linker combines the object file and additional necessary code (such as `printf`) to produce the final executable program. On many computer systems, separate commands are used to compile and link the program. In many PC-based systems, an integrated environment is provided, in which editing, compiling, linking, running, and even debugging all take place in the same environment.

A text editor is required to prepare a C program. On UNIX systems, there are essentially two text editors to choose from: `vi` and `emacs`. The `vi` text editor is a little antiquated, so unless you are an old-time `vi` expert, I recommend you expend the effort to learn `emacs`. Under MS-DOS, a variety of options are available, including MS-DOS's own (very basic) editor, various commercially available editors, and the editor that comes built into various C systems. I assume you are familiar with at least one editor.

Let's assume the above program has been stored in a file called `hello.c`. To compile the program under UNIX, we use the command `cc -o hello hello.c` (or perhaps we use `gcc` instead). Most MS-DOS C systems, such as Borland's Turbo C, provide an integrated environment, in which you invoke the compiler by carrying out a menu dialogue, or by pressing a "hot" (i.e., preprogrammed) key. You may also use the command line environment: the Borland Turbo C command to compile the program would be `tcc hello.c`. The executable code is written to file `hello.exe`. To run the program, we type `hello` (in UNIX), or we choose the proper menu item.

One of the most basic building blocks in C is the function, which acts like a subroutine or a procedure in other languages, but is also capable of returning a value, using the `return` statement. Every program *must* have one function named `main`. This function returns a value, usually taken by the operating system as a completion status code. In our above program, `return 0;` is used to signal to the operating system that the program terminated normally.

Statements are commands that are carried out as the program runs. In our program, we have two statements, each ending in a required semicolon. The compound statement, which is a collection of statements surrounded by braces, is the only statement that does not end in a semicolon. The `printf` statement is a *call* statement; it invokes the `printf` function. The string can be split up, using two calls to `printf`:

```
printf("Hello");  /* first  part of message */
printf("!\n");    /* second part of message */
```

Comments in C, as illustrated above, begin with `/*` and end with `*/`. They can cross line boundaries, allowing collections of comment lines to be "boxed" or otherwise highlighted. They cannot be nested, and you must be careful not to leave unclosed comments.

C has various ***data types***, including `int` (integer type, such as 23), `char` (character type, such as `'a'`), and `float` (floating-point type, such as `3.14159`). Any variables we use in a program must be declared. Declarations precede the statements in the main program and can include an initial value, such as `int a = 5, b = 6, c;`. Beware of uninitialized variables! Once declared, variable values can be changed with the assignment statement. For example, let's calculate a worker's net pay, by multiplying the number of hours he worked by his hourly rate and withholding Social Security and Medicare contributions for 7.65%, known as FICA (Federal Insurance Contributions Act.)

```
int hours_worked;
float hourly_rate, gross_pay, fica_deduction, net_pay;

gross_pay = hours_worked * hourly_rate;
fica_deduction = gross_pay * 0.0765;
net_pay = gross_pay - fica_deduction;
```

To print the values of variables, we use the `printf` function:

```
printf("Hours Worked: %d\n", hours_worked);
printf("Hourly Rate: $%5.2f\n", hourly_rate);
printf("Gross Pay:   $%5.2f\n", gross_pay);
printf("Deductions:  $%5.2f\n", fica_deduction);
printf("Net Pay:     $%5.2f\n", net_pay);
```

You are not limited to printing variables, but can also print ***expressions***:

```
printf("Deductions: $%5.2f\n", hours_worked * hourly_rate * 0.0765);
```

To obtain input, we use the `scanf` function. It requires a ***format string***, with which we specify the form the input will take. To read an `int`, we use `"%d"`; to read a `float` we use `"%f"`. For example, we can use the following two calls to `scanf` to read in the number of hours and the hourly rate:

```
scanf("%d", &hours_worked);
scanf("%f", &hourly_rate);
```

The `&` is required, except in the case of pointers, which we'll cover later.

Constants are defined in C using ***macro definitions***. For example, instead of using the percentage value of `0.0765`, we can define a macro:

```
#define FICA_PERCENTAGE 0.0765
```

Macro definitions are handled by the preprocessor. There's an established convention of using all uppercase letters for macro names.

Variable names are ***identifiers***, which contain letters, digits, and underscores, and must begin with a letter or an underscore. The C language is ***case-sensitive***: the difference between lower-case and upper-case letters *does* matter. A number of names are ***keywords*** (such as `int` and `float`) and can't be used as identifiers. In addition, you should not use the names of functions defined in the standard library, nor use names that begin with underscore. Long names are both allowed and encouraged; I recommend using underscores to delimit pieces of a name, as in `hours_worked`.

Program layout in C is a fairly significant issue. Every program can be viewed as a stream of ***tokens***: a sequence of characters that belong together as a unit. These include identifiers, keywords, operators, punctuation marks, and strings. Generally, the amount of space (including the space character, the tab character, and the new-line character) is immaterial between tokens, but not within tokens. Spaces can be deleted almost anywhere, except

1. whenever deleting the space would cause two tokens to merge—`inti` instead of `int i`;
2. whenever the space occurs inside a string—`"HiThere"` instead of `"Hi There"`;
3. for preprocessor directives, which must appear on separate lines, although a comment may appear on the same line as the directive.

Similarly, spaces can generally be inserted anywhere except

1. in the middle of a token—`ma in()` instead of `main()`; or

2. in the middle of a string—`printf("C blues");` instead of `printf("Cblues");`.

A string can cross the boundary between one line and the next, but only using a special trick, which will be covered later. It's a very good idea to use spaces and empty lines systematically, to separate blocks of code and improve the program's appearance and readability. Some criteria for doing this are:

1. Insert spaces before and after operators.
2. Indent declarations and statements within functions.
3. Use empty lines to divide programs into subsections; that is, separate preprocessor directives from declarations and declarations from statements.

2.2 Solved Exercises

As a first exercise, I thought I would guide you through the complete development process of a program. Before we begin, here's a useful observation:

Programs are NOT developed in the order in which they appear.

Whenever you read a program, whether you wrote it or someone else did, please keep in mind that you are reading *the end result* of someone's thought processes. Generally, this is the reason documentation and comments are necessary: the program code itself describes little or nothing about the thought process that led to it. Also, please don't fall into the temptation of thinking, "Well, it's my own program, and I'm the only one who's going to use or modify it." Even after only a short period of time (sometimes just a few minutes!), your own program can be as alien as a program written by someone else. I hope you are already a believer in the need to sprinkle programs generously with comments. If you aren't, I assure you that soon you'll be staring at your own program, wondering, "What was I thinking here?"

2.2.1 Solved Exercise 1: Calculating Net Pay

Let's develop a complete program that will read the number of hours worked and the worker's pay rate, then calculates and prints the worker's net pay. We have already shown some of the statements required for this earlier in this chapter; the real trick is to put these components together *systematically*. The issue is similar to playing chess: anyone can learn fairly quickly how each individual piece moves, but playing chess involves strategy, attack and defense, openings, and so on.

We begin by determining the input and the output of the program. It's also a good idea to document these in the form of C comments.

```
/*****************************************************************/
/* This program reads in a worker's total hours and hourly  */
/* rate of pay, and calculates the worker's gross and       */
/* net pay by deducting the required FICA contributions.    */
/*****************************************************************/
```

This also raises a fairly significant question: should we write the program out on paper and then type it into the computer, or should we develop the program on-line? This is a difficult question. Composing a program on-line increases the temptation to "hack now, document later." On the other hand, virtually everything we would write by hand on paper would have to be typed in eventually. Most programmers these days use paper only for sketches and diagrams that are difficult to elaborate on the computer. We suggest you do the same, but pay special attention to documentation of your programs.

One advantage of composing at the computer is that it's easier to develop the program in successive refinement steps. Our first version looks like this:

```
#include <stdio.h>

/****************************************************************/
/* This program reads in a worker's total hours and hourly    */
/* rate of pay, and calculates the worker's gross and         */
/* net pay by deducting the required FICA contributions.      */
/****************************************************************/

main()
{
  int hours_worked;
  float hourly_rate, gross_pay, net_pay;

/****************************************************************/
/* Read in hours worked and hourly rate of pay.               */
/****************************************************************/


/****************************************************************/
/* Calculate and print gross pay and net pay.                 */
/****************************************************************/
}
```

Although there is little code so far, quite a bit of the program's design has been accomplished. The program has been broken down into two tasks: obtaining the input, and calculating and printing the results. Let's elaborate on the part that obtains the input.

```
#include <stdio.h>

/****************************************************************/
/* This program reads in a worker's total hours and hourly    */
/* rate of pay, and calculates the worker's gross and         */
/* net pay by deducting the required FICA contributions.      */
/****************************************************************/

main()
{
  int hours_worked;
  float hourly_rate, gross_pay, net_pay;

/****************************************************************/
/* Read in hours worked and hourly rate of pay.               */
/****************************************************************/

  printf("Simple Payroll Program:\n");
  printf("----------------------\n\n");
  printf("Enter the number of hours worked: ");
  scanf("%d", &hours_worked);
  printf("Enter the hourly rate of pay: ");
  scanf("%f", &hourly_rate);

/****************************************************************/
/* Calculate and print gross pay and net pay.                 */
/****************************************************************/
}
```

This second version illustrates two healthy programming practices:
1. Always have your program identify itself from the start, and
2. Always provide a descriptive prompt for input.

A third healthy practice consists of echo-printing, printing the data immediately after reading it in to allow the user to verify it. You can even prompt the user for verification, continuing only when the user acknowledges that the data are correct.

Now, for the final step, we need a few assignment statements. To calculate the FICA deductions, we define a constant using the `define` preprocessor directive. This makes the program easier to modify in the future. We need a new variable, `fica_deduction`, which is subtracted from `gross_pay`. This variable is added to the list of variables declared. Some variables appear sooner in the the program development process, and others appear later, as needed. In the end, we print out all five data items, each one with a suitable caption. In printing, we add new-line characters and spaces so that the output looks nice. Aligning the decimal points vertically can also be done, as we shall see later. Below is the final version of the program.

```
#include <stdio.h>

#define FICA_PERCENTAGE 0.0765

/*******************************************************/
/* This program reads in a worker's total hours and hourly  */
/* rate of pay, and calculates the worker's gross and       */
/* net pay by deducting the required FICA contributions.    */
/*******************************************************/

main() {
  int hours_worked;
  float hourly_rate, gross_pay, net_pay, fica_deduction;

/*******************************************************/
/* Read in hours worked and hourly rate of pay.        */
/*******************************************************/

  printf("Simple Payroll Program:\n");
  printf("-----------------------\n\n");
  printf("Enter the number of hours worked: ");
  scanf("%d", &hours_worked);
  printf("Enter the hourly rate of pay: ");
  scanf("%f", &hourly_rate);

/*******************************************************/
/* Calculate and print gross pay and net pay.          */
/*******************************************************/

  gross_pay = hours_worked * hourly_rate;
  fica_deduction = gross_pay * FICA_PERCENTAGE;
  net_pay = gross_pay - fica_deduction;

  printf("\nHours Worked:   %d\n", hours_worked);
  printf("Hourly Rate:    $%5.2f\n", hourly_rate);
  printf("Gross Pay:      $%5.2f\n", gross_pay);
  printf("FICA Deduction: $%5.2f\n", fica_deduction);
  printf("Net Pay:        $%5.2f\n", net_pay);
  return 0;
}
```

Here's a sample run of the program:

```
        Simple Payroll Program:
        -----------------------

        Enter the number of hours worked: 21
        Enter the hourly rate of pay: 12.5

        Hours Worked:   21
        Hourly Rate:    $12.50
        Gross Pay:      $262.50
        FICA Deduction: $20.08
        Net Pay:        $242.42
```

It is often necessary to interrupt a program while it is running. Under most systems, `control-c` will do the trick. It is also often necessary to signal an end-of-file to a running program. Under UNIX, this is done with `control-d`; under MS-DOS `control-z` is used.

2.3   Programming Exercises

1. Modify the simple payroll program so it can handle fractions of hours.

2. Write a program that reads in two integers and outputs their sum, difference, and product.

3. Compile and run the "dimensional weight of a box" program shown in the main text, page 21. Change the program so it reads all three box dimensions using a single call to `scanf`.

4. Write a complete, well-written, documented program that reads an integer n, then prints n, its square, its cube, and the sum of all three.

5. Write a complete, well-written, documented program that calculates the final price of a truck, given that the truck's list price is $20,000, the sales tax is 8.2%, and the car dealer is offering a 5% discount. The license tag costs $150.00 and does not pay sales tax, but is discounted 5% as well.

6. What (if anything) is wrong with the following program?

    ```
    main() {
       int While;
       While = 0;
    }
    ```

7. Which of the following are legal identifiers in C? `35number`, `Symbol_Table`, `Name-And_Address`, `_digit`, `_digit__`, `_dig__it___`.

8. In the program shown, identify all the errors that would be detected by an ANSI C compiler.

    ```
    #include <stdio.h>
    #define COUnt    10

    main(
    )               {  int i, j, k; flaot l, m;
       scan(%d, &i) ;     scan("%f", &l)
       printf("%f', l);
       j = i * COUNT:
       printf("%d", j, k) printf("%d", i);
       printf("\n"));
    }
    ```

9. Rewrite the following program by inserting spaces and formatting it better in order to make it more readable.

    ```
    #include <stdio.h>
    main() { int i, j, k, 1; float a, b , c; i = 0; j=5;k=6;
       j=j+1;l=k*j;i=i+1;
       a=20.0;b=30.0;c=2.0*a+b; a = a + 1.0;b=b+2.0;}
    ```

10. Modify the program that calculates the dimensional weight of a box (main text, page 21) to print the overall dimensions of the box (height + length + width).

11. Write `printf` statements that will produce the following output:

```
Name      Social      Birth      Phone #      Grade
          Security    Date                    Point
          Number                              Average
====      ========    =====      =======      =======
```

12. Modify the simple payroll program so it processes an additional data item, the number of overtime hours worked. Assume the worker makes one and a half times his hourly rate for overtime hours.

13. Write a program that will print a large letter C, like the one shown below.

```
CCCCCCCCCCCCC
CCCCCCCCCCCCC
CC
CC
CC
CC
CC
CC
CCCCCCCCCCCCC
CCCCCCCCCCCCC
```

14. Display the output of the following C code fragment. Show how to change the program to make it produce "You Must Terminate Comments."

```
/* Display the sentence ...
printf("You Must ");
printf("Terminate ");       /* the second line */
printf("Comments\n");
```

15. Change the "dimensional weight of a box" program (main text, page 21) to calculate the surface area of the box instead. Match the following output:

```
The height is: 10
The length is: 5
The width  is: 2
The surface area is: 160
```

16. What (if anything) is wrong with the following program?

```
main(){
    int While, printf;

    While = 0;
    printf = While;
}
```

17. Modify the "Fahrenheit to Celsius" program (main text, page 22) to perform the reverse conversion from Celsius to Fahrenheit. Make sure that you redefine the scaling factors and the freezing points to fit correctly in the equations.

18. Swap the first two nonempty lines in the program pun.c (main text, page 10). What happens? Must the #include <stdio.h> directive appear at the beginning of the file? Now move the #include statement further down, so it appears after the printf statements. What happens? Why? In general, where can/should the #include statements appear?

3 Formatted Input/Output

3.1 Chapter Summary

3.1.1 The `printf` function

The `printf` function takes one or more arguments, the first of which is the format string. The remaining arguments are expressions. `printf` processes the format string, replacing *conversion specifications* in it with the values of the expressions and converting each such value from its internal (binary) form to a character form suitable for printing. The final result is a format string ready for printing, which `printf` sends to standard output. The process of scanning and filling in the format string proceeds from left to right, independently of how many arguments there are in the call to `printf`. The format string (not the expressions) "drives" the process. C compilers will not complain if there too few or too many arguments: if there are too few, meaningless values will be printed; any extra arguments will be ignored. The compiler will attempt the conversion faithfully and quite blindly: no warning is given for inappropriate conversions, which usually result in garbage output.

The general form of a conversion specification is `%[-][m][.p]X`. *m* and *p* are integer constants, and *X*, the conversion specifier, is (for now) one of the letters d, e, f, or g. The square brackets indicate optionality: the minus sign is optional, as well as the `.p` (precision) and the *m* (minimum field width). The conversion places the printable value into at least *m* columns, taking more than *m* if necessary and justifying if fewer than *m* are needed. Justification is by default to the right; the minus sign causes left justification. The first four conversion specifiers (more to come later) are:

- `%d`: Display in decimal form; *p* is the minimum number of digits to display (the default is 1).
- `%e`: Display in exponential format (scientific notation); *p* is the number of digits after the decimal point.
- `%f`: Display in "fixed decimal" format; *p* is the same as for *e*.
- `%g`: Display in fixed decimal or exponential format, depending on the size of the floating-point number; *p* is the maximum number of significant digits to be displayed.

Ordinary characters (those that are not part of a conversion specification) are printed as they appear in the format string. The one exception is `%` itself, which must be doubled within the format string to be printed: `printf("%%");`.

Other characters may need an escape sequence to be printed, usually of the form `\X`. Examples include `\n`, `\a`, `\b`, `\t`, and `\\`. Two other noteworthy examples are `\"`, to get the `"` character inside a string, and `%%`, to get the `%` character inside the format string without the compiler's mistaking it for a conversion specification.

3.1.2 The `scanf` function

In many respects the `scanf` function is similar to `printf`: the first argument is a format string, and the remaining items are variables to be read in. The format string contains ordinary characters and conversion specifications (although ordinary characters are much less common than with `printf`), and the types of conversions allowed are essentially the same as for `printf`. The conversion process is driven by the format string: it's possible to have too few or too many items, and type mismatches between a variable and its corresponding conversion specification will go unnoticed by the compiler.

One major difference is that the second and subsequent arguments of `scanf` must be preceded by `&` (not always, but more on that later). Omitting the `&` is a major hazard: the results are unpredictable. Don't count on the compiler to catch the error. Most compilers can't always catch it, and some compilers don't even try.

`scanf` processes the format string from left to right, acting on the conversion specifications it encounters, assembling values from the input (which it views as a stream of characters), and storing those values in the variable arguments. As it progresses, three positions are tracked:

■ The current position in the format string. If this is an ordinary character, it is matched with the input in one of two ways: (1) a white-space character (i.e., space, tab, and new-line character) is matched against any sequence of white-space characters on the input; and (2) a non-white-space character is matched against *the very next character* on the input. If the current position in the format string is a conversion specification, then an item is "scanned" on the input, beginning with

■ the current position in the input. Starting from this position, scanf first skips any white space (for d, f, e, and g conversion specifications, but not necessarily for others we'll cover later), and then attempts to scan an item of the specified type on the input. This scanning process runs until an input character is reached that cannot be fit into the ongoing item. This last character is returned to the input, as if it hadn't been read. The characters that were read in are converted to a value of the appropriate type, and that value is stored in the variable in

■ the current position in the variable argument list. This variable should have the & in front of it.

Judicious use of white-space characters in the scanf function can allow for fairly sophisticated pattern matching. For example, if we wish to read in three integer values, and our intent is to allow some flexibility in the input while requiring the integers to be separated by commas, we might write

```
scanf("%d ,%d ,%d", &a, &b, &c);
```

which will allow the commas to be placed anywhere in between the integers, and the integers to be spaced out over several lines, so long as all other intervening characters are limited to white spaces. However, you must be very careful. The statement

```
scanf("%d, %d, %d", &a, &b, &c);
```

will not work: after the first integer, the very next character must be a comma. If it isn't, scanf terminates prematurely without reading values for b and c.

3.2   Solved Exercises

3.2.1   Solved Exercise 1: Calculating Travel Time

We're going on a trip. Let's develop a program that will help us estimate the time of arrival at our destination. The program reads in the distance to be traveled, the speed at which we'll travel, and the departure time. It will calculate the amount of time the trip will take and give us our estimated arrival time. Our first version of the program looks like this:

```
#include <stdio.h>

/********************************************************/
/*  This program reads in the distance to be covered on a  */
/*  trip, our average speed, and our departure time.       */
/*  It calculates and prints our travel time and estimated */
/*  arrival time.                                          */
/********************************************************/

main()
{
  int depart_hours, depart_mins;
  float distance, speed;

/********************************************************/
/* Read in the distance, speed, and departure time.       */
/* Departure time is in the form hh:mm.                   */
/********************************************************/


/********************************************************/
/*  Calculate travel time and arrival time.              */
/********************************************************/
```

```
/**************************************************************/
/*  Print results.                                           */
/**************************************************************/
}
```

So far, we know that we need to break down the departure time into two int variables: depart_hours, and depart_mins. Let's refine our program by writing the printf and scanf statements to read the input data.

```
#include <stdio.h>

/**************************************************************/
/*  This program reads in the distance to be covered on a    */
/*  trip, our average speed, and our departure time.         */
/*  It calculates and prints our travel time and estimated   */
/*  arrival time.                                            */
/**************************************************************/

main()
{
  int depart_hours, depart_mins;
  float distance, speed;

/**************************************************************/
/* Read in the distance, speed, and departure time.         */
/* Departure time is in the form hh:mm.                     */
/**************************************************************/

  printf("Travel calculation program:\n\n");
  printf("Distance to be traveled (miles): ");
  scanf("%f", &distance);
  printf("Speed of travel (mph): ");
  scanf("%f", &speed);
  printf("Departure (military) time (hh:mm): ");
  scanf("%d:%d", &depart_hours, &depart_mins);

/**************************************************************/
/*  Calculate travel time and arrival time.                 */
/**************************************************************/

/**************************************************************/
/*  Print results.                                           */
/**************************************************************/
}
```

Now we're ready to perform the calculations. To calculate travel_time, we divide distance by speed. Then we break down travel_time into hours and mins, so they can be added individually to the departure times (held in depart_hours and depart_mins). Calculating hours is easy: simply assign travel_time (a float) to hours. This removes any fractional part, leaving only the integer part. Your compiler may give you a warning, since information is lost. Calculating mins is a little more involved: subtracting hours from travel_time yields what we want, but in the form of a fraction of hours. For example, if travel_time is 10.5, then hours is 10, and travel_time - hours is 0.5. To obtain the number of minutes, we first multiply by 100 (in our case yielding 50, and then adjust to the scale of minutes, multiplying by 60/100. The net effect is to evaluate (travel_time - hours) * 60. We define a constant named MINS_PER_HOUR with value 60 for this purpose.

Next, we calculate arrival_hours by adding hours to depart_hours. In addition, we must add a possible extra hour produced by the minutes adding up to more than 60. For example, if the departure time is 15:45, and the travel time is 10.5, then arrival_hours would be 26, not 25, since the minutes add up to 75. Also, the hours could spill over into the next day, so we calculate the excess over 24 hours, using the remainder (%) operator. Finally, arrival mins is calculated in a similar manner: we use the % (remainder) operator (discussed in more detail later) to obtain the remainder of dividing 75 by 60, yielding 15.

Note that in this analysis, we found the need for additional variables, which are now added to the declarations at the top of the program. Here's the second version of the program.

```
#include <stdio.h>

#define MINS_PER_HOUR 60

/*********************************************************/
/*  This program reads in the distance to be covered on a  */
/*  trip, our average speed, and our departure time.       */
/*  It calculates and prints our travel time and estimated */
/*  arrival time.                                          */
/*********************************************************/

main()
{
    int depart_hours, depart_mins, hours, mins, arrival_hours,
        arrival_mins;
    float distance, speed, travel_time;

/*********************************************************/
/* Read in the distance, speed, and departure time.      */
/* Departure time is in the form hh:mm.                  */
/*********************************************************/

    printf("Travel calculation program:\n\n");
    printf("Distance to be traveled (miles): ");
    scanf("%f", &distance);
    printf("Speed of travel (mph): ");
    scanf("%f", &speed);
    printf("Departure (military) time (hh:mm): ");
    scanf("%d:%d", &depart_hours, &depart_mins);

/*********************************************************/
/*  Calculate travel time and arrival time.              */
/*********************************************************/

    travel_time = distance / speed;
    hours = travel_time;
    mins = (travel_time - hours) * MINS_PER_HOUR;
    arrival_hours = (depart_hours + hours
                    + (depart_mins + mins) / MINS_PER_HOUR) % 24;
    arrival_mins =  (depart_mins + mins) % MINS_PER_HOUR;

/*********************************************************/
/*  Print results.                                       */
/*********************************************************/
}
```

Lastly, we print the results. To print a time in the format hh:mm, the conversion specification "%2d:%2d" doesn't quite do it: each number is printed in two columns, but leading zeroes are replaced with spaces, e.g. 3: 2. Instead we want something like 03:03. Although we cover this in more detail later, the conversion specification can be preceded by the *precision*, in this case .2, to indicate that there is a minimum of 2 digits, and that leading zeroes are to be printed. Here's the complete program and a sample session running it.

```
#include <stdio.h>

#define MINS_PER_HOUR 60
```

```
/**********************************************************/
/*  This program reads in the distance to be covered on a  */
/*  trip, our average speed, and our departure time.       */
/*  It calculates and prints our travel time and estimated */
/*  arrival time.                                          */
/**********************************************************/

main()
{
    int depart_hours, depart_mins, hours, mins, arrival_hours,
        arrival_mins;
    float distance, speed, travel_time;

    /**********************************************************/
    /* Read in the distance, speed, and departure time.       */
    /* Departure time is in the form hh:mm.                   */
    /**********************************************************/

    printf("Travel calculation program:\n\n");
    printf("Distance to be traveled (miles): ");
    scanf("%f", &distance);
    printf("Speed of travel (mph): ");
    scanf("%f", &speed);
    printf("Departure (military) time (hh:mm): ");
    scanf("%d:%d", &depart_hours, &depart_mins);

    /**********************************************************/
    /*  Calculate travel time and arrival time.               */
    /**********************************************************/

    travel_time = distance / speed;
    hours = travel_time;
    mins = (travel_time - hours) * MINS_PER_HOUR;
    arrival_hours = (depart_hours + hours
                    + (depart_mins + mins) / MINS_PER_HOUR) % 24;
    arrival_mins =  (depart_mins + mins) % MINS_PER_HOUR;

    /**********************************************************/
    /*  Print results.                                        */
    /**********************************************************/

    printf("\nDistance: %5.2f miles.\n", distance);
    printf("Speed: %5.2f mph.\n", speed);
    printf("Departure time: %.2d:%.2d.\n",
            depart_hours, depart_mins);
    printf("Travel time: %.2d:%.2d.\n", hours, mins);
    printf("Arrival time: %.2d:%.2d.\n",
            arrival_hours, arrival_mins);
    return 0;
}
```

Here's a sample run of the program:

```
Travel calculation program:

Distance to be traveled (miles): 147.5
Speed of travel (mph): 58.6
Departure (military) time (hh:mm): 12:38

Distance: 147.50 miles.
Speed: 58.60 mph.
Departure time: 12:38.
Travel time: 02:31.
Arrival time: 15:09.
```

3.3   Programming Exercises

1. Write a program that takes two measurements in feet (width, length) and prints the number of square yards of carpet required. Remember to prompt for values.

2. Write a program that prints a simple pattern, such as the triangle shown below.

3. Write a program that reads in three numbers and then prints them in reverse order.

4. Write a program that reads in information about a military officer: age, rank, serial number, base pay, and number of years in service. Use integers to code the various ranks: 1 = enlisted, 2 = sergeant, 3 = captain, etc. Print out a nicely formatted statement detailing the information.

5. You're a lawyer, and you need a program that will print an invoice so your victim (ahem, client) can pay you. Write a program that will take as input the number of hours you worked for the client, and your hourly rate, and prepares a nicely formatted invoice.

6. Write a program that will read in five `float` numbers, calculate their average, and print them out along with their average.

7. Write a program that asks you for your age in years, months, and days, and displays your age in days. Assume every month has exactly 30 days.

8. Modify the program in the previous exercise to calculate the total number of heartbeats in your life so far. On average, people's hearts beat at the rate of 73 beats per minute.

9. Write a program that calculates a light-year, the distance light travels in one year. Light travels at the speed of 186,000 miles per second.

10. Write `scanf` statements that will result in the values 20, 10, and 5 to be stored in the integer variables x, y, and z respectively, for each of the following input lines:

    ```
    abc 20 34 10            5
          20 10 5
       20       5    10
      20 abc 10 5 abc
    20 10 5 abc
    ```

11. Write a program that displays the value of *pi*, 3.141592. Display it to 5 decimal places, right-justified, in 9 columns.

12. Display the values `30`, `62.7`, `25.037`, `133.666`, and `-18.7` in a vertical column. Display each number with an accuracy of 2 decimal places and make the decimal points line up vertically.

13. Write a program that will take as input a distance in miles and will print out the corresponding number of kilometers (1 mile = 1.609 kilometers).

14. An acre contains 43,560 square feet. How many square meters does this represent? (A square yard has 9 square feet, and a square yard is 0.8361 square meters). Write a program to compute this.

15. Write a program that will read in two fractions (such as 3/7), then print each fraction, and their sum and product, both as fractions and as floats. To refresh your memory, $a/b + c/d = (ad + bc)/bd$, and $a/b * c/d = ac/bd$. You don't have to reduce fractions to their simplest form.

16. Modify the program in the previous exercise to display the fractions over several lines, using dashes to separate numerators from denominators, like so:

```
  3       6      3 * 7 + 4 * 6        45
 ---  *  ---  =  -------------    =   ----  = 1.60714
  4       7          4 * 7            28
```

17. In the old British monetary system, there were 20 shillings to a pound and 12 pence to a shilling. Thus 12.4.3 meant 12 pounds, 4 shillings, and 3 pence. In the new system, a pound contains no shillings, only 100 pence. Write a program that will read a monetary value such as 12.4.3 and will print the equivalent value in the new British system. (*Note*: printing the British pound sign, £, is something you will learn to do later.)

18. Write a program to do the reverse of the previous exercise: convert a new British monetary value into an old one.

19. Write a program that reads in someone's height in feet and inches, using a single quotation mark for feet, and the double one for inches (i.e. 5′4″), and prints that person's height in inches.

20. Write a program that will read the number of miles driven and the number of gallons of gasoline used, and will print the fuel efficiency (miles per gallon). Look up the necessary conversions and print the result also in liters per kilometer.

4 Expressions

4.1 Chapter Summary

C is known as an *imperative* language, one in which the *modus operandi* of the programmer is to give instructions to the computer, which the computer will execute faithfully and blindingly fast. Thus in a typical scenario, we will instruct the computer to

1. read in some input data by executing `scanf` statements,
2. perform some calculations—which involves evaluating expressions—and perhaps store the results in certain variables by executing assignment statements, and
3. output the results by executing `printf` statements.

Chapter 3 focused on how to get the information in and out of the computer (items 1 and 3 above); Chapter 4 now focuses on item 2. You calculate values by combining constants and variables with *operators* to form expressions. The C language has a remarkably rich and powerful collection of operators. Some of them have been used in earlier chapters, such as the addition operator +.

Operators are classified according to the following attributes:

- The *arity*, or the number of operands the operator requires. Unary operators have arity one (e.g., the unary minus in the expression −3), binary operators have arity 2 (e.g., the binary multiplication in the expression 3 * 7), and ternary operators have three operands. There is one ternary operator in C, which we will see in a later chapter.
- The operator's location with respect to its operands. *Prefix* operators appear before their operands; *infix* operators appear in between their operands; *postfix* operators appear after their operands. The unary minus is a prefix operator (e.g., −3); the binary division / is an infix operator (e.g., 3 / 7), and the increment operator comes in a postfix (as well as prefix) variety (e.g., i++).
- The operator's *precedence*, or the priority that the operator receives when it appears along with other operators in an expression. For example, in the expression a * b + c, the fact that * has higher precedence than + indicates that in this expression, the intent is to add c to the product a * b, not to multiply a by the sum b + c. The precedence rules compartmentalize the operators into little families with one family per level of priority.
- The operator's *associativity*, or the priority that an operator receives when it appears along with other operators of the same precedence. Associativity can be thought of as a tie-breaking rule. In the expression 3 − 2 − 1, where both operators (binary minus) have the same precedence, we need a tie-breaking rule to determine whether to perform the left minus first and subtract 1 from 3 − 2 (yielding zero), or to perform the right minus first and subtract 2 − 1 from 3 (yielding 2). In C, the binary minus operator is left associative, so the value of the expression is zero. Most binary operators in C are left associative and all operators of the same precedence always have the same associativity.
- The order of evaluation of the operands. For unary operators, this is not an issue, because there is only one operand to evaluate. For most other operators in C, this issue is implementation-defined: in the expression (a + b) * (c − d), the compiler decides whether (a + b) is evaluated before (c − d) or vice versa.

It's extremely important not to confuse precedence with order of evaluation. For example, in the expression a * b + c, precedence indicates that the multiplication will take place between a and b, not between a and b + c. Quite independently of this, c could be evaluated before or after a * b is, and similarly, we don't know whether a or b will be evaluated first. Thus, the precedence rules indicate which operand will be operated with which, whereas the order of evaluation indicates when such operations will take place. This becomes particularly significant when some of the subexpressions have *side effects*, when evaluating one subexpression can change the value of a variable and affect the evaluation of another subexpression. For example, assuming i has the value 3, the expression ++i + i can yield 7 or 8, depending on whether subexpression i is evaluated before subexpression ++i, or vice versa. To reiterate, this situation is independent of the fact that the ++ applies to i, not to i + i.

Often the result of the operation itself is also implementation-defined. For example, when dividing integers, the result is a truncated integer, but if the result is negative, the truncation may be carried out by rounding up or down, depending on the particular C implementation being used.

In many languages, the assignment is a statement. In C, the assignment is in fact an operator with the attributes listed above: its arity is two, it is an infix operator with precedence level 5 (at least for now, according to the table on page 54 of the main text), its associativity is to the right, and its order of evaluation is implementation-defined. The assignment is of the form *v = e*, where (for now) *v* is a variable name and *e* is an expression. In general, *v* is an expression that must have an *lvalue*, a location in the machine's memory. Thus assignments such as i + j = 0 are illegal, because i + j has no lvalue, or no place in which to store the zero.

In an expression of the form *v = e*, expression *e* is evaluated and its value is assigned to *v* (destroying the value stored there previously, if any). The assignment produces a result, which is the value of *v* after the assignment. Thus an assignment can occur anywhere an ordinary value can, including:

- in a printf statement: printf("%d", a = 3);
- in the control expression of a while statement: while ((a = a + 1) <= 7) { ... }; here the parentheses around a = a + 1 are necessary because the <= operator has higher precedence than the assignment operator;
- in a subexpression of another assignment: a = 3 + (b = 7);
- as the expression in another assignment: a = (b = 4). Here we have parenthesized the assignment of 4 to b (unnecessarily, because = is right associative); the value of that assignment, namely 4, is assigned to a.

Normally, it is not such a great idea to use assignments in this way. You may be wondering, then, why are these seemingly bizarre possibilities allowed? As we shall see later, some possibilities exhibit code that is very compact, powerful, and expressive, and therefore elegant and worth using. They're known as *idioms*, and we'll see quite a bit of them later. In making the assignment *v = e*, a type conversion will have to be made if the type of *v* disagrees with that of the expression *e*. This will be covered later.

Compound assignments combine the effect of the assignment operator with another operator, producing a short notation. The quintessential situation is when we wish to increment a variable x by a certain amount y: the expression x += y has the same effect as x = x + y. In general, however, you must be careful: the expression *v op= e* carries out operation *op* between *v* and *e* (note that this is not the same as evaluating the expression *v op e*), and assigns the resulting value to *v*, without evaluating *v* a second time. *v* is evaluated only once because (in general) it might have a side effect. How can *v* have a side effect? So far, we have thought of *v* as only a variable name, but as we'll see later, *v* can be a complex expression (including side effects!), as long as it has an lvalue. Compound operators are all right associative, and so far we have five of them: +=, -=, *=, /=, and %=; there are five others that will be covered later.

Yet another way to increment a variable is using the ++ (*increment*) and -- (*decrement*) operators. Both come in the prefix and postfix forms, which means that ++i and i++ both increment i by 1, but their resulting values are different. The value of ++i is the value of i *after* the increment has taken place; the value of i++ is the value of i *before* the increment. Thus ++i is the *pre-increment* operator (increment first, then fetch); i++ is the *post-increment* operator (fetch first, then increment). The -- operator has similar properties, but decrements by 1.

Any expression can be used as a statement in C if you place a semicolon after it. The effect of the semicolon is to discard the value of the expression. Thus the assignment *expression* n = 1 (no semicolon), becomes the assignment *statement* n = 1;. In fact, we have done this before, perhaps without realizing it. The printf function actually returns an integer value, which is the number of characters in the formatted string being printed. In earlier chapters we have been discarding this value using the semicolon:

```
printf("%d", 3);
```

We certainly don't have to discard that value. It can be treated like any other value: it can be operated upon, assigned to a variable, or even printed:

```
printf("%d\n", i = printf("%d\n", n) + printf("%d\n", m));
```

This statement first prints integers n and m. We can't tell which of the two is printed first, because the order of evaluation of the operands of + is implementation-defined. Then the number of characters printed by the two `printf` statements are added, assigned to i, and printed. For example, if n = 34 and m = 456, the output could be

```
34
456
7
```

Please note that this kind of programming is *not* normally recommended[1], although there are situations in which it is useful to keep track of how many spaces have been used up by `printf`.

4.2   Questions and Answers

In this chapter our solved exercises will consist of a few questions and their answers.

Q: How does the compiler interpret two or more consecutive operators, as in the expression a+++b? Does this add b to a++, or does it add a to ++b?

A: To explore this issue, let's start with a simple example. Write and compile a short program that calculates the expression b - (-3), for some value of b. According to the rules of precedence, the unary minus has priority over the binary minus, so the parentheses around -3 are *not* necessary. Now remove the parentheses and recompile the program. You should get a syntax error, because the compiler now interprets the expression as if it were (b--) 3, which is clearly ill formed. To illustrate further, replace b with a numeric value, such as 4. You should now get an error message such as `invalid lvalue in decrement`, in addition to the original message. Now insert spaces between all characters, i.e., 4 - - 3 and recompile. The errors should disappear. What's going on? The C compiler is a computer program—albeit a large computer program—that reads in its input data (your program), one character at a time, and translates your program into machine language so it can be executed. Part of its job is to collect the input characters into tokens or lexical units. Tokens include operators (++, %), separators ({, }, ;), identifiers (xyz, n2), reserved words (while, float) and constants (37, 2.3E+3). *The C compiler collects the characters from left to right, and always forms the longest possible token.* Thus, in the expression 4 - - 3, only the space after the first minus is required: in 4- -3 the space separates the minus signs into two tokens. Note that the compiler will act this way even if it causes illegal expressions, and even if other interpretations of the input are legal. Thus b--3 is interpreted as (b--) 3.

Q: How do you tell whether a set of parentheses is necessary in an expression?

A: Generally, you examine the expression operators on either side of the subexpression in question, and determine whether these operators have precedence that is high enough to change the structure of the expression if the parentheses were removed. For example, consider the fully parenthesized expression

```
(a = (b += (((c++) - d) * ((--e) / (-f)))))
```

First, consider the subexpression (c++). Its immediate neighbors are parentheses to the left (which we defer until it's time to consider that set of parentheses) and binary minus to the right. Since the binary minus has lower precedence than the postfix ++, we are safe in eliminating the ()'s in (c++). Similarly, the parentheses in both (--e) and (-f) are unnecessary, because both -- and unary - have higher precedence than /. We now have

```
(a = (b += ((c++ - d) * (--e / -f))))
```

---

1 The situation with legal but convoluted statements in C reminds me of the following quotation, attributed to Sir Winston Churchill: "This is the sort of English up with which I will not put!"

Now consider eliminating the ()'s in (c++ - d). To the left of this subexpression is (, which we defer. To the right we have a binary *, which has higher precedence than the binary -. We cannot eliminate the ()'s in (c++ - d), since the left operand of * would become d instead of (c++ - d). Thus that set of ()'s must remain in the expression. Now consider the subexpression (--e / -f). The binary * to its left has the same precedence as the /; the ()'s in question override the left associativity of * and /. If the ()'s were removed, the right operand of * would become --e instead of (--e / -f). Thus so far the expression remains the same as above.

Next consider the subexpression ((c++ - d) * (--e / -f)). To its left we find +=. We compare the precedence of += with the precedence of any operator inside the parentheses (excluding operators inside nested parentheses, in this case ++, -, --, /, and -). We conclude that since += has lower precedence than *, the ()'s are unnecessary. Thus we have

$$(a = (b += (c++ - d) * (--e / -f)))$$

Next, the = operator has the same precedence as the +=, and lower precedence than *. Thus the outer ()'s in (b += (c++ - d) * (--e / -f)) are unnecessary. Finally, we're left with one final set of ()'s surrounding the entire expression, which are clearly unnecessary. Thus our final expression is

$$a = b += (c++ - d) * (--e / -f)$$

Q: How does one "construct" expressions in C?

A: Generally, programmers write expressions in separate pieces, roughly from the inside out (certainly not from left to right!), so that the operations are carried out in the order desired. Along the way, attention is paid to the precedence and associativity rules, and parentheses are introduced where needed. For example, suppose you're taking a college course in C programming (a distinct possibility, since you are reading this!) According to the syllabus, there are two midterms (variables mt1 and mt2), each counting for 20% of the grade. The final exam is worth 25%, and there are five programming assignments (pa1 through pa5), each worth 7%. We assume all the above variables are floats, on a scale of 0 to 10. Late in the term, you know your grades on the midterms and programming assignments, and you begin to wonder how well you need to perform on the final exam to earn a point total of, say, 80.0 (hopefully a grade of B). We first write expressions to calculate and add the point totals for midterms and programming assignments:

```
0.4*(mt1 + mt2) + 0.35*(pa1 + pa2 + pa3 + pa4 + pa5)
```

Next, noting that 0.4 * midterms + 0.35 * assignments + 0.25 * final = 80, we subtract the above expression from 80.0, yielding the point total for the final exam (we distributed the minus sign among the two sum terms, so no extra parentheses are required):

```
80.0 - 0.4 * (mt1 + mt2) - 0.35 * (pa1 + pa2 + pa3 + pa4 + pa5)
```

Finally, we divide the above expression by 0.25 (or alternatively multiply by 4) to obtain the desired (and anticipated!) grade on the final exam. Note that the parentheses are necessary.

```
(80.0 - 0.4 * (mt1 + mt2) - 0.35 * (pa1 + pa2 + pa3 + pa4 + pa5)) * 4
```

4.3   Programming Exercises

1.   Determine the output produced by each of the following printf statements.

```
printf("%d\n", 3-2/4);
printf("%d\n", -27/-5+4/3);
printf("%d\n", 16%-5+7*6);
printf("%d\n", -12*3%2*-23/+6-5*2);
```

2. Determine the output produced by each of the following `printf` statements.

```
printf("%d\n", d += ++a + b++ - --c);
printf("%f\n", x-- *2 + 5);
printf("%d\n", (3%5) / (5%3) );
```

3. Write a program that reads in a number of days, hours, minutes, and seconds, and calculates the total number of seconds.

4. Write a program that will calculate the number of bytes per square inch on a floppy disk. Assume the disk is single-sided. The disk's diameter is 3.5 inches, and it holds 1.4 million bytes. The formula for calculating the area of a circle is $A=\pi r^2$, where r is the radius of the circle, or one-half the diameter.

5. Write a program that will convert the weight of an object from grams to ounces. *Hint*: 35.27 ounces equals 1000 grams.

6. You're taking a computer course. According to the syllabus, there are two midterms, each counting for 20% of the grade. The final is worth 25%, and there are five programming assignments, each worth 7%. Write a complete program that will prompt you for the grade you received on each of these parts of the course (midterms, programming assignments, and final, each on a scale of 0 to 10.0), and will calculate and print your final numerical grade in the course.

7. Modify the previous program as follows. You're about to take the final exam in the course. You know your grades in the two midterms and the five programming assignments. You wish to earn a certain numerical grade, say 90. Modify your program so it will read in the desired total numerical grade and will calculate the grade you need on the final to earn your desired overall total.

8. Write a program to solve the linear equation $ax + b = 0$. The equation's solution is as follows:

$$x = \frac{-b}{a}$$

What happens if we attempt to use a value of zero for *a*?

9. Write a program that will read in a `float` amount and print it as a dollar figure, using a comma to separate thousands, as in $23,456.78. *Hint*: the number of thousands is x / 1000, and x − x / 1000 is what's left.

10. Write a program that will calculate the area for a right-angle triangle, given the lengths of the sides *a* and *b*:

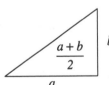

11. How does the C compiler evaluate the expression a+++++a? Specifically, determine the output of
`a=3; printf("%d", a+++++a);`

12. Write a program that will read in the number of seconds since, say, a given Space Shuttle mission began, and will print the number of days, hours, minutes, and seconds into the mission. For example, 397941 seconds amounts to 4 days, 14 hours, 32 minutes, and 21 seconds.

13. An employee is entitled to an annual pension of one-fifth of his last annual salary for each five complete years' service to the company. Thus, after 25 years' service, the pension is 100% of his last salary. Write a program that reads in the last salary, the year and month the employee began work, and the year and month of retirement. The program should calculate and print the annual pension.

14. Implement a simple weekly payroll program. The input will consist of the employee number (an `int`), the number of hours worked (`int`), the hourly rate (a `float`), the federal withholding rate (a `float` representing a percentage, e.g., 15%), the number of overtime hours (an `int`), and the overtime rate (a `float`, e.g., 1.5 times regular pay). Assume one input item per line. Your program should calculate the total gross pay, the FICA (Social Security and Medicare) deduction of 7.65%, the Income Tax Withholding[2], and the net pay (if any!). Here's a suggested output layout for such an employee:

```
C's Payroll:

Employee Number: 34567

Hourly rate of Pay:              $  18.66
Hours Worked:          40
Total Gross Pay:                 $ 746.40
Deductions:
FICA                   $ 53.37
Federal Tax (15%)      $111.96
_____

TOTAL Deductions       $165.33

Net Pay                          $ 581.07
```

_____

2 Feel free to include State Income Tax Withholding in your calculations. Here in Florida we don't have it, and we like to gloat about it!

5   Selection Statements

5.1   Chapter Summary

In programming, we often need the ability to choose between two or more alternatives. C provides *selection* statements to do this. Before examining them, however, we must first discuss logical expressions.

5.1.1   Logical Expressions

A logical expression such as a < b typically appears in a statement (such as the if) that tests the value of the expression and chooses a course of action based on whether the value is "true" or "false." C has no boolean or logical data type for these values. Instead, the numerical values of 0 (false) and 1 (true) are used.

The *relational* operators (<, >, <=, and >=) have their usual mathematical meanings, but they produce 0 or 1 as indicated above. These are binary infix operators, have lower precedence than the arithmetic operators, are left associative, and their order of evaluation is implementation-defined. They don't always behave the way you expect[1]: i < j < k does not test whether j lies between i and k. Instead, the value of i < j (0 or 1) is compared against k.

The *equality* operators (==, !=) are also binary infix, left-associative operators with an implementation-defined order of evaluation. Their precedence is lower than that of the relational operators. Thus a == b < c is equivalent to a == (b < c). Keep in mind that these are integer values, and any arithmetic operation applies to them. For example, assume that variables a, b, and c are expected to have values 1, 2, and 3, respectively. Then the expression (a == 1) + (b == 2) + (c == 3) will produce a count of the variables that have their "correct" value (0, 1, 2, or 3). This kind of programming trick is generally not a good idea: the program is hard to understand, and there are better ways to accomplish what's desired.

The *logical* operators (!, &&, and ||) are used to combine simple logical expressions into more complex ones. ! is a unary prefix, right-associative operator, with the same precedence as the unary + and – operators. && and || are binary infix, left-associative operators, with lower precedence than the equality operators (see the operator precedence table in the main text, page 595). The negation operator ! "toggles" the value of its operand from zero to 1 or from any nonzero value to zero. The "and" operator && produces the value 1 if both its operands are nonzero, and produces zero otherwise. The "or" operator || produces the value 1 if either of its operands is nonzero, and produces zero otherwise. Both && and || have left-to-right order of evaluation: the left operand is evaluated first, and the right operand is evaluated *only if necessary*. For example, (3==4) && expn produces zero (false), without evaluating expn. Similarly, (3==3) || expn produces 1, again without evaluating expn. Whenever using these *short-circuit* operators, you must be careful not to have side effects in the right operand, as those side effects might not take effect.

5.1.2   The if Statement

The if statement comes in two forms:

> if (*expression*) *statement*
> if (*expression*) *statement* else *statement*

These are sometimes called the *one-armed if* and the *two-armed if*. In both cases the first statement is executed if the control expression's value is nonzero; if it's zero, the one-armed if does nothing further, and the two-armed if executes its second statement. In an earlier example, variables a, b, and c were expected to have values 1, 2, and 3, and we wished to count the number of those variables that have the

---

1 By now, you should expect the unexpected in C!

expected values:

```
count = 0;
if (a == 1) count++;
if (b == 2) count++;
if (c == 3) count++;
```

Beware of the following common mistake: writing `if (a = 1) ...` instead of `if (a == 1) ...`. The expression `a = 1` evaluates to 1, causing `count` to be incremented even if a is not 1. In addition, this statement changes a to 1, which was probably not intended.

The statement controlled by the one-armed `if` is *one* statement. Likewise, the two statements controlled by the two-armed `if` are each an individual statement. In C, however, any group of statements can be enclosed in braces (as in { *statements* }), and the result will be treated as one **compound** statement. For example, a program that expects to process a minimum of 10 input items, and return a nonzero completion code if fewer than 10 are processed, might end as follows:

```
if (n < 10) {
  printf("Fewer than 10 items processed!");
  return 1;
} else {
  printf("A minimum of 10 items were processed.");
  return 0;
}
```

The compound statement does not end with a semicolon and can contain statements of any kind inside, including **nested** `if` statements, usually used to further subdivide courses of action. In our last example, we may want to subdivide the case in which fewer than 10 items have been processed, into two subcases: one in which no items were processed at all (return code 2), and one in which at least one item was processed.

```
if (n < 10)
  if (n == 0) {
    printf("No items processed at all !!");
    return 2;
  } else {
    printf("Fewer than 10 items processed!");
    return 1;
  }
else {
  printf("A minimum of 10 items were processed.");
  return 0;
}
```

In programming, courses of action often take on the form of a cascade of conditions, in which we move on to the next condition if the current one is false, and stop as soon as a condition is true. Our example can be reformulated as follows:

```
if (n >= 10) {
  printf("A minimum of 10 items were processed.");
  return 0;
} else
  if (n > 0) {
    printf("Fewer than 10 items processed!");
    return 1;
  } else {
    printf("No items processed at all !!");
    return 2;
  }
```

Like many other languages, C has the *dangling else* problem: if an `else` clause occurs nested inside two or more `if`'s, which `if` does the `else` belong to? The answer, in general, is that the `else` belongs to the most recent `if` statement that hasn't been paired with an `else`, *regardless of indentation*. Braces can be used to override this convention.

In C there is not only a conditional statement (the `if`, used to choose between two statements), but also a conditional operator, which is used to choose between two expressions. Its general form is *expr1* ? *expr2* : *expr3*. This is the only **ternary** operator in C, and it is right associative. The conditional expression's value will be either *expr2* (if *expr1* evaluates to nonzero) or *expr3* (if *expr1* evaluates to zero). Note that only the expression chosen is evaluated; any side effects in the other expression will not take effect.

Finally, in C there is no boolean type, and the numeric values of 0 and 1 for "false" and "true" can be confusing. It is a good idea to define macros for these values, with names like FALSE and TRUE.

5.1.3 The `switch` Statement

Cascades of `if` statements are useful, but often we need to compare the value of one particular expression against several different values, so we can carry out a different task for each value. For example, we might offer the program user a menu of choices. Once the user enters his or her choice, the program must determine which choice was selected by the user, and act accordingly. The *switch* statement in C is a good choice for this type of situation. Its general form is

```
switch ( expression ) {
    case constant-expression : statements
        ...
    case constant-expression : statements
    default : statements
}
```

The `switch` statement operates as follows. First the (integer) control expression is evaluated. Its value is compared with the integer values of the constant expressions, which must all be different. If no match occurs, the `default` statements (if any) are executed. If the control expression's value matches one of the constant expressions, the statements in that case are executed, *as well as the statements for all subsequent cases*, unless a `break` statement is used to "quit" the switch statement. In this sense C differs from some languages you may have encountered before. In other languages, statements similar to `switch` select one alternative, execute that alternative, and quit (i.e., transfer control to the end of the selection statement). In C, once an alternative is selected, the `switch` statement merely transfers control to that alternative. Quitting is the responsibility of the code in that alternative.

The `break` statement is used to quit the current `switch` statement. Normally the last statement in a given case is a `break` statement, so control will transfer to the end of the `switch`. If that case is selected, and its statements contain no `break`, control simply falls through to the next case, ignoring the case label there. If no `break` (or other jump statement) occurs there either, control continues to fall through. The process continues until a `break` is encountered, or all the remaining alternatives are executed. "Falling through" like this is sometimes done deliberately, so several alternatives can share code. Since it is not done very often, it is good idea to document such situations well.

5.2 Solved Exercises

5.2.1 Solved Exercise 1: A Grading Program

We are taking a college course in which we have the following items counting towards the final grade: three homework assignments, each worth 15%; two midterms, each worth 15%; and a final exam worth 25%. We wish to have a menu-driven interaction with the user, through which the user can enter all but one of these grades, and calculate the score necessary on the remaining item. Aside from the usual calculation of the final grade, the program offers the option, say, of calculating the grade needed on the final exam to get the desired final grade. Our first version of the program would look like this:

```
#include <stdio.h>

/***************************************************/
/* This program allows the user to perform grade   */
```

```
/* calculations, based on the following:          */
/*                                                 */
/*    Three homework assignments, each worth 15%.  */
/*    Two midterm examinations, each worth 15%.    */
/*    One final exam, worth 25%.                   */
/*                                                 */
/* The program calculates any one of these items,  */
/* or the final grade, in terms of the other six.  */
/*                                                 */
/***************************************************/

main()
{
/***************************************************/
/* Print menu and obtain user choice for the item */
/* to be calculated.                               */
/***************************************************/

/***************************************************/
/* Input all items except the one chosen.          */
/***************************************************/

/***************************************************/
/* Calculate and print the item chosen.            */
/***************************************************/
}
```

Let's print the menu and obtain the user's choice for the item to be calculated. We'll also check the user's choice and use the exit function if it's out of range.

```
#include <stdio.h>

/***************************************************/
/* This program allows the user to perform grade   */
/* calculations, based on the following:           */
/*                                                 */
/*    Three homework assignments, each worth 15%.  */
/*    Two midterm examinations, each worth 15%.    */
/*    One final exam, worth 25%.                   */
/*                                                 */
/* The program calculates any one of these items,  */
/* or the final grade, in terms of the other six.  */
/*                                                 */
/***************************************************/

main()
{
  int choice;

/***************************************************/
/* Print menu and obtain user choice for the item */
/* to be calculated.                               */
/***************************************************/

  printf("Grade Calculation Program\n\n");
  printf("Please select the item to be calculated:\n");
  printf("  (you'll be asked to enter the others).\n\n");
  printf("Homework #1: (1)\n");
  printf("Homework #2: (2)\n");
  printf("Homework #3: (3)\n");
  printf("Midterm  #1: (4)\n");
  printf("Midterm  #2: (5)\n");
  printf("Final Exam : (6)\n");
  printf("Final Grade: (7)\n\n");
```

```
      printf("Please enter your choice: ");
      scanf("%d", &choice);
      if ((choice < 1) || (choice > 7)) {
        printf("Incorrect Choice !\n");
        return 1;
      }

      /***************************************************/
      /* Input all items except the one chosen.          */
      /***************************************************/

      /***************************************************/
      /* Calculate and print the item chosen.            */
      /***************************************************/
      }
```

Next, to input all items except the one chosen, we could use a switch statement. In each case, we would prompt for, and read, all items except the one for that case. The switch statement might look like this:

```
      switch (choice) {
        1: /* prompt and read homework 2  */
           /* prompt and read homework 3  */
           /* prompt and read midterm 1   */
           /* prompt and read midterm 2   */
           /* prompt and read final exam  */
           /* prompt and read final grade */
        2: /* prompt and read homework 1  */
           /* prompt and read homework 3  */
           /* prompt and read midterm 1   */
           /* prompt and read midterm 2   */
           /* prompt and read final exam  */
           /* prompt and read final grade */
        3: /* prompt and read homework 1  */
           /* prompt and read homework 2  */
           /* prompt and read midterm 1   */
           /* prompt and read midterm 2   */
           /* prompt and read final exam  */
           /* prompt and read final grade */
        4: /* prompt and read homework 1  */
           /* prompt and read homework 2  */
           /* prompt and read homework 3  */
           /* prompt and read midterm 2   */
           /* prompt and read final exam  */
           /* prompt and read final grade */
        /* cases 5, 6 and 7  */
      }
```

Pretty repetitive and monotonous, isn't it? Anytime your code begins to look repetitive like that, it's time to rethink it. One solution would consist of defining seven boolean variables, initialized to TRUE (indicating that all will be read). Then, after the user enters her choice, the one variable chosen is set to FALSE to prevent it from being read. This is done with a switch statement. While that's being done, we can print a nice message confirming to the user the choice she has made. We then proceed to read every item, if it's corresponding flag is TRUE. Finally, we calculate and print the item requested by the user. Here's the final version of the program:

```
#include <stdio.h>

#define TRUE 1
#define FALSE 0
#define HW_PERC 0.15
#define FIN_PERC 0.25
```

```
/*****************************************************/
/* This program allows the user to perform grade    */
/* calculations, based on the following:            */
/*                                                  */
/*     Three homework assignments, each worth 15%.  */
/*     Two midterm examinations, each worth 15%.    */
/*     One final exam, worth 25%.                   */
/*                                                  */
/* The program calculates any one of these items,   */
/* or the final grade, in terms of the other six.   */
/*                                                  */
/*****************************************************/

main()
{
  int choice, hw1_flag = TRUE, hw2_flag = TRUE,
      hw3_flag = TRUE, mt1_flag = TRUE, mt2_flag = TRUE,
      fin_flag = TRUE, grd_flag = TRUE;
  float homework_1, homework_2, homework_3,
     midterm_1, midterm_2, final_exam, final_grade;

/*****************************************************/
/* Print menu and obtain user choice for the item */
/* to be calculated.                              */
/*****************************************************/

  printf("Grade Calculation Program\n\n");
  printf("Please select the item to be calculated:\n");
  printf("   (you'll be asked to enter the others).\n\n");
  printf("Homework #1:  (1)\n");
  printf("Homework #2:  (2)\n");
  printf("Homework #3:  (3)\n");
  printf("Midterm  #1:  (4)\n");
  printf("Midterm  #2:  (5)\n");
  printf("Final Exam :  (6)\n");
  printf("Final Grade:  (7)\n\n");
  printf("Please enter your choice: ");
  scanf("%d", &choice);
  if ((choice < 1) || (choice > 7)) {
    printf("Incorrect Choice !\n");
    return 1;
  }

/*****************************************************/
/* Input all items except the one chosen.           */
/*****************************************************/

  printf("You have chosen to calculate ");
  switch (choice) {
    case 1: hw1_flag = FALSE;
            printf("Homework 1."); break;
    case 2: hw2_flag = FALSE;
            printf("Homework 2."); break;
    case 3: hw3_flag = FALSE;
            printf("Homework 3."); break;
    case 4: mt1_flag = FALSE;
            printf("Midterm 1."); break;
    case 5: mt2_flag = FALSE;
            printf("Midterm 2."); break;
    case 6: fin_flag = FALSE;
            printf("the Final Exam."); break;
    case 7: grd_flag = FALSE;
            printf("the Final Grade."); break;
```

```
      }
      printf("\nYou'll now be asked to enter the other items.\n\n");

      if (hw1_flag) {
        printf("Please Enter Homework #1: ");
        scanf("%f", &homework_1);
      }
      if (hw2_flag) {
        printf("Please Enter Homework #2: ");
        scanf("%f", &homework_2);
      }
      if (hw3_flag) {
        printf("Please Enter Homework #3: ");
        scanf("%f", &homework_3);
      }
      if (mt1_flag) {
        printf("Please Enter Midterm #1: ");
        scanf("%f", &midterm_1);
      }
      if (mt2_flag) {
        printf("Please Enter Midterm #2: ");
        scanf("%f", &midterm_2);
      }
      if (fin_flag) {
        printf("Please Enter Final Exam: ");
        scanf("%f", &final_exam);
      }
      if (grd_flag) {
        printf("Please Enter Final Grade: ");
        scanf("%f", &final_grade);
      }

   /******************************************************/
   /* Calculate and print the item chosen.            */
   /******************************************************/

      switch (choice) {
        case 1:
          homework_1 = (final_grade -
            (homework_2 + homework_3 + midterm_1 + midterm_2) * HW_PERC
            - final_exam * FIN_PERC) / HW_PERC;
          printf("Homework #1 = %5.2f\n", homework_1);
          break;
        case 2:
          homework_2 = (final_grade -
            (homework_1 + homework_3 + midterm_1 + midterm_2) * HW_PERC
            - final_exam * FIN_PERC) / HW_PERC;
          printf("Homework #2 = %5.2f\n", homework_2);
          break;
        case 3:
          homework_3 = (final_grade -
            (homework_1 + homework_2 + midterm_1 + midterm_2) * HW_PERC
            - final_exam * FIN_PERC) / HW_PERC;
          printf("Homework #3 = %5.2f\n", homework_3);
          break;
        case 4:
          midterm_1 = (final_grade -
            (homework_1 + homework_2 + homework_3 + midterm_2) * HW_PERC
            - final_exam * FIN_PERC) / HW_PERC;
          printf("Midterm #1 = %5.2f\n", midterm_1);
          break;
        case 5:
          midterm_2 = (final_grade -
```

```
          (homework_1 + homework_2 + homework_3 + midterm_1) * HW_PERC
          - final_exam * FIN_PERC) / HW_PERC;
        printf("Midterm #2 = %5.2f\n", midterm_2);
        break;
      case 6:
        final_exam = (final_grade -
          (homework_1 + homework_2 + homework_3 + midterm_1 + midterm_2)
          * HW_PERC ) / FIN_PERC;
        printf("Final Exam = %5.2f\n", final_exam);
        break;
      case 7:
        final_grade =
          (homework_1 + homework_2 + homework_3 + midterm_1 + midterm_2)
          * HW_PERC + final_exam * FIN_PERC;
        printf("Final Grade = %5.2f\n", final_grade);
        break;
    }
  return 0;
}
```

Below are the results from a sample run of this program. In this case, we intend to find out our final grade.

```
Grade Calculation Program

Please select the item to be calculated:
  (you'll be asked to enter the others).

Homework #1: (1)
Homework #2: (2)
Homework #3: (3)
Midterm  #1: (4)
Midterm  #2: (5)
Final Exam : (6)
Final Grade: (7)


Please enter your choice: 7
You have chosen to calculate the Final Grade.
You'll now be asked to enter the other items.

Please Enter Homework #1: 78
Please Enter Homework #2: 82
Please Enter Homework #3: 80
Please Enter Midterm #1: 93
Please Enter Midterm #2: 75
Please Enter Final Exam: 87
Final Grade =  82.95
```

Here's a second run. This time, we're close to the end of the term, and we'd like to find out what grade we need on the final exam in order to earn a final grade of 83.0.

```
Grade Calculation Program

Please select the item to be calculated:
  (you'll be asked to enter the others).

Homework #1: (1)
Homework #2: (2)
Homework #3: (3)
Midterm  #1: (4)
Midterm  #2: (5)
Final Exam : (6)
Final Grade: (7)
```

```
Please enter your choice: 6
You have chosen to calculate the Final Exam.
You'll now be asked to enter the other items.

Please Enter Homework #1: 78
Please Enter Homework #2: 82
Please Enter Homework #3: 80
Please Enter Midterm #1: 93
Please Enter Midterm #2: 75
Please Enter Final Grade: 83
Final Exam =  87.20
```

5.3   Programming Exercises

1. Modify the grade calculation program so that it checks against values that are out of range. Have the user specify the range of values, e.g., 0 to 100.

2. Write a program that will read in five values and write them out in ascending order.

3. Write a program that will print a truth table for the logical operators !, &&, and | |. Use two variables and lay out the table as follows:

X	Y	!X	!Y	X&&Y	Y||Y
0	0				
0	1				
1	0				
1	1				

4. The 1996 Federal Income Tax Rate Schedules were as follows:

Condition	Tax
	Filing Status **Single**
$0<TI\le\$24,000$	15% of TI
$\$24,000<TI\le\$58,150$	$\$3,600.00 + 28\%$ of $(TI-\$24,000)$
$\$58,150<TI\le\$121,300$	$\$13,162.00 + 31\%$ of $(TI-\$58,150)$
$\$121,300<TI\le\$263,750$	$\$32,738.50 + 36\%$ of $(TI-\$121,300)$
$\$263,750<TI\le$ -----	$\$84,020.50 + 39.6\%$ of $(TI-\$263,750)$
	Filing Status **Married filing jointly**
$0<TI\le\$40,100$	15% of TI
$\$40,100<TI\le\$96,900$	$\$6,015.00 + 28\%$ of $(TI-\$40,100)$
$\$96,900<TI\le\$147,700$	$\$21,919.00 + 31\%$ of $(TI-\$96,900)$
$\$147,700<TI\le\$263,750$	$\$37,667.00 + 36\%$ of $(TI-\$147,700)$
$\$263,750<TI\le$ -----	$\$79,445.00 + 39.6\%$ of $(TI-\$263,750)$
	Filing Status **Married filing separately**
$0<TI\le\$20,050$	15% of TI
$\$20,050<TI\le\$48,450$	$\$3,007.50 + 28\%$ of $(TI-\$20,050)$
$\$48,450<TI\le\$73,850$	$\$10,959.50 + 31\%$ of $(TI-\$48,450)$
$\$73,850<TI\le\$131,875$	$\$18,833.50 + 36\%$ of $(TI-\$73,850)$
$\$131,875<TI\le$ -----	$\$39,722.50 + 39.6\%$ of $(TI-\$131,875)$
	Filing Status **Head of Household**
$0<TI\le\$32,150$	15% of TI
$\$32,150<TI\le\$83,050$	$\$4,822.50 + 28\%$ of $(TI-\$32,150)$
$\$83,050<TI\le\$134,500$	$\$19,074.50 + 31\%$ of $(TI-\$83,050)$
$\$134,500<TI\le\$263,750$	$\$35,024.00 + 36\%$ of $(TI-\$134,500)$
$\$263,750<TI\le$ -----	$\$81,554.00 + 39.6\%$ of $(TI-\$263,750)$

Write a program that will take Taxable Income (TI) as input, allow the user to select a filing status through a menu, and calculate the amount of tax due (ugh!).

5. Modify the grade calculation program so that the percentages of the various items are input by the user, rather than being fixed.

6. Modify the linear equation program (Exercise 8, Chapter 4) so that it can detect when no solution exists, i.e., when the value of the coefficient *a* is zero. When this happens, print a message saying so.

7. Write a (very) simple calculator program. Take two float numbers as input. Then use a menu to let the user choose between addition, subtraction, multiplication, and division, and print the result. Remember to check for special conditions, such as division by zero.

8. Extend the calculator program in the previous exercise into a "C" calculator, i.e., a program that can perform any of the operations provided by the C language. Specifically, extend the program to handle values of type `int` or `float` (as appropriate), and to handle the following operators: <, >, <=, >=, ==, !=, !, &&, ||, %. Remember to check for problems, such as division by zero, or the fact that the % operator requires integer operands. *Hint:* store all values as `floats`. Whenever an `int` is required, determine whether the fractional part of the number is zero.

9. Extend further the "C" calculator to handle simple expressions, involving three values and two operators, e.g., a *op1* b *op2* c.

10. Modify the grade calculation program so that the `final_grade` variable is a letter: A = 90–100, B = 80–89, C = 70–79, D = 60–69, F = 0–59. Whenever this item is requested, print it as a letter. Whenever some other item is requested, use a menu to input the final grade and print a range (low and high) for the requested item. For example, suppose the user inputs a B (via a menu) as the value of `final_grade` and specifies the following:

    Homework #1: 78
    Homework #2: 82
    Homework #3: 80
    Midterm #1: 93
    Midterm #2: 75

The output should be:

       The Final Exam Grade ranges from 75.20 to 111.20.

This would indicate that a grade of A is impossible, no matter how well the student does on the final exam.

11. Write a program that reads in a positive integer and transforms that integer to binary. This is done by successively dividing the number by 2 and recording the remainder. For example, 13 in binary is 1101, because 13 = 6 * 2 (with remainder 1), 6 = 3 * 2 (with remainder 0), 3 = 1 * 2 (with remainder 1), and 1 = 0 * 2 (with remainder 1). Collecting the remainders in reverse order yields 1101. Assume that there will be at most 8 binary digits.

12. Write a program that will convert a binary number (maximum 8 binary digits) to decimal. From right to left, the binary digits represent the amounts 1, 2, 4, 8, 32, etc. In each position, the amount is added to the total only if the binary digit is 1. For example, 10110 represents (from right to left) 0 + 2 + 4 + 0 + 16 = 22.

13. Write a program that reads in a number and prints that number's absolute value, i.e., –x if x is negative, and x otherwise.

14. Write a program that reads in an integer value and prints a message indicating whether the number is odd or even.

15. Write a program that will take a dollar amount, such as $2436.37, and break it down into bill and coin amounts, i.e., bills for $1000, $100, $50, $20, $10, $5, and $1, and coins: quarters, dimes, nickels, and pennies. Assume a maximum amount of $9999.99. Express the denominations in English, e.g., One $1000 bill, Three $100 bills. Use the conditional expression to print bill or bills.

16. Write a program that reads in a four-digit year and determines whether that year is a leap year. First make sure the number indeed has four digits. Generally, a leap year is divisible by four, with the exception of century years (1800 and 1900 are not leap years). However, century years divisible by 400 *are* leap years (such as 1600 and 2000).

17. Write a program that reads in the lengths of the three sides of a triangle. First, verify that the lengths do form a triangle: adding any two sides should yield a number that exceeds the third. Next, determine if the triangle is equilateral: all sides would have equal length. Next, determine if the triangle is isosceles: two sides have equal length, which is different from the third. Finally, determine if the triangle is right-angled: the sum of the square of two sides would yield the square of the third.

18. Write a program that will read in a large dollar amount and print it using a comma to separate the millions and the thousands, as in $1,437,692.53.

6 Loops

6.1 Chapter Summary

C has three *iteration* or *loop* statements: `while`, `do`, and `for`. All three have a *controlling* expression and a *loop body*. Each is appropriate for different situations, depending on whether there is a counting variable of some kind, and whether it is appropriate to test the controlling expression before or after the loop body. In this chapter we also discuss the `break` statement again (because it works in loops as well in the `switch` statement), the `continue` statement, the `goto` statement, the comma operator, and the null statement.

6.1.1 The `while` Statement

This is the simplest iteration statement in C. Its general form is

> `while` (*expression*) *statement*

The controlling expression is evaluated first. If it is nonzero, the loop body (a single statement, possibly compound) is executed, and the expression is evaluated and tested again. If the expression's value is zero, the loop ends. The iteration will continue as long as the expression continues to evaluate to a nonzero value; if it never becomes zero, then the program will continue looping indefinitely. Loop termination can depend on the controlling expression, the loop body, both, or neither. Consider

> `while (--n) printf("%d\n", n);`

Here the loop body changes nothing, particularly n; the expression itself changes n with each iteration. Assuming n starts out as a positive value, this loop will terminate after printing 1; if n starts as zero or less, the loop will go on forever (or at least until the next power failure!). This vulnerability to the infinite loop can be removed by explicitly testing for a positive value:

> `while (--n > 0) printf("%d\n", n);`

Now the value tested is the 1 or 0 that results from comparing n (after decrementing it) with zero. If n starts out as a negative number or zero, the loop will do nothing—it will iterate zero times. Thus, regardless of the initial value of n, this loop will terminate eventually.

Sometimes an infinite loop is written deliberately, as in the idiom `while (1) { ... }`. In these cases we usually rely on some other statement (or function call) to break out of the loop, such as `break`, `goto`, or `return`. The `while` statement is known as a *top-tested* loop, and it works well in situations where the iteration could take place as few as zero times. For example, we might want to read integers until a zero is read:

```
scanf("%d", &n);
while (n) {
    ...
    scanf("%d", &n);
}
```

This loop might do nothing, if the first input value is zero.

6.1.2 The `do` Statement

The do statement is similar to the `while` statement:

> `do` *statement* `while` (*expression*)

The loop body is executed first, and thus at least once. Then the expression is evaluated and tested: if zero, the loop quits; if nonzero, the loop body is executed again and the expression re-evaluated for another test. This is known as a *bottom-tested* loop. It works well in situations where the iteration

should take place at least once. In particular, it is a good way to read integers until the value zero (or some other *sentinel* value) is read:

```
do {
   scanf("%d", &n);
   ...
} while (n != 0);
```

6.1.3   The `for` Statement

This is the most powerful iteration statement in C. It works well when the iteration has a "counting" variable. Its general form is:

$$for \ (\ expr1 \ ; \ expr2 \ ; \ expr3 \ ) \ statement$$

expr1 is the *initialization* expression, which usually assigns an initial value to a "counter." It is evaluated only once, and its value discarded, before the iteration begins. *expr2* is top tested: if it is "true" (nonzero) then the loop body (*statement*) is executed, followed by *expr3* and a return to test *expr2* again. If *expr2* evaluates to "false" (zero), the loop terminates. The value of *expr3* is also discarded; its purpose is normally to increment or decrement the counter.

A number of common forms of the `for` statement are often used; they are called idioms. Here's one that "counts up" from n to m:

```
for (i = n; i <= m; i++) { }
```

If it's not possible to count "up" from n to m (i.e., if n > m) the loop will execute zero times. If n and m have the same value, the loop will execute once. We assume that the loop body doesn't change i or m. Although it is legal to change these values in the loop body, it is generally not a good idea, because the effect upon the iteration can be drastic: incrementing i could make the loop "skip" values; changing i to a value greater than m could "abort" the loop; decrementing i would produce an infinite loop. Changing m in the loop body could have similar effects. In all these cases, there are better (and clearer) ways to get the job done. In fact, some languages (most notably Pascal) prohibit modification of the loop counter. There are no such prohibitions in C. This is yet another reason C is known as an error-prone language, in which you can easily shoot yourself in the foot. Aim carefully.

All three expressions in the `for` statement are optional, but not the semicolons that separate them. If *expr1* is absent, then no initialization takes place. If *expr3* is absent, then either the loop body or *expr2* will have to increment or decrement the counter. Finally, if *expr2* is absent, we assume a default value of 1 (true), which causes an infinite loop. A common form is `for (;;) { }`; to break out of the infinite loop we'll need a `break`, `return`, or `goto` statement.

The comma operator is a binary, infix, left-associative operator, whose precedence is the lowest of all operators and whose order of evaluation is left to right. Its general form is

$$expr1 \ , \ expr2$$

expr1 is evaluated first and its value is discarded. Then *expr2* is evaluated, and its value is the result of the comma operation. Normally *expr1* has side effects, otherwise its evaluation serves no purpose. Its most common use is in `for` loops, to initialize or increment/decrement more than one variable. For example, we may wish to count from 1 to n with one variable, and simultaneously from n to 1 with another variable:

```
for (i = 1, j = n; i <= n; i++, j--) { ... }
```

6.1.4   Exiting from a Loop

There are a number of ways to exit from a loop. The `break` statement transfers control out of the innermost `while`, `do`, `for`, or `switch` statement. Note that I said "*the* innermost," meaning that if these statements are nested, the `break` escapes from only one level of nesting. The `break` statement is a good way to abort an iteration—much better, for example, than fiddling with variables that are used in the loop's controlling expression.

The `continue` statement is similar to the `break` statement, but its use is restricted to loops (`while`, `do`, `for`, but not `switch`), and its purpose is to abort only the current iteration, not the entire loop. It transfers control to a point *just before* the end of the loop body. In our previous example, we counted simultaneously from 1 to n with `i`, and from n to 1 with `j`. We might wish to skip the iteration in which `i` matches `j` (which, incidentally, happens only if n is odd):

```
for (i = 1, j = n; i <= n; i++, j--) {
  if (i == j) continue;
  ...
}
```

The `goto` statement transfers control to any statement in the current function[1] as long as that statement has been identified with a *label*. This is in contrast with the `break` and `continue` statements, which transfer control to specific points in the program. A label is allowed on any statement:

identifier : statement

The `goto`'s general form is:

goto identifier ;

Use of the `goto` statement is rarely justified. It has few restrictions and can therefore wreak havoc. For example, a `goto` can transfer from the outside of a compound statement, a loop statement, or an `if` statement, to a point anywhere inside that statement, bypassing initializations and causing a great deal of confusion. Even if one avoids such nasty situations, most of the time one of the other, more disciplined control transfer statements (`break` and `continue`) is better suited to one's needs. In certain situations, the `goto` *can* be helpful. It can be used to break out of nested loops, whereas the `break` cannot. Still, good programmers use the `goto` only as a last resort. Too many `goto`s cause the program to look like a bowl of spaghetti, making it almost impossible to understand.

6.1.5 The Null Statement

A statement can be *null*, or empty except for the semicolon. The most common use for the null statement is to use it as a loop body. For example, in the loop

```
for (sum = 0, i = 1; i <= N; sum += i, i++)
  ;
```

we accomplish both initializations with a comma, and both the sum and the increment in the third expression. This leaves nothing to be done in the loop body; hence the null statement.

Null statements can cause problems. Since they are legal anywhere a nonnull statement could appear, a stray semicolon can change the program's meaning considerably. C programmers usually take steps to let any null statement stand out, such as placing it on a separate line (as above), or replacing the null statement with a dummy `continue` statement or an empty compound statement.

6.2 Solved Exercises

6.2.1 Solved Exercise 1: Loan Amortization

Let's develop a program that will help us decide whether to lease or buy a car. Now of course this is not just a matter of dollars and cents: if we absolutely love the car, we'll find a way to afford it, won't we? There's a beautiful model XXX (fill in your dream model) that's worth $16,999.00. Under the lease option, we can lease the car for two years or for three years, paying $300.00 a month. At the end of two years, if we so desire, we can pay $12,749.25 (75% of the original purchase price) and keep the car. After three years, keeping it will cost $11,049.35 (65% of purchase price). Under the purchase

---

1 So far, our only function is `main`.

option, we would borrow 100% (our bank really likes us and requires no down payment), and we can finance the car over four years, or five years. Our friendly banker tells us that to finance $16,999.00 over four years, at today's interest rate of 9.0%, the monthly payment will be $423.03. The five-year loan will have a monthly payment of $352.87.

So, the question is, is it worth it to make a higher monthly payment and purchase the car instead of leasing it? Before we decide, we need to know the loan balance at the end of two years and three years for each of the two types of loans. For this, we need to write a computer program. We begin by determining the input and the output of the program, and the major steps.

```c
#include <stdio.h>

/**************************************************************/
/* This program reads in a loan amount, an interest rate,   */
/* and a monthly payment, and prints an amortization table, */
/* listing the loan balance at the end of each period.      */
/**************************************************************/

main()
{
    float balance, interest, payment;

/**************************************************************/
/* Read in balance, interest rate, and payment.             */
/**************************************************************/


/**************************************************************/
/* Loop to calculate and print the remaining balance at     */
/* the end of each period.                                  */
/**************************************************************/
}
```

In refining the program, we read in the balance, the interest, and the monthly payment. Then, in the final step, we need a while loop to calculate the remaining balance at the end of each period. In each iteration, we calculate the actual interest charged with the expression (balance * interest / 12), because we assume the interest was entered as an annual rate. We add this interest amount to balance and subtract payment from the result to obtain the new balance, which we print out. We use an integer variable to count the periods and to format the output nicely. The loop goes on until the balance becomes zero or less. Below is the final version, along with a test run for each of the two types of loans.

```c
#include <stdio.h>

/**************************************************************/
/* This program reads in a loan amount, an interest rate,   */
/* and a monthly payment, and prints an amortization table, */
/* listing the loan balance at the end of each period.      */
/**************************************************************/

main()
{
    float balance, interest, payment;
    int i;

/**************************************************************/
/* Read in balance, interest rate, and payment.             */
/**************************************************************/

    printf("Amortization Table Program:\n\n");
    printf("Enter starting balance: ");
    scanf("%f", &balance);
    printf("Enter interest rate: ");
```

```
   scanf("%f", &interest);
   printf("Enter monthly payment: ");
   scanf("%f", &payment);

/****************************************************************/
/* Loop to calculate and print the remaining balance at     */
/* the end of each period.                                   */
/****************************************************************/

   i = 0;
   printf("\nAmortization Table:\n\n");
   printf("Period    Balance\n");
   printf("-------------------\n");
   while (balance > 0) {
      i++;
      balance = balance + (balance * interest / 12) - payment;
      printf("%5d  %10.2f\n", i, balance);
   }
   return 0;
}
```

Amortization Table Program:

Enter starting balance: 16999
Enter interest rate: 0.09
Enter monthly payment: 423.03

Amortization Table:

Period	Balance
1	16703.46
2	16405.71
3	16105.72
4	15803.48
5	15498.98
6	15192.19
7	14883.10
8	14571.70
9	14257.96
10	13941.86
11	13623.39
12	13302.54
13	12979.28
14	12653.59
15	12325.46
16	11994.88
17	11661.81
18	11326.24
19	10988.16
20	10647.54
21	10304.37
22	9958.62
23	9610.28
24	9259.32
25	8905.74
26	8549.50
27	8190.59
28	7828.99
29	7464.68
30	7097.64
31	6727.84
32	6355.27
33	5979.90
34	5601.72
35	5220.70
36	4836.83
37	4450.07
38	4060.42
39	3667.84
40	3272.32
41	2873.83

Amortization Table Program:

Enter starting balance: 16999
Enter interest rate: 0.09
Enter monthly payment: 352.87

Amortization Table:

Period	Balance
1	16773.62
2	16546.55
3	16317.78
4	16087.30
5	15855.08
6	15621.13
7	15385.41
8	15147.93
9	14908.67
10	14667.62
11	14424.76
12	14180.07
13	13933.55
14	13685.18
15	13434.95
16	13182.84
17	12928.85
18	12672.94
19	12415.12
20	12155.36
21	11893.66
22	11629.99
23	11364.34
24	11096.71
25	10827.06
26	10555.39
27	10281.69
28	10005.93
29	9728.11
30	9448.20
31	9166.19
32	8882.07
33	8595.81
34	8307.41
35	8016.85
36	7724.10
37	7429.16
38	7132.01
39	6832.63
40	6531.01
41	6227.12

```
   42     2472.36              42     5920.95
   43     2067.87              43     5612.49
   44     1660.35              44     5301.71
   45     1249.77              45     4988.61
   46      836.12              46     4673.15
   47      419.36              47     4355.33
   48       -0.53              48     4035.12
>                              49     3712.52
>                              50     3387.49
>                              51     3060.03
>                              52     2730.11
>                              53     2397.71
>                              54     2062.83
>                              55     1725.43
>                              56     1385.50
>                              57     1043.02
>                              58      697.97
>                              59      350.34
>                              60        0.09
>                              61     -352.77
>                   >
```

The balances at the end of the loan periods are not zero, because the monthly payment is specified only to two decimal places. This caused one of the runs to produce one extra iteration.

We now have the answers to our questions: the balances after two years are \$9,259.32 and \$11,096.71. The balances after three years are \$4,836.83 and \$7,724.10. It would appear that the slightly higher monthly payments for buying the car are worth it.

6.2.2   Solved Exercise 2: The Chess Knight's Moves

Let's develop a program that will draw a chess board and plot the legal positions that a chess knight could move to. In chess, the knight is one of the most versatile pieces. It is the one piece that can "jump" over other pieces (of either color, in fact). The knight's move is L-shaped: one or two squares horizontally, plus one or two squares vertically. It must travel farther in one direction than the other, so that after moving two squares horizontally, it can move only one square vertically. Obviously, moving to positions off the board is not allowed. Our program will read the knight's position (two integers, each between 1 and 8), and plot the entire chess board, including the knight, and the (maximum) eight legal positions it can move to. We'll assume the board is otherwise empty. For example, if we input values 3 and 7, we'd get the following:

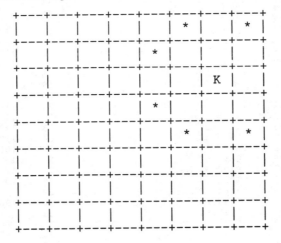

The knight is indicated by a K in row 3, column 7, and each of the legal positions it can move to are indicated with stars. Two of the eight maximum positions are off the board and not displayed. Our first design decision has to do with how to print a table like the one above. We have two options:

```
/* Print the first row of +---+'s       */
for (line = 1; line <= NROWS; line++) {
   /* Print one row of vertical bars,       */
```

```
      /* with stars or a K where appropriate  */
      /* Print one row of +---+'s              */
   }
```

In this first option, we have the disadvantage of having to write twice the code to print one row of +---+'s. Changing the for to a do or while won't help much. In the second option, the loop controlling the rows iterates from 1 to 17, not from 1 to 8. Inside the loop, odd-numbered rows contain +---+'s, and even-numbered rows contain vertical bars, stars, and the K. This alternative has the disadvantage of row not being the actual row number, which we will have to compute in each iteration. We'll stick with the second alternative. Here's the first version of the program:

```
#include <stdio.h>

#define NROWS 8
#define NCOLS 8

main()
{
   int knight_row, knight_col;
   int line, row, col;

   printf("Chess Knight Program\n");

   /*********************************/
   /* Read knight_row, knight_col   */
   /* until they are both in range. */
   /*********************************/

   /*********************************/
   /* Print 2 * NROWS + 1 rows      */
   /*********************************/

   for (line = 1; line <= 2 * NROWS + 1; line++) {
      row = line / 2;
      if (line % 2 != 0) {
         /**********************************************/
         /* Odd line number: print one row of +---+'s  */
         /**********************************************/
      }
      else {
         /**********************************************/
         /* Even line number: print one row of vertical*/
         /* bars, with '*'s and a K where appropriate. */
         /**********************************************/
      }
   }
   return 0;
}
```

Obtaining the knight's row and column from the input offers a good opportunity to use the do loop. To print a row of +---+'s, we first print one + and then repeatedly print ---+. A line of vertical bars is handled in a similar way, using a for loop to iterate through the columns. In each column, we will determine whether to print a *, a K, or leave that square empty. At this stage the program would be expected to print an empty chess board; it would be prudent to test the program thoroughly before refining it further. Thus the second version:

```
#include <stdio.h>

#define NROWS 8
#define NCOLS 8

main()
```

```
{
  int knight_row, knight_col;
  int line, row, col;

  printf("Chess Knight Program\n");

  /*********************************/
  /* Read knight_row, knight_col   */
  /* until they are both in range. */
  /*********************************/

  do {
    printf("Enter knight's coordinates: ");
    scanf("%d %d", &knight_row, &knight_col);
  } while ((knight_row < 1) || (knight_row > NROWS) ||
           (knight_col < 1) || (knight_col > NCOLS));

  /*********************************/
  /* Print 2 * NROWS + 1 rows      */
  /*********************************/

  for (line = 1; line <= 2 * NROWS + 1; line++) {
    row = line / 2;
    if (line % 2 != 0) {
      /**************************************************/
      /* Odd line number: print one row of +---+'s  */
      /**************************************************/
      printf("+");
      for (col = 1; col <= NCOLS; col++)
        printf("---+");
      printf("\n");
    }
    else {
      /**************************************************/
      /* Even line number: print one row of vertical*/
      /* bars, with '*'s and a K where appropriate. */
      /**************************************************/
      printf("|");
      for (col = 1; col <= NCOLS; col++) {

        /*******************************************/
        /*   If a K belongs here, print it.        */
        /*******************************************/

        /*******************************************/
        /*   If a '*' belongs here, print it.      */
        /*******************************************/

        /*********************************************/
        /*  Print a vertical bar if slot not filled. */
        /*********************************************/
      }
      printf("\n");
    }
  }
  return 0;
}
```

Finally, we reach the heart of the matter. Inside the last `for` loop, we have the *current* position on the board, given by `row` and `col`. First, we print K if these coordinates match those of the knight itself, which are `knight_row` and `knight_col`. Next, to determine whether the current position is a knight's move away from the knight, we need two nested for loops, each from −2 to 2. Inside the inner loop, we specifically exclude the cases in which the two indices are equal (excluding their sign), and whenever either index is zero. If a star or K is printed, we set a boolean variable `filled` to TRUE. If not, we print spaces. Here's the final version of the program:

```c
#include <stdio.h>

#define NROWS 8
#define NCOLS 8
#define FALSE 0
#define TRUE  1

main()
{
  int knight_row, knight_col;
  int line, row, col, i, j;
  int filled;

  printf("Chess Knight Program\n");

  /*******************************/
  /* Read knight_row, knight_col */
  /* until they are both in range. */
  /*******************************/

  do {
    printf("Enter knight's coordinates: ");
    scanf("%d %d", &knight_row, &knight_col);
  } while ((knight_row < 1) || (knight_row > NROWS) ||
           (knight_col < 1) || (knight_col > NCOLS));

  /*******************************/
  /* Print 2 * NROWS + 1 rows    */
  /*******************************/

  for (line = 1; line <= 2 * NROWS + 1; line++) {
    row = line / 2;
    if (line % 2 != 0) {
      /*********************************************/
      /* Odd line number: print one row of +---+'s */
      /*********************************************/
      printf("+");
      for (col = 1; col <= NCOLS; col++)
        printf("---+");
      printf("\n");
    }
    else {
      /*********************************************/
      /* Even line number: print one row of vertical*/
      /* bars, with '*'s and a K where appropriate. */
      /*********************************************/
      printf("|");
      for (col = 1; col <= NCOLS; col++) {
        filled = FALSE;

        /*********************************************/
        /*   If a K belongs here, print it.          */
        /*********************************************/
        if ((row == knight_row) && (col == knight_col)) {
          printf(" K |");
          filled = TRUE;
          continue;
        }

        /*************************************************/
```

```
          /*   If a '*' belongs here, print it.        */
          /*********************************************/
          for (i = -2; i <= 2; i++) {
            for (j = -2; j <= 2; j++) {
              if ((i == j) || (i == -j) || (i == 0) || (j == 0)) continue;
              if ((knight_row + i == row) && (knight_col + j == col)) {
                printf(" * |");
                filled = TRUE;
              }
            }
          }

          /***********************************************/
          /*  Print a vertical bar if slot not filled.  */
          /***********************************************/
          if (!filled) printf("   |");
        }
        printf("\n");
      }
    }
  return 0;
}
```

Here's some sample output of the knight program.

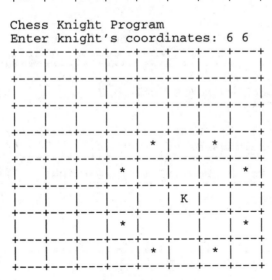

6.3   Programming Exercises

1. In this exercise, we'll try to achieve the simulation of a watch using integers.
    (a) Write a program that counts to 10,000.
    (b) Run your program a few times and use your watch to determine how long it takes for each run. Record your results.
    (c) Write a program to read in the numbers obtained in (b) and calculate the average time your computer takes to count to 10,000. *Note:* if you are working under a multi-user operating system such as UNIX, your timings may be skewed due to the presence and activities of other users. Try this exercise when no one's around. If you work on a PC, you have the machine to yourself!
    (d) Expand your program to calculate how many integers your machine can count in 1 second.
    (e) Write a timer program in C. The program should take as input the number of seconds to count. It should wait that many seconds, and then beep you several times. When you complete your program, reward yourself by using the value 1200 to take a 20-minute nap.
    (f) Extend your program to allow a "snooze" feature. After the requisite time has passed, and the user beeped, continue beeping at one-minute intervals. Use this feature to make sure you get back to work after your 20-minute siesta.

2. Write a program that will print the first n numbers in the Fibonacci sequence and their quotients. The first two Fibonacci numbers are 1 and 1. The third (and all subsequent) Fibonacci numbers are the sum of the previous two. Thus the Fibonacci sequence is 1, 1, 2, 3, 5, 8, 13,. . . . The quotient of a Fibonacci number is the result of dividing it by its predecessor in the sequence: 1.0, 2.0, 1.5, 1.666, 1.6, 1.625, ...This sequence is known to converge (i.e., to come arbitrarily close) to the "golden mean," which is $(1+\sqrt{5})/2$. Use your program to print this real number with at least 8 decimal digits.

3. Write a program that reads in a positive integer N and prints out all combinations of 3 numbers that add up to N. *Hint:* use 3 nested `for` loops.

4. The factorial function is defined by f(n) = n (n − 1)(n − 2) . . . (3) (2) (1). Write a program that will read in a positive integer n and calculate the factorial of n. Be careful. The factorial function can produce very large numbers.

5. Write a simple calculator program for complex numbers. Each complex number has two components of type `float`: the *real* part, and the *imaginary* part, as in 3.1 + 4.3*i*. *i* is the imaginary unit value, $\sqrt{-1}$. To add or subtract two complex numbers, add or subtract respectively their real and imaginary parts, i.e., $(a + bi) + (c + di) = (a + c) + (b + d)i$. To multiply, $(a + bi)(c + di) = (ac - bd) + (ad + bc)\,i$. Finally, to divide,

$$\frac{(a+bi)}{(c+di)} = \frac{(bd+ac)}{c^2+d^2} + \frac{(cb-ad)}{c^2+d^2}\,i$$

6. In the finals of the Olympic 100-meter race, qualifying times are used to allocate the eight available lanes for the runners. The runner with the fastest qualifying time races in lane 4, the second fastest in lane 5, the next in lane 3, the next in lane 6, then 2, etc. Write a program that will read in up to eight qualifying times, labeling the runners A through H in the order in which they are input. Your program should then print a schedule for the final race, showing each runner and his or her qualifying time in the correct lane.

7. Write a program that will print a variety of triangle-based shapes, each of a size specified by the user, such as these:

```
*       *           *       *  ***** *****  *           *  *********
* *     * *         * *      * *  *  *  * *  ** **  **       * *  **** ****
***     *  *        ***      *  *     *    *  *  *  ***       *** ***      ***
****    *  *        ****     *  *    *  *   ** **  ****  ****  **        **
*****  *****  *****  *****  *****  *****  *********  *           *
```

Here the size requested was 5. Use `for` loops to print these figures.

8. Write a program that will read in `float` numbers until the value read in is zero, then average the numbers.

9. A vending machine sells coffee or tea for $0.25. Cream, sugar, and extra sugar can be added for $0.05 apiece. Write a program that will simulate this vending machine. First, accept coins from the user (user enters integers 5, 10, or 25, which are verified), until the user enters zero. Then give the user a choice (with a menu) for coffee or tea. Then ask whether cream, sugar, or extra sugar are desired. If the amount deposited is sufficient, simulate dispensing the item, and give change if necessary. If the amount deposited is not sufficient, give the user a chance to add money.

10. Write a program that will print a truth table for three boolean variables. You'll need three nested loops. Use your program to ascertain whether the following are tautologies (propositions that are always true).

$$((p \ || \ q) \ \&\& \ r) \ == \ ((p \ \&\& \ r) \ || \ (q \ \&\& \ r))$$
$$((p \ || \ q) \ \&\& \ r) \ == \ ((p \ || \ q) \ \&\& \ (p \ || \ r))$$

11. Modify the chess knight program so that a board of any size (not just 8x8) will be handled. Also, insert two additional loops so the program will print the knight (and all its possible moves) for every position on the board, i.e., 64 boards in all. After printing each board, stop to read a dummy value from the input. Let the user press <Return> repeatedly and watch a "movie" of the knight taking a walk (row by row) through the board, surrounded by a cloud of stars, except when the knight is in the vicinity of the board's edges, where portions of the cloud disappear into the space outside the board!

12. In the knight program presented earlier, there are two `continue` statements. Remove each of them in turn. What happens? Are the `continue` statements necessary? What purpose do they serve?

13. A procedure known as the Newton-Raphson method allows us to calculate the square root of a positive real number a as follows: start with x = 1.0. Then set y = (x + a / x) / 2. If x and y are not yet close enough, then set x = y and recalculate y. Stop when the difference between x and y is small enough to be negligible. Write a program to calculate the square root of a given number this way. Your program should read both a and the desired tolerance, e.g., 0.0001.

14. Write a program similar to the knight program for the chess queen. In chess, the queen can travel any distance in any one direction.

15. Write a program that will take as input a sequence of single-digit integers, count how many times each digit occurs, and print a histogram of the results. For example, with the input:

```
3 1 4 2 6
9 6 7 1 6
3 1 9
6 7 0
```

the output should be:

```
                6
   1            6
   1    3       6 7      9
   1 2 3 4      6 7      9
   =================
   1 2 3 4 5 6 7 8 9
```

since there were three 1's, one 2, two 3's, etc. If any digit occurs more than ten times, print an error message and halt the program.

16. Write a program that will read in two integers n and m, and calculate two sums: all the odd numbers between n and m, and all the even numbers between n and m.

17. Write a program that reads an integer *n* and prints a triangle with *n* lines, like so:

You will need a double `while` loop for this.

18. Write a program that will input a number of items for an invoice as follows: quantity, item number, price, and discount percentage. Your program should read these items repeatedly, until quantity = 0 is read in, and then print an invoice. The program should add a 6% sales tax and compute a total. Here's a suggested layout:

```
C'S RETAIL MART

Quantity Item  Price   Ext. Price Discount  Total

    3      32  $24.50   $73.50      0.0%    $73.50
    1      68  $ 7.15   $ 7.15      2.0%    $ 7.01
    2      91  $16.99   $33.98      3.0%    $32.96

                        Sub-total  $113.47
                       Sales Tax (6%)  $   6.81

                           Total   $120.28
```

19. Write a program that will input a number *n* and will print a table of squares, cubes, and quartics from 1 to *n*. Arrange the numbers in neat columns. The output should look like this:

```
Number    Square    Cube    Quartic
-------------------------------------
  1          1         1         1
  2          4         8        16
  3          9        81       243
  .  .  .
```

20. Modify the program in the previous exercise to print a table of inverse powers, i.e.,

```
Number  1/Square  1/Cube   1/Quartic
-------------------------------------
  1       1.0      1.0       1.0
  2       0.25     0.125     0.0625
  3       0.11     0.012     0.0041
  .  .  .
```

21. Write a program that transforms a binary number to decimal. A binary number such as 10111 breaks down as follows:

$$1 * b^4 + 0 * b^3 + 1 * b^2 + 1 * b^1 + 1 * b^0 = 16 + 4 + 2 + 1 = 23,$$

where $b = 2$ is the base of binary numbers. To evaluate this without using exponentiation, we use Horner's rule, which results from factoring out b a number of times (in this case 4):

$$1 * b^4 + 0 * b^3 + 1 * b^2 + 1 * b^1 + 1 =$$
$$(1 * b^3 + 0 * b^2 + 1 * b^1 + 1) * b + 1 =$$
$$((1 * b^2 + 0 * b^1 + 1) * b + 1) * b + 1 =$$
$$(((1 * b + 0) * b + 1) * b + 1) * b + 1$$

Notice that in evaluating this expression from the inside out, we are processing the digits of the binary number from left to right. Below is the iterative scheme for doing this, written in *pseudocode*. You translate it into C!

> Total = Binary_digit_1;
> Total is multiplied by two, and Binary_digit_2 is added to it;
> Total is multiplied by two, and Binary_digit_3 is added to it;
> ...
> Total is multiplied by two, and Binary_digit_n is added to it;

22. Write a program that reads in an integer n and determines whether n is prime. A simple way to do this is to test every number i between 1 and n − 1, to see if i divides n (it will if i % n is zero). Try also the faster version of this algorithm, which stops examining values of i as soon as i * i exceeds n.

23. Modify your prime number program above to find out how many prime numbers there are between 2 and 1000. Is this number prime? Is the number of prime numbers between 2 and 10,000 prime?

24. Write a program that reads in an integer and produces the *prime decomposition* of that number. The prime decomposition of a number is the list of prime numbers that "multiply up" to it. For example, 19950 = 2 * 3 * 5 * 5 * 7 * 19. Notice that a prime number can appear more than once. Starting with i=2, determine whether i is in the prime decomposition of N: (i % N == 0). If it is, then divide N by i and try again. When i no longer divides N, increment it and continue. Stop when N becomes 1.

25. Write a program that will read in numeric grade values for a group of students. Ignore (but identify to the user) values that are not between 0 and 100. Count the values above or equal 90 (a grade of A), those between 80 and 90 (a B), those between 70 and 80 (a C), those between 60 and 70 (a D), and those below 60 (an F). Report the totals in each category, with the percentage of the total that each number represents.

7 Basic Types

7.1 Chapter Summary

The four principal basic types in C are int, float, double, and char. Additional basic types can be obtained by *qualifying* these types with qualifiers such as long, short, signed, and unsigned. The sizeof operator measures the amount of storage required for a given type. typedef is used to create new names for types.

7.1.1 Integer Types

Integer types are signed or unsigned, short or long. Any combination of these is allowed:

signed short int	signed int	signed long int
short int	int	long int
unsigned short int	unsigned int	unsigned long int

The three types on the first line of the above table are the same as those on the second line, because the default is signed whenever not specified. This leaves a total of six types. The range of values for these types is machine-dependent. On 16-bit machines, short and int typically occupy 16 bits, and long 32 bits. On 32-bit machines, typical sizes are 16 bits for short, and 32 bits for both int and long. Generally, if we have n bits, the range of values is from -2^{n-1} to $2^{n-1}-1$ for signed types, and from 0 to 2^n-1 for unsigned types. Typical actual ranges of these values are shown in the main text, page 111.

Integer constants can be written in decimal (no leading zeroes allowed), octal (begin with one zero) or hexadecimal (begin with 0x). It's important to note that numbers are stored internally in binary, regardless of the base in which we express them in C. A constant is normally of type int, if its value lies within that range; if not, it is taken to be of type long. You can force the constant to be of type long or unsigned by following the constant with any combination of the letters L, l, U, or u. To read or write these new types, there are special conversion specifiers in scanf and printf.

- To read or write an unsigned int, use the conversion letters u (unsigned), o (octal), or x (hexadecimal). The usual d is for signed integers.
- To read or write a short int, add h in front of the conversion letter: hd, hu, ho, or hx.
- To read or write a long int, add l in front of the conversion letter: ld, lu, lo, or lx.

7.1.2 Floating Types

There are three floating types: float, double, and long double. On most machines, float provides about 6 decimal digits of precision, and double about 15. This takes care of most needs. long double is rarely used, but typically provides between 80 and 128 bits, or some 16 to 30 decimal digits. The ANSI C standard says little about the precision required, but the above figures are typical for machines that comply with the IEEE Floating-Point Standard, a standard for computer hardware. Some specific typical values are shown in the main text, page 115.

Floating constants must contain at least one decimal point or an exponent. Thus 3E3 and 3000.0E0 denote the same value. The exponent is specified with the letter E (or e) and may optionally contain a sign (+ or −). By default, floating constants are of type double. To specify otherwise, add F (or f to indicate type float), or add L (or l, to indicate long double) to the end of the constant, e.g., 3.1E2L. To read a value of type double, use the conversion letters le, lf, or lg. This is *only* for scanf; in printf, conversions e, f, and g work with both float and double. To read or print a long double, use the letter L instead: Le, Lf, and Lg.

7.1.3 Character Types

The representation of characters in C is machine-dependent, although most computers today use the ASCII code. Character variables can be declared as signed, unsigned, or neither. Some compilers treat `char` as unsigned, with values normally ranging between 0 and 255. Other compilers treat `char` as signed, with values between -128 and 127. You should make no assumptions in this regard: non-portable programs can result. Character constants are specified using single quotes, as in `'a'` or `'#'`. In C, characters are treated as small integers, most often stored in one byte. For example, in the ASCII code, `'A'` has the value 65, and `'a'` has the value 97. Characters can appear anywhere that integers can; C simply uses the character's integer value. Thus, characters can be added, subtracted, compared, incremented, assigned, and so on. Expressions such as `'a' * '#'` make little sense but are legal. Often we wish to compare characters: the expression `('A' <= c) && (c <= 'Z')` yields true if c is an upper-case letter, but only if we assume that these letters have consecutive values in the character code being used. In the ASCII code, letters are indeed consecutive, but a better alternative would be to use the library function `isupper(c)`. Several other convenient functions are available in the character processing library; to access them, you need the include directive `#include <ctype.h>` at the top of your program. We also frequently increment characters: the statement `if (++c > 'Z') c = 'A';` will increment c and wrap around back to `'A'` if c has moved beyond `'Z'`.

There are a number of *escape sequences* that allow the specification of special characters. Earlier we used `'\n'`. A complete table of escape sequences is given in the main text on page 119. Still, these don't cover all the nonprinting ASCII characters, so C provides *numeric escapes*. These can be specified in octal (`'\44'` or `'\044'`) or hexadecimal (`'\x2C'`). To read and write characters, we can use `scanf` and `printf` with the `%c` conversion specification. C also provides `getchar` and `putchar`, which are considerably faster and are also available in the library header `<stdio.h>`. They are often more convenient, especially `getchar`, which returns the value of the single character it reads and is the basis of a number of idioms:

```
■ while (getchar() != '\n') ;  /*skips rest of line */
■ while ((ch = getchar()) == ' ') ;  /*skips spaces */
■ while (!isdigit(ch = getchar())) ; /*skips until first digit */
■ while (!isalpha(ch = getchar())) ; /*skips until letter*/
■ while (!isalnum(ch = getchar())) ; /*skips until alphanumeric*/
■ while ((ch = getchar() != EOF)) statement /* process every character*/
                                    /* until end of file */
```

The `isdigit`, `isalpha`, and `isalnum` functions examine the character given, return 1 if the character is a digit, a letter, or alphanumeric character, respectively, and return zero otherwise. To use these functions, you'll have to use the directive `#include <ctype.h>` at the beginning of your program. `getchar` is a function, about which more will be said later. It returns the value of the next character on the input. When there's no next character, `getchar` returns EOF, a macro (more on that later, too) whose value is -1.

7.1.4 The `sizeof` Operator

The `sizeof` operator may be used to determine the size of a data object or type, measured in storage units, which is defined as the amount of storage occupied by one character (1 byte). It has two general forms:

```
sizeof ( type-name )
sizeof expression
```

If the operand is an expression, the parentheses are not required, but it's a good idea to include them because of potential problems with operator precedence.

7.1.5   Type Conversion

C allows mixing of the basic types in operations. In doing so, however, conversions from one type to another are often necessary to enable the computer to perform the operation. A common situation is `'a' + 1`. Here adding a character and an integer poses no great problem, because the character is stored as an integer anyway. A more complex situation arises in the expression `3.6 + 4`, in which we are adding an `int` and a `float`. Since integers and floats are stored differently, an actual conversion will have to take place. Such conversions can be ***implicit*** (taken care of automatically), or ***explicit*** (specified by the programmer) using the ***cast*** operator. Implicit conversions are performed in the following two situations:[1]

1. The operands in an arithmetic or logical expression have different types. Here C will perform the usual arithmetic conversions.
2. The left side and the right side of an assignment have different types. Here C will convert the right operand into the type of the left operand.

The usual arithmetic conversions operate by ***promoting*** the narrower operand to the type of the other operand. We have three cases:

1. ***integral promotions***: a `char` or `short` is converted to `int`.
2. Either operand is a floating type. Here we promote the narrower operand (which could be an integer type) along the sequence `float` → `double` → `long double`.
3. Neither operand is a floating type. Here we first perform integral promotions and then promote the narrower operand along the sequence `int` → `unsigned int` → `long int` → `unsigned long int`.

In general, it's dangerous to mix signed and unsigned integers. Thus, unsigned integers should be avoided if possible. For assignments, C simply converts the right operand to the type of the left operand. If the left operand is wide enough, there will usually be no problem. For example, converting a `float` to an `int` usually means dropping the fractional part. However, if the `float` value is too large to fit in an `int`, you may get a meaningless value, or even a run-time error.

The programmer can specify conversions explicitly using the cast operator:

$$(\text{type-name}) \ \text{expression}$$

Casts are often used to document conversions that would take place implicitly anyway. More often, casts are used to force conversions that wouldn't normally take place. For example, if `x` is a float and `n = 13` is an `int`, the assignment `x = n/10` will not assign `1.3` to `x`. Instead, the result of `n/10` will be the integer 1, which is converted to 1.0, a floating number. To fix the problem, we must make sure that the floating division operator is carried out. Any of the following will do: `x = (float) n / 10;`, `x = n / (float) 10;`, `x = n / 10.0;`. The following will *not* do: `x = (float)(n / 10);`. Casts are also sometimes used to avoid overflow. For example, when multiplying two short integers, the result may be too large for a short. Casting one of the shorts into an `int` will avoid the problem.

7.1.6   Type Definitions

C provides a means for defining the name of a type as a synonym for an existing type:

`typedef` *old_type_name new_type_name*

Type definitions are used for a variety of purposes. One of them is to make programs more readable. In the same program, we may have floating values that represent currency and other floating values that represent interest rates. These could be identified separately with

```
typedef float Dollars;
typedef float Interest_rate;
```

---

1 There are actually four situations. The other two have to do with sending and returning values from functions, and will be covered in a later chapter.

Later, declarations are easier to understand:

```
Dollars balance, deposits;
Interest_rate Rate_6months, Rate_12months;
```

The type definition has another advantage. If in the future it becomes necessary to change the type of currencies, from `float` to `double`, for example, the change can be effected in one place in the program, without having to search through the entire program for all the places where such variables are declared. The need for such a change is by no means far-fetched: it happens quite often when porting a program to another computer installation.

7.2   Solved Exercises

7.2.1   Solved Exercise 1: A Word Analysis and Counting Program

Many programs (such as spell-checkers) take as input an entire text file. Such programs must divide up the input text into units, such as words, delimiters, and punctuation characters. A program of this nature is called a scanner. Let's write a program called "wac" (word analysis and count). When "wac" runs, it will print on a separate line each word it encounters in the input, discard delimiters and punctuation marks, handle comments, and count (a) the number of characters, (b) the number of words, and (c) the number of lines processed from the input file. When it has completed scanning the input file, "wac" will produce a report on the number of characters, words, and lines processed.

As happens often in computer programming, the above specification of the program we're about to write is quite vague and imprecise. We need some definitions.

- *word*: a sequence of length one or more characters, each of which is either a letter or a decimal digit.
- *letter*: characters `'a'` through `'z'` and `'A'` through `'Z'`.
- *decimal digits*: characters `'0'` thru `'9'`.
- *delimiter*: a space, a tab, or new-line character.
- *punctuation mark*: any of the following: , . : ; _ " - ? ! ( ) { } [ ]
- *comment*: a sequence of characters starting with a forward slash (`'/'`), and ending with a new-line character (`'\n'`).
- *illegal character*: any character not covered by the previous definitions.

Our definition of *word* doesn't exactly match that of *word* in the English language. For example, "hand-held bag" will be considered three words ("hand," "held," and "bag"). Comments are to be excluded from the scanning process: if we encounter `'/'` in the input file, we will then look for the next end-of-line character (`'\n'`). Every character between the `'/'` and the new-line, inclusive, should be included in our character count, but should be otherwise ignored. Thus, inside comments we do not count words, but we do count the line in which the comment occurs. Characters within a comment are not checked for validity by any other rule. For example, `'#'` is neither a letter nor a digit nor a delimiter, but is nonetheless okay in a comment. If we encounter an error (an invalid character, such as `'#'` or `'''`), we will not terminate the program. We will instead produce an error message such as "`ERROR! Illegal character (X).`," and skip the offending character.

The first issue in designing our program is how to handle the input characters systematically. According to the program specification, characters are handled in different ways depending on the situation. For example, a letter will be printed if it is part of a word, but will be discarded if it occurs inside a comment. Our first version of the program is as follows:

```
#include <stdio.h>

main()
{
  int inchar, nchars = 0, nwords = 0, nlines = 0;

  while ((inchar = getchar()) != EOF) {
  nchars++;
```

```
/************************************************/
/* Process inchar. If appropriate, print inchar or  */
/* new-line and increment nwords, nlines.            */
/************************************************/
}
/************************************************/
/* Report nchars, nwords, nlines.                   */
/************************************************/
}
```

The difficult part is to determine exactly when it is appropriate to increment variables, and especially when to print the current character and/or the new-line character, or an error message. A table covering all the possible combinations[2] should help us design our program. As we process the input characters, we will be at all times in one of three "states":

1. IN_WORD: currently processing a word. Sometime earlier a letter or digit was encountered, and nothing but letters and digits have been encountered since. Those characters have all been printed. If the next character is a letter or digit, it will form part of the current word. If not, the current word will be finished.
2. OUT_WORD: currently in between words. We are no longer in the middle of a word. The last character could have ended a comment, or ended a word, or been a delimiter or punctuation mark. If the next character is a letter or digit, it will begin a new word. If the next character is '/', it will mark the beginning of a comment. If it is a delimiter or punctuation mark, we will remain in our current state.
3. IN_COMMENT: currently in the middle of a comment. Sometime earlier a slash ('/') was encountered. Since then, every character encountered has been different from '\n' and has been ignored (except for counting it). If the next character is '\n', it will mark the end of the current comment. If not, the current comment will continue.

Given these three states, we can consider in turn the appropriate action for each of the various possibilities for the next character:

Input character	STATE		
	IN_WORD	OUT_WORD	IN_COMMENT
letter or digit	putchar(inchar) nc++ state=IN_WORD	putchar(inchar) nc++ state=IN_WORD	nc++ state=IN_COMMENT
.,:;[]{}() etc.	putchar(\n) nc++ nw++ state=OUT_WORD	nc++ state=OUT_WORD	nc++ state=IN_COMMENT
\n	putchar(\n) nc++ nw++ nl++ state=OUT_WORD	nc++ nl++ state=OUT_WORD	nc++ nl++ state=OUT_WORD
/	putchar(\n) nc++ nw++ state=IN_COMMENT	nc++ state=IN_COMMENT	nc++ state=IN_COMMENT
all others	putchar(\n) ERROR nw++ nc++ state=OUT_WORD	ERROR nc++ state=OUT_WORD	nc++ state=IN_COMMENT

This table confirms our earlier observation that `nchars` is to be incremented for every character.

The next design decision to be made consists of choosing the selection statements. We have two alternatives. The first alternative is to nest `if` statements within a `switch` statement.

---

2 This table encodes a mechanism called a finite-state automaton.

```
switch (state) {
  case IN_WORD:
    if (isalnum(inchar)) { /*...*/ }
    else if ((inchar == '.') || (inchar == ',')
             /* ... */      || (inchar == ')') { /*...*/ }
    else if ((inchar == '\n')) { /*...*/ }
    else if ((inchar == '/'))  { /*...*/ }
    else { /*...*/ }
  case OUT_WORD:
    if (isalnum(inchar)) { /*...*/ }
    else if ((inchar == '.') || (inchar == ',')
             /* ... */      || (inchar == ')') { /*...*/ }
    else if ((inchar == '\n')) { /*...*/ }
    else if ((inchar == '/'))  { /*...*/ }
    else { /*...*/ }
  case IN_COMMENT:
    if (isalnum(inchar)) { /*...*/ }
    else if ((inchar == '.') || (inchar == ',')
             /* ... */      || (inchar == ')') { /*...*/ }
    else if ((inchar == '\n')) { /*...*/ }
    else if ((inchar == '/'))  { /*...*/ }
    else { /*...*/ }
}
```

This alternative has the advantage of being fairly easy to read, but does nothing to take advantage of actions common to various alternatives. The second alternative (our preference) nests `switch` statements within an `if` statement. It is a little less compact, but it exploits commonalities between various actions.

```
if (isalnum(inchar))
  switch (state)  {
    case IN_WORD:
    case OUT_WORD:  /* ... */
    case IN_COMMENT:
  }
else if ((inchar == ',') /* ... */) || (inchar == ')'))
  switch (state) {
    case IN_WORD:
    case OUT_WORD:   /* ... */
    case IN_COMMENT:
  }
else if ((inchar == '\n'))
  switch (state) {
    case IN_WORD:
    case OUT_WORD:   /* ... */
    case IN_COMMENT:
  }
else if ((inchar == '/'))
  switch (state) {
    case IN_WORD:
    case OUT_WORD:   /* ... */
    case IN_COMMENT:
  }
/* Anything else must be an invalid character */
else
  switch (state)  {
    case IN_WORD:
    case OUT_WORD:   /* ... */
    case IN_COMMENT:
  }
```

Now to finish off the program. Some of the entries in the table are not necessary in the program (such as changing the state to IN_COMMENT when already there). For others, the entries across a row in

the table share common actions. For example, if inchar == '/', the state is changed to
IN_COMMENT regardless of its previous value, and the current word terminated only if we are currently
in a word. To encode the three possible values of the current state, we use symbolic constants, for which
we arbitrarily chose the values 1, 2, and 3. A program of this nature must be well documented: we've
added a thorough description at the beginning, including the state table. The three counting variables
are initialized to zero, and clearly, the initial state is OUT_WORD. Finally, reporting the values of the
three counting variables at the end of the program is a straightforward matter. Here's the final version of
the program.

```c
#include <stdio.h>
#include <ctype.h>

#define IN_WORD      1
#define OUT_WORD     2
#define IN_COMMENT   3

/***************************************************************/
/* Description: Program that loops to process all input       */
/* characters. Letters are formed into words while delimiters */
/* are ignored. Any invalid characters encountered are        */
/* reported as errors. Also ignored are any comments, denoted */
/* by a slash, up to the eol. Invalid characters within       */
/* comments are ignored, and do not produce an error message. */
/*                                                            */
/* The program itself is organized based on a finite-state    */
/* automaton structure, shown in the table below.             */
/*                                                            */
/* Note the abbreviations:                                    */
/*                                                            */
/* ch: inchar                                                 */
/* nc: number of chars                                        */
/* nw: number of words                                        */
/* nl: number of lines                                        */
/* st: state                                                  */
/***************************************************************/
/* Input         IN_WORD        OUT_WORD        IN_COMMENT     */
/* char                                                       */
/*------------------------------------------------------------*/
/* letter        putchar(ch)    putchar(ch)     nc++          */
/*   or          nc++           nc++            st=IN_COMMENT  */
/* digit         st=IN_WORD     st=IN_WORD                    */
/*------------------------------------------------------------*/
/* .,:;[]{}()    putchar(\n)    nc++            nc++          */
/* etc.          nc++ nw++      st=OUT_WORD     st=IN_COMMENT  */
/*               st=OUT_WORD                                  */
/*------------------------------------------------------------*/
/* \n            putchar(\n)    nc++            nc++          */
/*               nc++ nw++ nl++ nl++            nl++          */
/*               st=OUT_WORD    st=OUT_WORD     st=OUT_WORD    */
/*------------------------------------------------------------*/
/* /             putchar(\n)    nc++            nc++          */
/*               nc++ nw++      st=IN_COMMENT   st=IN_COMMENT  */
/*               st=IN_COMM                                   */
/*------------------------------------------------------------*/
/* all           putchar(\n)    ERROR           nc++          */
/* others        ERROR          nc++            st=IN_COMMENT  */
/*               nw++ nc++      st=OUT_WORD                   */
/*               st=OUT_WORD                                  */
/***************************************************************/
```

```
main()
{
  int inchar;
  int nchars = 0, nwords = 0, nlines = 0;
  int state;
  state = OUT_WORD;      /* initial state */

  /****************************************************************/
  /* Loop through input file, reading one character at a time.*/
  /****************************************************************/

  while ((inchar = getchar()) != EOF) {
    nchars++;
    /***********************************************/
    /* Check if inchar is a letter or digit.     */
    /***********************************************/
    if (isalnum(inchar))
      switch (state)  {
        case IN_WORD: case OUT_WORD:
          putchar(inchar);
          state=IN_WORD;
          break;
        case IN_COMMENT:
          break;
      }

    /***********************************************/
    /* Check if inchar is punctuator, space, or tab.*/
    /***********************************************/
    else if ((inchar == ',')  || (inchar == '.')  || (inchar == ':') ||
             (inchar == ';')  || (inchar == '_')  || (inchar == '"') ||
             (inchar == '-')  || (inchar == '?')  || (inchar == '!') ||
             (inchar == '(')  || (inchar == ')')  || (inchar == '{') ||
             (inchar == '}')  || (inchar == '[')  || (inchar == ']') ||
             (inchar == ' ')  || (inchar == '\t'))
      switch (state) {
        case IN_WORD:
          putchar('\n');
          nwords++;
        case OUT_WORD:
          state = OUT_WORD;
          break;
        case IN_COMMENT:
          break;
      }

    /***********************************************/
    /* Check if inchar is new-line.              */
    /***********************************************/
    else if ((inchar == '\n'))
      switch (state) {
        case IN_WORD:
          putchar('\n');
          nwords++;
        case OUT_WORD: case IN_COMMENT:
          nlines++;
          state = OUT_WORD;
          break;
      }

    /***********************************************/
    /* Check if inchar begins a comment.         */
    /***********************************************/
```

```
          else if ((inchar == '/'))
            switch (state) {
              case IN_WORD:
                putchar('\n');
                nwords++;
              case OUT_WORD: case IN_COMMENT:
                state = IN_COMMENT;
                break;
            }

          /***********************************************/
          /* Anything else must be an invalid character. */
          /***********************************************/
          else
            switch (state)  {
              case IN_WORD:
                putchar('\n');
                nwords++;
              case OUT_WORD:
                printf("ERROR!!! Illegal character (%c).\n", inchar);
                state = OUT_WORD;
                break;
              case IN_COMMENT:
                break;
            }
      }

    printf("\n\nNumber of characters: %d\n", nchars);
    printf("Number of words:      %d\n", nwords);
    printf("Number of lines:      %d\n", nlines);
    return 0;
}
```

Sometimes we wish to have a program take input from a file rather than the keyboard, and send output to a file rather than the screen. Most operating systems allow this, including UNIX and MS-DOS. If we place the input data for our program in a file called `data.in`, we can then run our program and send the output to a file called `data.out`, with the following command: *prog* `< data.in >` `data.out`.

7.3   Programming Exercises

1. Write a line-numbering program that will copy its own input to the output, character by character, except that it will insert a line number at the beginning of each line. Try your program on its own source code!

2. The phone company assigns three letters to each digit except 0 and 1 (ABC to 2, DEF to 3, etc.). There can be over two thousand combinations of letters that correspond to one seven-digit phone number, so we'll limit ourselves to the last four digits in the phone number. Write a program that translates a four-digit numeric phone number into all possible alphabetic forms. Translate 0 and 1 into a space. You'll need four nested loops for this, to generate all possible combinations. Print them out at the rate of ten combinations per line.

3. Write a program that copies its input to its output, but capitalizes all letters.

4. Write a program that will print the sizes (using `sizeof`) of the various integer, floating, and character types on your implementation of C.

5. Write a program that will read in numbers in decimal and print them out, including the sign, in octal and hex.

6. Modify the loan amortization program in Chapter 6 so it stops printing the amortization table every 20 lines and prompts the user with `Press <Enter> to Continue:`.

7.   Write a program that checks for proper capitalization in a piece of text. After each period, question mark, or exclamation point, your program should scan (skipping spaces, tabs, and new-line characters) until the next letter and print an error message if that letter is not capitalized. Include the current line number and character number in the error message.

8.   In cryptography, one of the simplest ciphers is known as a monoalphabetic shift cipher. In this cipher, each time a letter appears in the original message (called the *plain text*), it is replaced by a unique letter from the substitution alphabet, in which the letters are shifted to the right by a certain number of positions. For example, the alphabet may be shifted by 20 positions:

     Original alphabet: ABCDEFGHIJKLMNOPQRSTUVWXYZ
     Substitution alphabet: GHIJKLMNOPQRSTUVWXYZABCDEF

The resulting message is called the *cipher text*. To make things more difficult for an eavesdropper, punctuation is removed and the cipher text is written in groups of five letters to hide the spaces that indicate individual words. Write a program that will take its input (until EOF), remove all nonletters, and then print the cipher text equivalent using the above alphabets. For example, with the input

```
I came, I saw, I conquered!
```

the cipher text would be

```
Oigsk OygcO Iutwa kxkj.
```

Make sure the shift amount is handled as a symbolic constant, so the encryption scheme can be easily changed.

9.   Write a program that will decode the cipher text of the previous exercise.

10. Write a simple version of the more utility, which is used to display files one screenful at a time. After printing each screenful, use getchar to stop, and prompt for the next screenful. Quit if the user enters q.

11. Write a program that checks for double and triple keystrokes in a piece of text. Each character should be compared to its predecessor and to the character before that. Print out a warning message for any two consecutive identical characters and an error message for any three consecutive identical ones. Include the current line number in every message.

12. Write a program that reads in characters until the end-of-file and reports on the number of each kind of character encountered: letters, digits, punctuation marks, and others.

13. Explain the behavior of the following program:

```
#include <stdio.h>
main() {
    unsigned char c;
    c = EOF;
    if (c == EOF)
        printf("YES");
    else
        printf("NO");
}
```

Hint: what happens if we remove the unsigned qualifier?

14. Explain the behavior of the following program.

```
#include <stdio.h>
main() {
    printf("31+51 equals %d\n", 31 + 51);
}
```

15. Write a program that will print out the values of the following constants provided by limits.h:

CHAR_BIT,   SCHAR_MIN,   SCHAR_MAX,   UCHAR_MAX,

SHRT_MIN,   SHRT_MAX,   USHRT_MAX,   INT_MIN,

INT_MAX,   UINT_MAX,   LONG_MIN,   LONG_MAX,

ULONG_MAX,   CHAR_MIN,   CHAR_MAX

Extend your program so it can help you find out what happens when you go beyond these values. Use a menu to let the user choose one of these types, and then add (or subtract) first a small number, then a large number, to the limit value.

16. Consider the following program:

```
#include <stdio.h>
main() {
    char c;
    int a;
    printf("sizeof(c)       = %d\n", sizeof(c));
    printf("sizeof('c')     = %d\n", sizeof('c'));
    printf("sizeof(c = 'c') = %d\n", sizeof(c = 'c'));
    printf("sizeof(a + 7)   = %d\n", sizeof(a + 7));
    printf("sizeof(a + 7.2) = %d\n", sizeof(a + 7.2));
}
```

Write down the output you would expect from this program, and then run it.

17. Write a program that will help you determine the effect of casting a value of one basic type to another in your implementation. First, let the user choose the type to be cast, using a menu. Then read the value to be cast. Then let the user select the target type, and finally print the resulting value.

18. Consider the following program:

```
#include <stdio.h>
main() {
    unsigned short a, b;
    unsigned int   c, d;
             int   e, f;
    float diff;
    a = 1; c = 1; e = 1;
    b = 2; d = 2; f = 2;

    diff = a - b;
    printf("difference of unsigned shorts = %.1f\n", diff);
    diff = c - d;
    printf("difference of unsigned ints   = %.1f\n", diff);
    diff = e - f;
    printf("difference of          ints   = %.1f\n", diff);
}
```

Study this program and predict its output. Then run it.

8 Arrays

8.1 Chapter Summary

Arrays are our first example of **aggregate** variables: variables that can contain more than one value. Arrays are **homogeneous**, meaning every element in the array has the same type. In a later chapter we will discuss **structures**, which are **heterogeneous** aggregate variables that can contain values of different types.

8.1.1 One-Dimensional Arrays

An array is declared by giving the type of the array elements and their number. For example,

```
#define ARRAY_LENGTH 10
int a[ARRAY_LENGTH];
```

declares an array of 10 elements. The number of elements must be given by a constant expression; the use of a symbolic constant is a good idea in general. The elements of the array are numbered from 0 to N−1, where N is the number of elements declared:

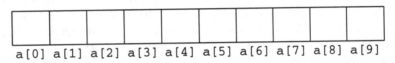

To refer to an individual array element, we use the expression a[*expr*], where *expr* has an integral value. The brackets [ ] constitute the **subscripting** operator, which has the highest precedence of all operators in C.[1] Each array element is a separate variable and can be handled in all the same ways as ordinary variables can, including assigning a value to it, comparing it, reading and printing it, and performing arithmetic operations as appropriate for the array type.

One of the most common activities with an array is to perform an activity for each element in it. The for loop is ideal for this, since the lower and upper bounds of the iteration are usually known in advance:

```
/* Print every other array element, backwards */
for (i = N - 1; i >= 0; i = i - 2)
  printf("%5d", a[i]);

/* Sum the array elements with odd values */
for (i = 0; i < N; i++)
  sum = sum + (a[i] % 2 ? a[i] : 0)

/* Shift the array elements to the right. */
/* a[N] is lost.                          */
for (i = 0; i < N - 1; i++)
   a[i+1] = a[i];
```

With arrays, you must always be careful about subscripts going out of range. In the last example above, if the loop condition had been i < N, then the assignment a[N] = a[N−1] would have taken place. Unfortunately, a[N] is one element beyond the end of the array. The assignment would obediently attempt to change whatever memory location is adjacent to the array, often with disastrous consequences. **Warning**: the result of accessing such out-of-bounds memory locations is *undefined*. Anything can happen, including a system crash. Quite often, however, the memory location in question holds some other variable. In that event, the behavior of the program may seem outright bizarre, with variables

---

1 Other operators we'll cover later, such as ->, have the same precedence as [ ].

seemingly changing at random. This type of error is very difficult to track down, so it's best to avoid it in the first place.

It is legal for the subscript expression to have side effects, but the side effects can easily take place at the wrong time and are best avoided if possible. For example, the above `for` loop that shifts the array elements could be rewritten as follows:

```
i = 0;
while (i < N - 1)
    a[i] = a[i++];
```

The intent is reasonable: evaluate `a[i++]`, which increments `i`, and then store the result in `a[i]` with the new value of `i`. However, recall that the order of evaluation of the operands of the assignment (=) operator is implementation-defined. The order of events could well be: evaluate `a[i]` on the left (thereby determining the location to be assigned), evaluate `a[i++]`, and increment `i`. The result is that each array element is copied to itself, a fantastic waste of time.

Arrays can be initialized when they are declared, with a list of constant values enclosed in braces:

```
int a[10] = {9,8,7,6,5,4,3,2}
```

If the list is shorter than the array, the rest of the array is filled with zeroes. In the example above, `a[0]` through `a[7]` get values 9 through 2; `a[8]` and `a[9]` are both initialized to 0. If we omit the length of the array, the length of the initializer is used to determine the length of the array.

The `sizeof` operator can be used to determine the number of bytes used by an array. When divided by the size of an array element, it yields the number of elements in the array without resorting to a symbolic constant:

```
sizeof(a) / sizeof(a[0])
```

This expression can be used in place of a symbolic constant.

8.1.2   Multidimensional Arrays

Arrays of any number of dimensions are allowed in C. A two-dimensional array is declared with

```
int a[3][5];
```

This array has three rows and five columns:

	0	1	2	3	4
0					
1					
2					

To access an individual array element, we use the expression `a[i][j]`, where $0 \leq i \leq 2$ and $0 \leq j \leq 4$. **Warning**: in many other languages, subscripting a two-dimensional array is done using a comma: `a[i,j]`. In C, the comma operator has a completely different meaning. In fact, `a[i,j]` is the same as `a[j]`, so beware.

In C, arrays are stored in *row-major* order; that is, the elements of the array are strung out in a single stream of memory locations, with the last dimension in the declaration varying first. Thus, the above array appears as

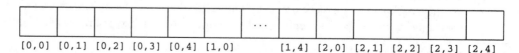

| | | | | | | ... | | | | | | |
| [0,0] | [0,1] | [0,2] | [0,3] | [0,4] | [1,0] | | [1,4] | [2,0] | [2,1] | [2,2] | [2,3] | [2,4] |

Multidimensional arrays can be initialized, with nested initializer lists:

```
int a[3,5]={ {1,0,1,0,1}, {0,1,0,1,0}, {1,0,1,0,1}}
```

Each nested initializer list corresponds to one row, as shown below.

	0	1	2	3	4
0	1	0	1	0	1
1	0	1	0	1	0
2	1	0	1	0	1

If a nested initializer list is not long enough, the rest of the row in question will be filled with zeroes. If there are not enough nested initializer lists, the remainder of the entire array will be filled with zeroes. Finally, if the the nested braces are not provided, the array will be simply be filled in row-major order, and if not enough values are provided, the rest of the array will be filled with zeroes.

Any array can be specified as a constant by preceding its declaration with the word const. This is a good idea if the array is not supposed to be modified by the program. For example, a sliding scale of commissions for salespeople might be described with two arrays:

```
const int volume[5] = {1000, 3000, 5000, 10000, 25000};
const float commission[5] = {1.0, 1.5, 2.0, 2.5, 3.5};
```

8.2 Solved Exercises

In this section we'll solve two exercises. The first exercise involves arithmetic on very large numbers, so large that none of the scalar types can represent them. We'll use arrays to store these numbers. In the second exercise, we'll write a program that sorts some numbers in ascending order.

8.2.1 Solved Exercise 1: Very Large Numbers

Here's a simple question: what exactly is the factorial of 1000? Recall that the factorial of n, denoted n!, is n (n − 1) (n − 2) . . . 1, and 1! = 1. Try this on a hand-held calculator: 1 * 1 = 1, 1 * 2 = 2, 2 * 3 = 6, 6 * 4 = 24, 24 * 5 = 120, etc. The factorial function grows very fast: you don't need to go very far before you begin to exceed your calculator's precision. For example, my calculator says 13! = 6.227020e+09, but the actual value is 6,227,020,800. A couple of digits have been lost already. In C, even with variables of type long double, we can aspire at most to some 30 digits. Surely 1000! has many more than that. So precisely how many digits does 1000! have, and what are they? Let's write a program to find out.

We will store our large number in an array of integers called large. Each array entry will hold one digit of the large number. The least significant digit will reside in large[0]. The "empty" portion of the array will be filled with zeroes. For example, the configuration below shows the result of calculating 8! = 40,320. The last nonzero digit is in large[last_digit], we have just incremented current_n from 8 to 9, and we are about to calculate 9!.

To calculate 9!, we must multiply the number residing in `large` by `current_n`. The method employed is the tried-and-true multiplication method taught in grammar school.[2] Starting at `large[0]`, and moving left, we multiply `current_n` by each digit in `large`, replacing the digit in `large` with the least significant digit in the product obtained, and carrying over an amount to the next column. The result is

```
MAXSIZE-1                                5   4   3   2   1   0
     +---+---+---+---+---+     +---+---+---+---+---+---+
     | 0 | 0 | 0 | 0 | 0 | ... | 3 | 6 | 2 | 8 | 8 | 0 |
     +---+---+---+---+---+     +---+---+---+---+---+---+


        +---+                                         +---+
        | 5 |                                         | 9 |
        +---+                                         +---+
       last_digit                                  current_n
```

This multiplication scheme still works when `current_n` goes beyond 10 or even 100: the carry is at most ten times the value of `current_n`, and thus fits in an `int`. In our first version of the program, we'll allocate an array of 1000 digits. Some systems may find this to be an array too large to handle. Some tests on your own system might be helpful.

```c
#include <stdio.h>

#define MAXSIZE 1000
#define MAXFACT 1000

/*******************************************************/
/* Program to calculate the factorial of MAXFACT.   */
/*******************************************************/

main()
{
  int large[MAXSIZE] = {0};
  int n, index, carry, product, last_digit;

  large[0] = 1;
  last_digit = 0;

  /*******************************************************/
  /*   Process each value of n, from 1 to MAXFACT.   */
  /*******************************************************/
  for (n = 1; n <= MAXFACT; n++) {

    /*******************************************************/
    /*   Calculate digits 1 through 'last_digit'       */
    /*******************************************************/
    carry = 0;
    for (index = 0; index <= last_digit; index++) {
      product = large[index] * n + carry;
      large[index] = product % 10;
      carry = product / 10;
    }

    /*******************************************************/
    /*   Take the carry past 'last_digit';  strip the */
    /*   digits off 'carry' until it becomes zero.    */
    /*   Careful: here we can exceed the array bounds.*/
    /*******************************************************/
    while (carry) {
```

---

2 Thought you'd never run into this stuff again, eh? In fact, just to bring back fond memories of digits carried to the left, the array is shown right to left, instead of the usual left to right.

```
        /***********************************************/
        /* Peel the least significant digit off carry, */
        /* place it in large[index], and increment     */
        /* 'index'. If index goes out of bounds, print */
        /* an error message and break out of the loop. */
        /***********************************************/
      }
      last_digit = index - 1;

        /***********************************************/
        /*   Print large number at 50 digits per line. */
        /***********************************************/


    }
    return 0;
}
```

To finish the program, we write the code in the loop that takes the carry past last_digit. Each time we increment index, we check it in case it's gone out of bounds. If it has, we break out of the loop, and set panic to TRUE, so the outer loop can tell when array bounds have been exceeded and abort the entire computation. Finally, we use line_counter to print the large numbers at the rate of 50 per line.

```
#include <stdio.h>

#define MAXSIZE 3000
#define MAXFACT 1000
#define FALSE 0
#define TRUE  1

/******************************************************/
/* Program to calculate the factorial of MAXFACT.    */
/******************************************************/

main()
{
  int large[MAXSIZE] = {0};
  int n, index, carry, product, last_digit, line_counter, panic;

  panic = FALSE;
  large[0] = 1;
  last_digit = 0;

    /*****************************************************/
    /*   Process each value of n, from 1 to MAXFACT.    */
    /*****************************************************/
  for (n = 1; n <= MAXFACT; n++) {

      /***********************************************/
      /*   Calculate digits 1 through 'last_digit'   */
      /***********************************************/
    carry = 0;
    for (index = 0; index <= last_digit; index++) {
      product = large[index] * n + carry;
      large[index] = product % 10;
      carry = product / 10;
    }

      /***************************************************/
      /*   Take the carry past 'last_digit';  strip the */
      /*   digits off 'carry' until it becomes zero.    */
      /*   Careful: here we can exceed the array bounds.*/
      /***************************************************/
```

```
    while (carry) {
      /************************************************/
      /* Peel the least significant digit off carry,  */
      /* place it in large[index], and increment      */
      /* 'index'. If index goes out of bounds, print  */
      /* an error message and break out of the loop.  */
      /************************************************/
      large[index] = carry % 10;
      carry = carry / 10;
      index++;
      if (index >= MAXSIZE) {
        printf("OUT OF SPACE\n");
        panic = TRUE;
        break;
      }
    }
    last_digit = index - 1;

    if (panic) break;

    /************************************************/
    /*  Print large number at 50 digits per line.   */
    /************************************************/
    line_counter = 0;
    printf("%d! has %d digits:\n", n, last_digit + 1);
    for (index = last_digit; index >= 0; index--) {
      printf("%1d", large[index]);
      line_counter++;
      if (line_counter % 50 == 0) printf("\n");
    }
    printf("\n\n");

  }
  return 0;
}
```

As you can see in the code, our initial estimate of 1000 digits was far from adequate for calculating 1000!. This program produces a prodigious amount of output. Here's the last large number it prints:

```
1000! has 2568 digits:
40238726007709377354370243392300398571937486421071
46325437999104299385123986290205920442084869694048
00479988610197196058631666872994808558901323829669
94459099742450408707375991882362772718873251977950
59509952761208749754624970436014182780946464962910
56393887437886487337119181045825783647849977012476
63288983595573543251318532395846307555740911426241
74743493475534286465766116677973966688202912073791
43853719588249808126867838374559731746136085379534
52422158659320192809087829730843139284440328123155
86110369768013573042161687476096758713483120254785
89320767169132448426236131412508780208000261683151
02734182797770478463586817016436502415369139828126
48102130927612448963599287051149649754199093422215
66832572080821333186116811553615836546984046708975
60290095053761647584772842188967964624494516076535
34081989013854424879849599533191017233555566021394
50399736280750137837615307127761926849034352625200
01588853514733161170210396817592151090778801939317
81141945452572238655414610628921879602238389714760
88506276862967146674697562911234082439208160153780
88989396451826324367161676217916890977991190375403
12746222899800519544441428201218736174599264296556
```

```
81746628302955570299024324153181617210465832036786
90611726015878352075151628422554026517048330422614
39742869330616908979684825901254583271682264580665
26769958652682272807075781391858178889652208164348
34482599326604336766017699961283186078838615027946
59551311565520360939881806121385586003014356945272
24206344631797460594682573103790084024432438465657
24501440282188525247093519062092902313649327349756
55139587205596542287497740114133469627154228458623
77387538230483865688976461927383814900140767310446
64025989949022222176590433990188601856652648506179
97023561938970178600408118897299183110211712298459
01641921068884387121855646124960798722908519296819
37238864261483965738229112312502418664935314397013
74285319266498753372189406942814341185201580141233
44828015051399694290153483077644569099073152433278
28826986460278986432113908350621709500259738986355
42771967428222487575867657523442202075736305694988
25087968928162753848863396909959826280956121450994
87170124451646126037902930912088908694202851064018
21543994571568059418727489980942547421735824010636
77404595741785160829230135358081840096996372524230
56085590370062427124341690900415369010593398383577
79394109700277534720000000000000000000000000000000
00000000000000000000000000000000000000000000000000
00000000000000000000000000000000000000000000000000
00000000000000000000000000000000000000000000000000
00000000000000000000000000000000000000000000000000
000000000000000000
```

8.2.2   Solved Exercise 2: Sorting

Let's develop a program for one of the simplest sorting algorithms: the bubble sort. First we need some housekeeping. We'll store input numbers in an array, always being careful about the array subscript staying in bounds. We will print out the numbers after reading them, and again after sorting them.

We read the numbers in using a do loop and stop as soon as a value of −1 is read. We read each value into a temporary variable, temp, and not directly into a[index], because index could be out of range. After ensuring that is not the case, we can assign temp to a[index].

Bubble-sorting consists of comparing (and swapping if necessary) adjacent pairs of values, from a[0] to a[last-1]. The first time this is done, the highest value in the array moves to the top position (last-1), floating up like a bubble in water, to its correct position in a[last-1], where we need consider it no further. During the second pass, the second highest value makes its way to a[last-2]. With each pass, the sorted (top) portion of the array grows by one, eventually encompassing the whole array. This is accomplished with two nested for loops, as shown in the program:

```c
#include <stdio.h>

#define MAXARRAY 100

main()
{
  int a[MAXARRAY];
  int last, index, top, temp;

  /***********************************************************/
  /* Read numbers into the array until a -1 appears.       */
  /* Check the array index so it doesn't go out of bounds. */
  /***********************************************************/
  index = 0;
  printf("Bubble Sort Program.\n");
```

```
      printf("Please enter integers, ending with -1\n");
      do {
        scanf("%d", &temp);
        if (index >= MAXARRAY) {
          printf("EXCEEDED ARRAY SIZE of %d!\n\n", MAXARRAY);
          break;
        } else {
          a[index] = temp;
          index++;
        }
      } while (temp != -1);

      last = index - 1;

      /*************************************************************/
      /* Print out the numbers that were read in.                */
      /*************************************************************/
      printf("NUMBERS READ IN: (%d)", last);
      for (index = 0; index < last; index++) {
        if (index % 10 == 0) printf("\n");
        printf("%5d", a[index]);
      }
      printf("\n\n");

      /*************************************************************/
      /* PERFORM THE BUBBLE SORT.                                */
      /*************************************************************/
      for (top = last - 1; top >= 1; top--)
        for (index = 0; index < top; index++)
          if (a[index] > a[index+1]) {
            temp = a[index];
            a[index] = a[index+1];
            a[index+1] = temp;
          }

      /*************************************************************/
      /* Print out the sorted numbers.                           */
      /*************************************************************/
      printf("SORTED NUMBERS:  (%d)", last);
      for (index = 0; index < last; index++) {
        if (index % 10 == 0) printf("\n");
        printf("%5d", a[index]);
      }
      printf("\n\n");

      return 0;
    }
```

Finally, here's the program's output on a random collection of numbers:

```
NUMBERS READ IN:  (50)
  349  124  541  978  457  565  942  313  583  288
   21  225  307  246  197  505  303  392  414  516
  596  413  544  448   35  401  363  207  908  249
  220  257  373  114  588  183   31  530  496  614
  170  869  191  477  115  388  335  419  132  749

SORTED NUMBERS (50):
   21   31   35  114  115  124  132  170  183  191
  197  207  220  225  246  249  257  288  303  307
  313  335  349  363  373  388  392  401  413  414
  419  448  457  477  496  505  516  530  541  544
  565  583  588  596  614  749  869  908  942  978
```

8.3 Programming Exercises

1. The first five rows of Pascal's Triangle appear like this:

$$
\begin{array}{ccccccccc}
 & & & & 1 & & & & \\
 & & & 1 & & 1 & & & \\
 & & 1 & & 2 & & 1 & & \\
 & 1 & & 3 & & 3 & & 1 & \\
 1 & & 4 & & 6 & & 4 & & 1 \\
 1 & 5 & & 10 & & 10 & & 5 & 1
\end{array}
$$

   In each row, every number (except the first and last) is the sum of the two numbers closest to it on the previous row. The significance of these numbers is that they are the binomial coefficients, or the coefficients in $(a + b)^n$. For example, $(a + b)^3 = a^3 + 3ab^2 + 2a^2b + b^3$. The coefficients are 1, 3, 3, and 1, which are found on row 3 of Pascal's Triangle. Write a program that will read n, then calculate and print n rows of Pascal's Triangle.

2. Rewrite the knight's program from Chapter 6 so that it uses a two-dimensional array to represent the chessboard.

3. The knight's tour problem is as follows: given an initial position for a single knight on an otherwise empty chessboard, find a sequence of 64 moves that will make the knight visit every square on the board exactly once. This seemingly impossible task can be accomplished using Warnsdorff's rule: at any time, with the knight at a given position, there are at most eight positions on the board to which the knight could move. Some are off the board; others have been visited earlier in the tour. *Choose the position that has the fewest open positions available to it.* If this criterion yields a tie, use the same criterion on each of the positions available from the current one, i.e., use a second-level tie-breaker. If there's a tie at the second level, choose arbitrarily. Write a program that will read in the starting position of the knight and produce a knight's tour beginning at that position. Is a knight's tour always possible, regardless of the starting position?

4. The *insertion sort* operates as follows. As each number (say, n) is read in, it is inserted into an array in its correct position. To do this, first traverse the array, comparing the numbers in it with n. After finding n's correct position in the array (say, in location k), insert it: shift all array elements at location k or higher up by one position (thereby opening up room for n at location k), and then place the number in a[k]. After each number is inserted, the array will be sorted. Write a program that will perform the insertion sort on its input, which consists of a collection of integers.

5. Consider a variation of the insertion sort: instead of sequentially traversing the array to find the correct location for a number n, use *binary search*, as follows. To perform binary search between locations low and high, calculate the middle point between low and high: mid = (low + high) / 2. Then compare n with a[mid]: if n > a[mid], then discard the bottom half the of the array, by setting low = mid + 1. If n < a[mid], then discard the top half. Repeat this process of cutting the array in half, until either n == a[mid] (found it), or low > high (n is not in the array).

6. Sets of numbers can be represented using arrays. The general idea is that a[i] != 0 if i is in the set, and a[i] == 0 if it is not. Array element a[i] can be thus treated as a boolean, and the array a as a boolean vector. Since the array has a fixed bound, say, N, the values in the set are restricted to the range 0 . . . N. For example, the array a[10]={0, 0, 1, 0, 1, 1} would represent the set {2, 4, 5}, because a[2], a[4], and a[5] have the value 1, and everywhere else a contains zeroes. Write a program that reads in two sets of numbers A and B, and calculates and prints their union (A ∪ B) and intersection (A ∩ B). Recall that A ∪ B is the set of elements that appear in either A or B, and that A ∩ B is the set of elements that appear in both A and B. *Hint:* the logical && and || operators are very useful for this.

7. Write a program that will read in two columns of floating-point data (the two vectors) and calculate vector sum, multiplication, and inner product. Vector sum is the entry-by-entry sum of the vectors. Vector multiplication is also the entry-by-entry multiplication of the vectors. Inner product is the sum of the products of the entries, i.e., for vectors $a_1 \ldots a_n$ and $b_1 \ldots b_n$, their inner product is $a_1 b_1 + a_2 b_2 + \ldots a_n b_n$.

8. Write a program that will read in a sequence of integers, average them, and print a histogram.

9. Exercise 11 in Chapter 5 consisted of writing a program that transforms decimal integers to binary. The algorithm, which successively divides the number by two, yields the binary digits in reverse order. Modify this program to use an array to store the digits. How large does the array need to be to accommodate any integer?

10. Write a program that will build and print a magic square. A magic square is an n×n array (n is odd), containing the values 1 through n^2, arranged in such a way that the sum of every row, the sum of every column, and the sum of each diagonal all yield the same value. For example, the 3×3 magic square looks like this:

6	1	8
7	5	3
2	9	4

To build a magic square, we consecutively place the numbers 1 through n^2. We begin by placing a 1 at the middle position of the top row. Generally, the next number is placed in the square diagonally above and to the left of the current square. If moving up this way exceeds the top row of the array (as it does when placing the 2), then we wrap around to the bottom row. To place the next number (3), we again move up and left; if doing so exceeds to left boundary of the array, we wrap to the rightmost column. If moving up and left would place us in a square that's already taken, then the new number is placed immediately below its predecessor; thus 4 is placed under 3. Finally, on the one occasion in which we exceed both the row and column boundaries, we will act as if that square were taken; thus 7 goes under 6.

11. A Karnaugh map is a 4×4 table of boolean values considered useful for expressing a boolean function. A prime implicant in a Karnaugh map is a rectangle containing 1's; the rectangle can contain 1, 2, 4 , 8, or 16 1's, and must be maximal (not contained within any larger such rectangular area). For example, in the Karnaugh map shown below, there are three prime implicants. Notice that prime implicants can wrap around the edge of the Karnaugh map, and they are allowed to overlap.

1	0	0	1
0	1	1	0
1	1	1	1
0	0	0	0

Write a program that will read in a Karnaugh map and identify and count all the prime implicants in it. Then extend your program to find out the largest number of prime implicants that any Karnaugh map can have. There are 65,536 Karnaugh maps to examine!

12. In cryptography, one of the simplest ciphers is known as a monoalphabetic permutation cipher. In this cipher, each time a letter appears in the original message (called the plain text), it is replaced by a unique letter from the substitution alphabet, in which the letters are permuted according to some fixed (and very secret!) arrangement. To specify the permutation, we need only give the alphabet in some random order:

> Original alphabet: ABCDEFGHIJKLMNOPQRSTUVWXYZ
> Substitution alphabet: EMNVDLWAUCPOKXQBIZJRYTGSHF

As in an earlier exercise in Chapter 7, punctuation is removed and the cipher text is written in groups of five letters to hide the spaces that indicate individual words. Write a program that will take its input (until EOF), remove all nonletters, and then print the cipher text equivalent using the above alphabets. For example, with the input

```
To err is human.
```

the cipher text would be

```
Rqdzz ujayk ex.
```

13. Write a program that will play the game of tic-tac-toe. *Hint:* a 3×3 magic square might be useful.

14. In computer communications, messages are exchanged using binary codes. A Hamming code is used to pad a message with additional "check" bits, so that a single error in the transmission can be detected and corrected. Let's assume we have 4 bits at a time to transmit. We place those 4 bits in a 7-bit word, in locations 3, 5, 6, and 7. Bits 1, 2, and 4 will be the check bits, calculated as follows:

$$b_1 = (b_3 + b_5 + b_7) \bmod 2$$
$$b_2 = (b_3 + b_6 + b_7) \bmod 2$$
$$b_4 = (b_5 + b_6 + b_7) \bmod 2$$

For example, if the data bits are 1101, the complete 7-bit Hamming code is 1010101. If the check bits look redundant, they are. Having this many check bits allows the Hamming code to detect and correct a single error in *any* of the seven bits. Now assume these seven bits are transmitted (say, through the Internet), and that an error occurs during transmission. Errors are in fact quite common, due to electrical surges, sunspots, gremlins, etc. Suppose our 7-bit message is received as 1010111. To find the location of the error, we check the above equations to see if they are satisfied, and record three results, named c_1, c_2, and c_4.

$$c_1 = (b_1 + b_3 + b_5 + b_7) \bmod 2$$
$$c_2 = (b_2 + b_3 + b_6 + b_7) \bmod 2$$
$$c_4 = (b_4 + b_5 + b_6 + b_7) \bmod 2$$

The resulting values, if read as a binary number, yield the index of the error. In our case, $c_4 c_2 c_1 = 110$, which in binary is 6. The error occurred in bit 6! Write a series of C programs that will simulate this process. First, write a program that will read any number of characters from the input, and convert each character into two 7-bit Hamming codes, one for the first four bits of the character, one for the other four bits. Recall our earlier exercises on conversion from decimal to binary. The output of this first program should be a number of lines, each containing 14 bits. The second program should copy its input to the output, except that it will randomly introduce errors. Be sure not to introduce more than one error for each 7-bit sequence. Finally, the third program would read each 14-bit sequence, correct errors if necessary, and reconstruct the original character message.

15. An n×m matrix can be transposed by swapping matrix elements $a_{i,j}$ and $a_{j,i}$. For example, the following two matrices are transpositions of each other:

$$\begin{bmatrix} 1 & 3 & 7 \\ 2 & 6 & 4 \end{bmatrix} \begin{bmatrix} 1 & 2 \\ 3 & 6 \\ 7 & 4 \end{bmatrix}$$

A (square) matrix is symmetric if it is identical to its transposition. Write a program that will read in a matrix, one row per line. Print a message if the matrix is symmetric; if it isn't, print out its transposition.

16. A maze can be represented with a two-dimensional array in which nonzero entries are walls and zero entries are passages. When printing a maze, nonzero entries could be printed as X's, and zero entries as spaces. As a path is being traced through the maze, it could be represented with 0's. For example, a 30×20 maze would look like this:

```
* * * * * * * * * * * * * * * * * * * * * * * * * * *
00**                    ***              *
*0** **********      *******  *
*0000**     ** *******       * *
* **0** ** ** **      * ** *** *
***0** **     ** ** * *    * *
**000**0*****  ** ** ** ***     *
*00***0**      ** ** ** *******
*0*****0** ***** ** **         *
*0000000** ***** ** ** *******
********** ***** ** **      **
** * * ***        ** ******* **
** * * ************     *** **
**                  ***** *** **
***** **********      *** **
*        ****    ******  *** **
*  ******* ***       ****** **
*  *     ** ** ***    *** **
**** ***     ** ******     **
**** ***********************
```

Write a program that will read in such an array, and repeatedly prints it so the user can select the direction in which to move next. The user's requested move can prompt a number of responses:

- A wall blocks the way.
- A step forward from the current cell to one not visited before.
- A step backward from the current cell to one visited previously.
- A giant step forward: found the exit!

17. Extend the very large integer arithmetic program so that very large integers can be read in from the input, added, subtracted, and multiplied. To read in a very large integer, read in its digits one at a time, all in one line. Addition and subtraction should be fairly straightforward. Multiplication of two very large numbers is done using the same grade-school algorithm; use a double `for` loop. Be sure to check ahead of time to ensure the result of the operation will fit in the arrays involved: if the two very large numbers have n_1 and n_2 digits, their sum (and difference) will have at most $\max(n_1, n_2) + 1$ digits, and their product will have at most $n_1 + n_2$ digits.

18. The game of Life was invented by mathematician John Conway and has become something of a cult classic among programmers. It is played on a two-dimensional board. Each cell on the board can either be empty or contain one "creature." Initially, in generation zero, the board contains some predetermined (or randomly generated) configuration of creatures. The next generation is computed from the previous one, in accordance with two rules:

- An empty cell experiences a birth if three or more of its neighboring cells were alive in the previous generation.
- A live cell continues to live in the next generation if either two or three of its neighboring cells are alive.

These rules crudely simulate the behavior of colonies of live organisms regarding growth, isolation, and overcrowding. It is important to note that each generation appears instantly: all births and deaths take place at the same time. This means that for each generation, you must make two passes through the two-dimensional array: one to count live neighbors, and another to effect births and deaths. Write a program to play the game of Life on a board of a reasonable size, say, one that can be printed entirely on your screen. You may deal with the "end of the world" (the edge of the board) in either of two ways: consider off-board cells as perennially empty, or wrap around to the other side of the world.

19. Extend the simple weekly payroll program that was given as an exercise in Chapter 4. Read and store in arrays the data for each employee: employee number, number of hours worked, hourly rate, federal and state withholding rates. Use additional arrays to store the gross pay, the Social Security deduction of 7.65%, the actual amounts withheld for federal and state taxes, and net pay. Print out a pay stub for each employee. Here (again) is a suggested layout:

```
Employee Number: 34567
Hourly rate of Pay:              $  18.66
Hours Worked:         40
Total Gross Pay:                 $ 746.40
Deductions:
FICA                  $ 53.37
Federal Tax (15%)     $111.96
                                _____
TOTAL Deductions      $165.33
NET PAY                          $ 581.07
```

Accumulate totals for all employees: gross pay, FICA deductions, federal withholding, total deductions, and net pay. Then print out a complete payroll report, one line per employee, with the totals at the bottom.

20. The Greek mathematician Eratosthenes developed an algorithm for calculating prime numbers, known as the Sieve of Eratosthenes, around 450 B.C. It works as follows. Assume we wish to determine which numbers between 2 and 1000 are prime. Fill an array with 1000 1s: initially every number between 2 and 1000 is considered prime. Consider 2: it is prime, so cross out every second number (4, 6, 8, etc.). Then come back to the beginning of the array and move (from 2) on to the next prime number, the next one not crossed out: 3. Cross out every third number: 6, 9, 12, etc. Continue this process, advancing to the next prime number and crossing out all its multiples until you exceed 1000. At this point, every number not crossed out is prime. Write a program that will implement the Sieve of Eratosthenes and print out all the prime numbers between 2 and N, where N is a symbolic constant.

21. The 15-puzzle is a children's game in which 15 interlocking tiles, numbered 1 through 15, can slide horizontally and vertically past each other on a 4×4 grid that leaves one slot open. Given an initial configuration of the tiles, the object of the game is to move the tiles around one at a time to arrive at the solved puzzle, which looks like this:

1	2	3	4
5	6	7	8
9	10	11	12
13	14	15	

Write a program that will allow its user to play the 15-puzzle game. After determining the initial configuration, repeatedly display it and request input from the user, to move the empty space up, down, left, or right. To determine the initial configuration, a random sequence of moves from the solution is probably best. Don't determine the initial configuration by placing the tiles randomly; it may yield an initial configuration that is impossible to solve.

22. Extend the bubble-sorting program to a bidirectional bubble sort: the first pass works from array locations 1 through N and "carries" the largest element to a[N]. The second pass processes elements downward, from N−1 to 1, and carries the smallest element to a[1]. The third pass goes up, from 2 to N−2, and so on. After 2×k passes, the bottom k elements of the arrays contain the k smallest numbers (sorted), and the top k elements of the array contain the k largest numbers (also sorted). Run some experiments with programs and determine which one is faster.

9 Functions

9.1 Chapter Summary

Functions are the building blocks of C programs. Their principal value to the programmer is as a means to divide a large program into manageable, understandable, modifiable, reusable pieces. Functions in C, unlike functions in mathematics, don't necessarily have arguments, nor do they necessarily produce values. Thus, functions in C can act like "procedures" do in other languages. Functions must be *declared* and *defined* so that they can be *called*.

9.1.1 Defining and Calling Functions

The general form for function definitions is

> *return-type function-name* (*parameters*)
> {
>   *declarations*
>   *statements*
> }

The return type can be `void` if the function is not meant to return a value. The function name is an identifier, and the parameters, as we'll see, act like locally declared variables. Every function has a *body*, the block enclosed in braces. Inside this block (as in any other block), variables can be declared and statements can be executed.

A C program consists of as many function definitions as we want, as long as one of those is the definition of `main`. Function definitions by themselves don't accomplish much; to use a function we must call it. The general form of a function call is the expression

> *function-name* (*arguments*)

The arguments are expressions, separated by commas. More specifically, the arguments are *assignment* expressions: they can contain any operator except the comma operator. Thus the commas that separate the expressions in the function call are not instances of the comma operator. Except for this restriction, arguments are indeed expressions, and can be as large and complex as desired. Arguments can even contain function calls! A function call can be placed in any place where an ordinary expression could go. When program execution reaches the function call, the following steps take place:

1. The arguments are evaluated and their values are passed to the function.
2. Control is passed to the function. The parameters are initialized to the values of the arguments that have been passed in. The function's body is executed.
3. Presumably, at some point in the execution of the function's body, a `return` statement is executed. The value to be returned, if any, is passed back to the function call.
4. Execution resumes at the point of call; the function call is complete.

During the execution of a function call, if the program reaches the bottom of the function body without executing a `return` statement, a "free" return is executed and control is returned to the point of call. However, it's not a good idea to count on this free `return`; the value returned by the function is undefined, which can have disastrous consequences.

There are two principal scenarios in which functions are used. In the first, the function is used as a mathematical function, i.e., as a "black box" that receives information, processes it, and returns a result. As an example, consider the `is_prime` function in Chapter 9 of the main text, page 162:

```
Bool is_prime(int n)
{
  int divisor;
```

```
    if (n <= 1) return FALSE;
    for (divisor = 2; divisor * divisor <= n; divisor++)
      if (n % divisor == 0)
        return FALSE;
    return TRUE;
}
```

The `is_prime` function is a self-contained, independent *process* for determining if a given number is prime. Most importantly, its internal details, the algorithm used, are irrelevant to the rest of the program. The main program can be written (and was!) by considering `is_prime` as a black box, with no knowledge of its internal workings—*as if it were a scalar variable*. Thus, if we decide to change the internal workings of the function, the remainder of the program is completely unaffected. For example, here's another version of `is_prime`.

```
Bool is_prime(int n)
{
  int divisor = 1;

  if (n <= 1) return FALSE;
  while (1) {
    divisor++;
    if (divisor * divisor > n) return TRUE;
    if (n % divisor == 0) return FALSE;
  }
}
```

As if it were a replacement part in a car, this new version of the function can replace the old one, if we so desire. Note how convenient the `return` statement is: we use it not only to return the appropriate value to `main`, but also to abort the `while` loop.

The second principal scenario involving functions is one in which the function is viewed as a task or a procedure. In this scenario, the black box returns nothing but accomplishes a well-defined task. The function call is a statement, where no return value is expected. This is illustrated by the following program, which prints a triangle of asterisks that resembles a Christmas tree.

```
#include <stdio.h>

void print_tree(int rows)
{
  int i, j;

  for (i = 1; i <= rows; i++) {
    for (j = 1; j <= rows - i; j++)
      printf(" ");
    for (j = 1; j <= 2 * i - 1; j++)
      printf("*");
    printf("\n");
  }
}

main()
{
  int n;

  printf("How many rows ? ");
  scanf("%d", &n);
  print_tree(n);
  return 0;
}
```

Note how the `print_tree` function is fairly complex, but its internal details do not matter to its "client," the main program, whose only concern is to read a value and pass that value along to `print_tree`.

In summary, there are two principal ways in which to use functions: as mathematical functions and as procedures. In the former case, the central purpose of the function is to produce a value of some type; in the latter, the purpose is to accomplish a task. In either case, good programming practice dictates that functions hide internal details from their clients.

9.1.2 Function Declarations

So far, we have arranged the function definitions so that they all precede their calls. Unfortunately, this is not always realistic, and sometimes it is simply impossible. When the compiler encounters a call to a function that appears before that function's definition, it knows nothing about that function (number of parameters, return type). Rather than reporting an error, it is forced to make some assumptions.

1. It assumes that the return type of the function is `int`.
2. It assumes the call is supplying the correct number of parameters.
3. It assumes that if the arguments are promoted appropriately, their types will match those of the parameters.

Depending upon the situation, these assumptions could be very wrong. To avoid this problem, C allows us to *declare* functions. Function declarations (also known as prototypes) consist essentially of the first line of the function definition:

return-type function-name (parameters) ;

The purpose of the declaration is to inform the compiler about the function. The definition of the function (its body) can be postponed. Armed with a function's declaration, the compiler can analyze each call to that function and verify (among other things) that the number of parameters and their types are correct. Once a function is declared, its definition can appear anywhere (except, of course, inside another function). This gives considerable flexibility to the programmer, who is free to collect together the definitions of functions that might be related in some way.

9.1.3 Arguments

C has only one mechanism for passing arguments to functions: *pass by value*.[1] This means that when an argument is passed to a function, a copy of the value is made, so that any changes to the corresponding parameter do not affect the argument. Consider the following program.

```
void double_increment(int n)
{
    n++; n++;
}

main()
{
    int n = 3;

    double_increment(n);
    printf("n is %d\n", n);
    return 0;
}
```

Here an attempt is made to change the n in `main` by passing it to `double_increment`. However, the n in `main` will remain unchanged, because it is a completely separate variable from the n in the `double_increment` function. Arrays can be passed as arguments. For one-dimensional arrays, the norm is to leave the length of the array unspecified in the parameter declaration, and transmit the array length through an additional parameter:

---

1 Other languages, such as Pascal and Fortran, have the *pass by reference* mechanism. In C, the effect of pass by reference can be achieved using pointers, which will be covered later.

```
void f(int b[], int n) { ... }
```

Later, when calling this function, no brackets should be used: `f(a, MAXLENGTH);`. There is no good way for the function to verify it has received the correct number of array elements. If the value of argument n is too small, or too large, bad things can happen. For multidimensional arrays, the length of every array dimension must be given, except for the first dimension:

```
void f(int a[][MAX], int n) { ... }
```

Here the number of columns is MAX and the number of rows is given by n.

9.1.4   The `return` Statement

The return statement has the general form

```
return expression ;
```

The expression is optional, but should be present if the function has a nonvoid return type. Conversely, if the function has a `void` return type, there should be no expression. Functions return automatically after their last statement is executed, so sometimes a `return` statement is not needed at all. However, in nonvoid functions, you should be careful to ensure the following: 1) at least one `return` statement appears in the function, 2) every `return` statement has an expression, and 3) a `return` statement is guaranteed to be executed. Item 3) is especially important, because the compiler is of no help with it, and in a large complex function it can be very difficult to guarantee.

9.1.5   Program Termination

The default return type of `main` is `int`. In some computer systems, the value returned by `main` can be tested once the program's execution ends. Conventionally, this is used to establish a status code at the completion of the program: zero for normal completion, nonzero for abnormal completion. You can use the `return` statement inside `main`, but another way to terminate the program, which can be used anywhere (in other functions) is the `exit` function in `<stdlib.h>`. It requires an argument, and here are some examples:

```
exit (0);   /* normal termination */
exit (1);      /* abnormal termination */
exit (EXIT_SUCCESS); /* normal termination */
exit (EXIT_FAILURE); /* abnormal termination */
```

9.1.6   Recursive Functions

A function that calls itself is said to be ***recursive***. The classical example of recursion is the factorial function, denoted $n!$, which is given by the recursive formula $n! = n \times (n - 1)!$. Another example would be the following recursive function for calculating the GCD (greatest common divisor) of two numbers.

```
#include <stdio.h>

#define TRUE 1

int gcd(int n, int m)
{
   if (m == 0) return n;
   return gcd(m, n % m);
}

int main()
{
   int n, m;
```

```
        while (TRUE) {
          printf("Enter n: ");
          scanf("%d", &n);
          if (n == 0) break;
          printf("Enter m: ");
          scanf("%d", &m);
          printf("GCD(%d,%d) = %d\n", n, m, gcd(n, m));
        }
      }
```

Here's what happens if we enter n = 34, m = 6:

$$
\begin{aligned}
&\quad \texttt{gcd(34,6)}\\
&= \texttt{gcd(6,34\%6)}, \text{ since } \texttt{6!=0}.\\
&= \texttt{gcd(6,4)}\\
&= \texttt{gcd(4,6\%4)}, \text{ since } \texttt{4!=0}\\
&= \texttt{gcd(4,2)}\\
&= \texttt{gcd(2,4\%2)}, \text{ since } \texttt{2!=0}\\
&= \texttt{gcd(2,0)}.\\
&= 2
\end{aligned}
$$

Note the simplicity of the function. In spite of this, it has all the elements of recursion: a check for the base case (the recursion stops when m reaches zero) and the recursive call. In our case, we take advantage of the fact that if m is nonzero, gcd(n, m) = gcd(m, n mod m).

9.2   Solved Exercises

We will develop two programs in this section. In the first, we will illustrate functions as procedures, or tasks to be carried out. In the second example, we will use functions to return values and illustrate recursion as well.

9.2.1   Solved Exercise 1: Plotting the Sine Function

Let's develop a program that will display on the screen a plot of the values of the mathematical *sine* function (a function used in trigonometry) over some specific interval. The sin function takes float values (called radians, actually) and returns values between −1.0 and 1.0. It is available in the standard C library called <math.h>. The program will read in the interval end values x1 and xu, and the increment value delta. Suppose, for example, that x1 is 0.7, xu is 4.0, and delta is 0.1. That will give us a plot from 0.7 to 4.0, in increments of 0.1, of the value of the sin function.

The *y*-axis is to be displayed horizontally on the screen. The *x*-axis will be displayed vertically. This "sideways" orientation of the plot is much easier to produce than the more common one with the *x*-axis displayed vertically. For the example above, the output should look like the figure shown on the next page.

Notice that there are exactly sixty columns in the *y*-axis (displayed horizontally), and that the number of lines in the *x*-axis (displayed vertically) is given by the expression 1 + (xu - x1) / delta, which in this case yields 34. The *y*-axis has a plus sign marking every unit on its scale. The leftmost, middle, and rightmost values of *y* are shown above the *y*-axis (−1.0, 0.0, and 1.0 in the above example). Each value of *x*, in the range from x1 to xu, is displayed to the left of the *x*-axis, as shown above; vertical separator characters are used to draw the *x*-axis. Each data point is marked with an asterisk, and the entire plot is preceded by a header and followed by a footer. We begin by determining the major activities of the program and formulating them as functions that are called from the main program, shown below.

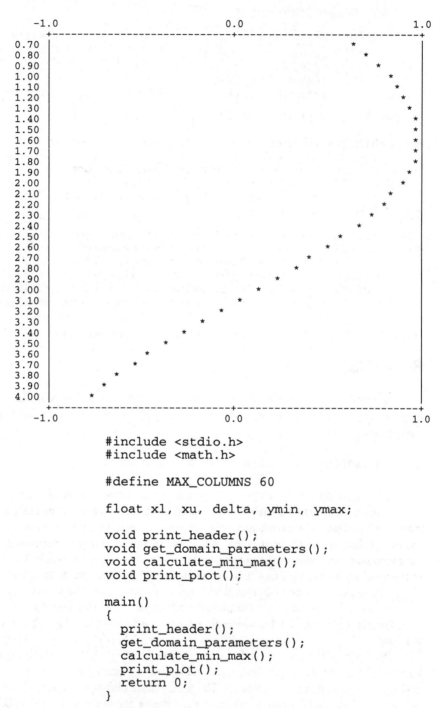

```
#include <stdio.h>
#include <math.h>

#define MAX_COLUMNS 60

float xl, xu, delta, ymin, ymax;

void print_header();
void get_domain_parameters();
void calculate_min_max();
void print_plot();

main()
{
    print_header();
    get_domain_parameters();
    calculate_min_max();
    print_plot();
    return 0;
}
```

print_header is self-descriptive. get_domain_parameters gets the user input: the lower bound and upper bounds for the *x*-axis (xl and xu), and the interval desired on the plot (delta). Function calculate_min_max calculates the largest and smallest values of the sine function in the interval specified by the user (ymin and ymax). These values are used by other functions, so we have made them global, declared outside of main.

In this program, some variables are declared outside of all the functions. They are called *external* variables, and they are discussed in Chapter 10. Ideally, we would like to avoid them, but a function can return only one value at a time. In a later chapter we will see how functions can return multiple values through their parameters by using pointers.

```
void print_header()
{
  printf("\n==============================================\n");
  printf("              Sine Function Plotting Program\n");
  printf("==============================================\n");
  printf("\n");
}

void get_domain_parameters()
{
  printf("Please enter lower bound for domain: ");
  scanf("%f", &xl);
  printf("Please enter upper bound for domain: ");
  scanf("%f", &xu);
  printf("Please enter interval over domain: ");
  scanf("%f", &delta);

  printf("\nYou entered the following domain parameters:\n");
  printf("  ==========================================\n");
  printf("    Lower bound for domain: %f\n", xl);
  printf("    Upper bound for domain: %f\n", xu);
  printf("    Increment value       : %f\n", delta);
  printf("  ==========================================\n\n");
}

void calculate_min_max()
{
  float x, y;

  ymin = sin(xl);
  ymax = sin(xl);
  for (x = xl; x <= xu; x += delta) {
    y = sin(x);
    if (y < ymin) ymin = y;
    if (y > ymax) ymax = y;
  }
}
```

Finally, there is the `print_plot` function. It requires two functions, `print_plot_header` and `print_plot_footer`. The main loop processes values `xl` through `xu`, with an increment of `delta`, printing a line of the plot for each value. We use an array of 60 characters (initialized to white spaces) to print each line of the plot. In each iteration, we calculate the proper location for the asterisk, set the previous location of the asterisk to white space, and print the entire array.

```
void print_plot_header()
{
  printf("     %3.1f", ymin);
  printf("                           %3.1f", (ymin + ymax) / 2);
  printf("                          %3.1f\n", ymax);
  printf("         +");
  printf("----------------------------+");
  printf("----------------------------+\n");
}

void print_plot_footer()
{
  printf("         +");
  printf("----------------------------+");
  printf("-----------------------------+\n");
  printf("     %3.1f", ymin);
  printf("                           %3.1f", (ymin + ymax) / 2);
  printf("                          %3.1f\n", ymax);
}
```

```
void print_plot()
{
  int scale_index, i, previous;
  float x;
  char A[MAX_COLUMNS];

  for (i = 0; i < MAX_COLUMNS; i++)
    A[i] = ' ';
  x = xl;
  previous = 0;
  print_plot_header();

  /**************************************************************/
  /* Loop through values of x in the domain, in incs of delta  */
  /**************************************************************/
  while (x <= xu) {

    /**********************************************************/
    /* Calculate scale_index: number of spaces to the left of */
    /* the asterisk. Keep track of previous location of the   */
    /* asterisk.  In each iteration, place a space in the     */
    /* previous location, and an asterisk in the current one. */
    /**********************************************************/
    scale_index = (sin(x) - ymin) * MAX_COLUMNS / (ymax - ymin) - 0.5;
    A[previous] = ' ';
    A[scale_index] = '*';
    previous = scale_index;
    printf("%5.2f |", x);
    for (i = 0; i < MAX_COLUMNS; i++)
      putchar(A[i]);
    printf("|\n");
    x = x + delta;
  }
  print_plot_footer();
}
```

I'll leave the assembly of the complete program to you. I suggest placing the functions in the order in which they appear above, except for the main program, which would go first. Don't forget to add prototypes for the two new functions `print_plot_header` and `print_plot_footer`.

The `#include <math.h>` directive is required; otherwise the compiler won't know about the `sin` function. Under UNIX systems, there's an additional complication: unlike the standard I/O library, the library of math functions is not always automatically included during the linking phase, because of its size and fairly infrequent use. This program must then be compiled using the command

`gcc plot.c -lm`

The `-lm` option indicates to the linking loader that the math library is to be linked in with the program. The `-lm` goes at the end of the `gcc` command to indicate that it is an option to the linker, not the compiler. If you compile the plot program without the `-lm` option, you might get a message like this:

```
/tmp/cca098381.o(.text+0x3ca): undefined reference to `sin'
```

The fact that the message does not refer to a source file (but instead to `/tmp`), and that it mentions an "undefined reference" rather than an undeclared function, are clear indications that the problem is during linking, not compilation.

A sample run of the program is shown below. The plot covers the interval between zero and 2π (π = 3.141592 . . .). Notice the wave shape of the sine function; it repeats itself every interval of length 2π.

```
================================================
                Sine Function Plotting Program
================================================

Please enter lower bound for domain: 0
Please enter upper bound for domain: 6.28
Please enter interval over domain: 0.2

You entered the following domain parameters:
==========================================
     Lower bound for domain: 0.000000
     Upper bound for domain: 6.280000
     Increment value        : 0.200000
==========================================
```

```
         -1.0                          0.0                          1.0
        +------------------------------+------------------------------+
0.00    |                              *
0.20    |                                  *
0.40    |                                       *
0.60    |                                          *
0.80    |                                             *
1.00    |                                               *
1.20    |                                                *
1.40    |                                                 *
1.60    |                                                 *
1.80    |                                                *
2.00    |                                               *
2.20    |                                             *
2.40    |                                          *
2.60    |                                       *
2.80    |                                   *
3.00    |                              *
3.20    |                          *
3.40    |                      *
3.60    |                  *
3.80    |              *
4.00    |          *
4.20    |       *
4.40    |*
4.60    |*
4.80    |*
5.00    |*
5.20    |   *
5.40    |      *
5.60    |         *
5.80    |             *
6.00    |                 *
6.20    |                     *
        +------------------------------+------------------------------+
         -1.0                          0.0                          1.0
```

9.2.2   Solved Exercise 2: Recursive Sorting

Let's write a program to sort some numbers in ascending order. There are many types of sorting algorithms. Let's assume there are n numbers to be sorted, in an array a[], in locations 0 through n−1. The sort proceeds as follows:

1. Find the largest element among elements 0 through n−1.
2. Swap that element with a[n−1]. Now the largest element is at the top of the array.
3. Recursively sort the first n−1 elements, i.e those stored in elements 0 through n−2.

We first develop the main program, in which we declare the array a, read in the data, print it, sort it, and print it again. We also develop the prototypes for the other four functions in the program.

```
#include <stdio.h>

#define ARRAY_SIZE 30

int get_input(int a[]);
void print_array(int a[], int n);
void sort(int a[], int n);

main()
{
  int n;
  int a[ARRAY_SIZE];

  n = get_input(a);
  print_array(a, n);
  sort(a, n);
  print_array(a, n);
  return 0;
}
```

Next, we develop the `get_input` and `print_array` functions:

```
int get_input(int a[])
{
  int index = 0, temp;

  printf("Please enter integers, ending with -1.\n");
  do {
    scanf("%d", &temp);
     if (index >= ARRAY_SIZE) {
       printf("EXCEEDED ARRAY SIZE of %d!\n\n", ARRAY_SIZE);
       break;
     } else {
       a[index] = temp;
       index++;
     }
  } while (temp != -1);

  return index - 1;
}

void print_array(int a[], int n)
{
  int i;

  printf("Array a:\n");
  printf("    +----+\n");
  for (i = 0; i < n; i++)
    printf("%3d|%4d|\n", i, a[i]);
  printf("    +----+\n");
}
```

Finally, we develop the sort function itself. According to our strategy, we need an auxiliary function (`max`) to find the index of the largest element in the portion of the array being considered. In the `sort` function, we use that index to swap the largest element with the one at the top of the array. Then we recursively sort the rest of the array, excluding the top element, which is now where it belongs.

```
int max (int a[], int n)
{
  int max_value, max_index = 0, i;

  max_value = a[max_index];
  for (i = 0; i <= n; i++)
    if (a[i] > max_value) {
```

```
            max_value = a[i];
            max_index = i;
        }
    return max_index;
}

void sort(int a[], int n)
{
  int largest, temp;

  if (n <= 1) return;
  largest = max(a, n - 1);
  temp = a[largest];
  a[largest] = a[n - 1];
  a[n - 1] = temp;
  sort(a, n - 1);
}
```

Once again I leave the assembly of the program to you. Assume the following input:

```
25    4   65   32   12   23   45    8    4    9   13   34   -1
```

Here's the corresponding output:

```
Array a:
    +----+
  0|  25|
  1|   4|
  2|  65|
  3|  32|
  4|  12|
  5|  23|
  6|  45|
  7|   8|
  8|   4|
  9|   9|
 10|  13|
 11|  34|
    +----+
Array a:
    +----+
  0|   4|
  1|   4|
  2|   8|
  3|   9|
  4|  12|
  5|  13|
  6|  23|
  7|  25|
  8|  32|
  9|  34|
 10|  45|
 11|  65|
    +----+
```

9.3   Programming Exercises

1.   Write a function max, and another named min, that take two float numbers and return the larger and smaller, respectively, of them.

2.   Write two functions square and cube, which return their arguments squared and cubed respectively. Write a third function called print_values, to print a table of squares and cubes for values between 1 and a value supplied by the user.

3. Modify the plot program so it will plot any one of the following functions: sin, cos, tan (all from <math.h>), x^2, and $3x^2 + 2x - 7$. The function is to be chosen by the user via a menu. Use a function to evaluate the function selected.

4. Modify the plot program so that it uses no global variables. *Hint:* use one function to input each domain parameter, such as get_lower_bound, get_upper_bound, and get_inc_value.

5. Write a function that prints the first n Fibonacci numbers. The first Fibonacci number is 0. The second Fibonacci number is 1. The third (and all subsequent) Fibonacci numbers are the result of adding the previous two Fibonacci numbers. Thus $F(n) = F(n-1) + F(n-2)$.

6. Assume the + operator is not available. Write a function add (int n, int m) that will add two numbers using only recursion and the increment and decrement operators. *Hint:* add(n, m) = add(++n, --m), if m is positive, and add(n, 0) = 0.

7. Write a function that will take an array of floats and an integer n, and will return the sum of array elements 0 through n.

8. Write a function that will add two arrays, element by element. The function should take as parameters the two arrays a and b, and an integer n. Place the results in b.

9. Write a function that will take an array of integers and an integer n and will calculate some simple statistics. The *mean* of the n numbers is their sum divided by n. The *median* among n values is the *midpoint* value (half of the values are above it, and half are below it). To calculate the median, the array must be sorted. The *mode* is the value that occurs most frequently. To calculate the mode, an extra array to count the occurrences of each value will be needed.

10. The Towers of Hanoi problem is a classical exercise in recursion. We have three pegs, labeled peg_a, peg_b, and peg_c, and n disks. The first disk is of diameter 1, the second disk is of diameter 2 (larger than disk 1), etc. Each disk has a hole in the middle so it will fit over a peg. Initially, all n disks are on peg_a, with the smallest disk on top and the largest on the bottom. The object of the game is to move all n disks from peg_a to peg_b, by only moving disks from one peg to another, moving them one at a time, and never placing a larger disk over a smaller one. *Hint:* here's an informal description of the recursive solution.

    To move n disks from peg_a to peg_b, using peg_c as a placeholder:
    1. Move n-1 disks from peg_a to peg_c, using peg_b as a placeholder.
    2. Move the bottom disk from peg_a to peg_b.
    3. Move n-1 disks from peg_c to peg_b, using peg_a as a placeholder.

11. Write a function that will take an array a of integers, an integer n, and an integer value v, and will search the array sequentially for v. If found, the function should return the index in which v is located in the array. If not found, the function should return −1.

12. Write a function that will take an array of integers, an integer n, and an integer value v to be searched. Assume the array is sorted in ascending order and use binary search to search for the array. Your function should return the index in the array where v is located, if present, and −1 otherwise. Binary search works as follows:
    1. Initially, we have a lower bound l = 0 and an upper bound u = n.
    2. Calculate the midpoint in the array: m = (u−l)/2.
    3. Compare v against a[m]. If v < a[m], then v is definitely not in the upper half of the array. Adjust u by setting it to m − 1, and repeat the process. If v > a[m], then v is not in the lower half, so adjust l: set it to m + 1, and repeat. If v == a[m], you found it!
    4. Continue this process of cutting the interval in half until either v is found, or until l and u cross over, in which case v is not in the array.

13. Reimplement the binary search function of the previous exercise using recursion.

14. Write a function that calculates the square root of a `float` number x using Newton's method. In Newton's method, we begin with an initial guess of the square root, say, `guess = 1.0`. Then we repeatedly improve our guess, until it is good enough. To improve the guess, we average it with `x/guess`; that is, we calculate `guess=(guess + x / guess) / 2`. To determine if guess is good enough, we compare `guess * guess` against x. If the difference between them (in absolute value) is less than, say, 0.0001, then guess is good enough, and the function should return guess.

15. Write a recursive version of the square root function in the previous exercise.

16. Goldbach's conjecture states that every even number greater than two is the sum of two prime numbers. For example, 4 = 2 + 2, 6 = 3 + 3, 8 = 3 + 5, etc. Extensive computer experiments have found no counterexample, but no proof has been found. Write a program that will confirm this conjecture for all even numbers between n and m, where n and m are input by the user. *Hint:* use a function to determine whether a number is prime.

17. Redo Exercise 17 in Chapter 6 using functions—write a function that will take an argument n and print the nth line of the triangle.

18. Redo Exercise 18 in Chapter 6 using arrays and functions. Use arrays to read in and store the quantity, the item, the price, the extended price, the discount percentage, the discount amount, and the total for each line.

19. Redo Exercise 15 in Chapter 3 using a function to reduce each fraction to its simplest form. *Hint:* the GCD function is quite useful for this.

20. Modify the plot program so that instead of plotting the function, the program performs numerical integration. The method works as follows. The input parameters are the same. In each iteration, (i.e., for each value of x between xl and xu), calculate the value of the function at the midpoint of the interval: `sin(x + delta / 2)`. This is the height of a narrow rectangle whose width is `delta`. The product of these two is the area of the rectangle. In numerical integration, we wish to add up the area of all such rectangles between the lower and upper bounds xl and xu.

10   Program Organization

10.1   Chapter Summary

In this chapter we discuss various issues that arise when a program has more than one function, including local and global variables, blocks and scope rules, and the placement of function prototypes, function definitions, and variable declarations in a program.

10.1.1   Local Variables

In general, a variable has *extent* and it has *scope*. The extent of a variable is the portion of execution time during which the variable exists. The scope of a variable is the portion of the program's text in which the variable can be used or referenced.

A variable declared inside the body of a function is said to be *local* to that function. Local variables have *automatic* extent: they are automatically allocated when their enclosing function is called and are automatically deallocated when the function returns. Local variables have *block* scope: they are visible from their point of declaration until the end of the enclosing function body. Parameters have the same extent and scope as local variables and only differ in the way they are initialized.

The `static` qualifier (`static int i;`) makes a local variable have *static* extent. This means it will have a permanent storage location, which will exist throughout the entire program execution.

10.1.2   External Variables

External variables (also known as global variables) are those that are declared outside of any function. Their duration is static and they have *file* scope: they are visible from their point of declaration to the end of the file. Any function declared after the variable can access it. An external variable seems like a good idea when more than one function needs to use it. However, external variables pose a variety of problems: functions that use them are not completely self-contained (and therefore less reusable), and they make programs harder to read, understand, and modify.

10.1.3   Blocks and Scope

Compound statements (or blocks) in C are of the form

```
{
    declarations
    statements
}
```

By default, any variable declared inside the block has automatic storage extent and block scope. In particular, the body of any function is a block. Blocks can be nested, which is useful to hide temporary variable names from the rest of the program and to reduce the potential for name conflicts. Variables that have block scope obey the following scope rule: inside a block, the declaration of a name x temporarily "hides" any declaration of x that is already visible, whether due to a global declaration, or a declaration in an enclosing block.

10.1.4   Organizing a C Program

There are fairly few rules regarding the order in which the various components of a C program must appear. One of them is that preprocessor directives don't take effect until the line in which they appear. Another is that variable and type names must be declared before they are used. Functions don't have to be declared before they are used, but it is highly recommended. One possible order of components is as follows:

```
#include directives
#define directives
Type definitions
External variable declarations
Function prototypes (other than main)
Definition of main
Function definitions
```

This order of program components ensures that preprocessor directives (constant definitions and library inclusions) hold throughout the program, as well as type definitions and global variables. Prototypes for all functions are not required, but supplying them allows the function definitions to appear later in whichever order is convenient.

10.2 Solved Exercises

10.2.1 Solved Exercise 1: Sets of Numbers

As an exercise in program organization, we'll implement a facility for manipulating sets of positive numbers. C is frequently criticized for its lack of a set data type. However, like stacks, sets can be implemented in most languages. In our case, we will use arrays to hold the set elements. We will develop the program using no external variables by declaring the sets in the main program and passing them around as parameters. Then, we'll discuss the possibility of declaring the sets externally. We first specify the various operations we'll need by writing their prototypes.

We choose to represent sets as arrays of integers. The zeroth element of each array will have a special meaning: it will indicate the number of elements in the set, say, N. The set elements themselves will be located in array elements 1 through N. Thus create_set simply stores a zero in a[0]. Function read_set reads integers from standard input and uses enter_set to add them to the set, avoiding repeated entries. print_set prints out the contents of the set, in the traditional mathematical notation, as a list of items separated by commas, surrounded by braces. The functions union_set and intersect_set carry out the well-known operations on sets a and b, storing the results in set c. Finally, enter_set adds a value to the set (unless it's already there), and element_of returns TRUE or FALSE depending on whether the element is in the set. We've organized the program in the order suggested earlier. Here's the program.

```c
#include <stdio.h>

#define MAX_SET_SIZE 50
#define TRUE   1
#define FALSE  0

void create_set(int a[]);
void read_set(int a[]);
void print_set(int a[]);
void union_set(int a[], int b[], int c[]);
void intersect_set(int a[], int b[], int c[]);
void enter_set(int v, int a[]);
int  element_of(int v, int a[]);

main()
{
  int a[MAX_SET_SIZE];
  int b[MAX_SET_SIZE];
  int c[MAX_SET_SIZE];

  read_set(a);
  read_set(b);
```

```
      printf("Set A: ");
      print_set(a);
      printf("Set B: ");
      print_set(b);
      union_set(a, b, c);
      printf("Set C: Union of A and B: ");
      print_set(c);
      intersect_set(a, b, c);
      printf("Set C: Intersection of A and B: ");
      print_set(c);
      return 0;
}

void create_set(int a[])
{
   a[0] = 0;
}

void read_set(int a[])
{
   int value;

   create_set(a);
   printf("Enter set values, ending with -1.\n");
   scanf("%d", &value);
   while (value != -1) {
      enter_set(value, a);
      scanf("%d", &value);
   }
}

void print_set(int a[])
{
   int i;

   printf("{");
   if (a[0] >= 1) printf("%d", a[1]);
   for (i = 2; i <= a[0]; i++)
      printf(",%d", a[i]);
   printf("}\n");
}

void union_set(int a[], int b[], int c[])
{
   int i;

   create_set(c);
   for (i = 1; i <= a[0]; i++)
      enter_set(a[i], c);
   for (i = 1; i <= b[0]; i++)
      enter_set(b[i], c);
}

void intersect_set(int a[], int b[], int c[])
{
   int i;

   create_set(c);
   for (i = 1; i <= a[0]; i++)
      if (element_of(a[i], b))
         enter_set(a[i], c);
}
```

```
void enter_set(int v, int a[])
{
  if (a[0] == MAX_SET_SIZE)
    printf("MAX SET SIZE EXCEEDED\n");
  else if (!element_of(v, a)) {
    a[0]++;
    a[a[0]] = v;
  }
}

int element_of(int v, int a[])
{
  int i;

 for (i = 1; i <= a[0]; i++)
   if (a[i] == v) return TRUE;
 return FALSE;
}
```

Here is a sample run of the program.

```
Enter set values, ending with -1.
1
3
5
-1
Enter set values, ending with -1.
2  3  5  6
-1
Set A: {1,3,5}
Set B: {2,3,5,6}
Set C: Union of A and B: {1,3,5,2,6}
Set C: Intersection of A and B: {3,5}
```

Now, consider the alternative of declaring the three sets externally. If the three variables a, b, and c were declared outside of all the functions, presumably the functions wouldn't have to take them on as parameters. However, the functions create_set, read_set, print_set, enter_set, and element_of all operate on different sets at different times, and thus need to know which specific set to work on. In this case, it is (as it is most of the time) a bad idea to insist on having external variables.

10.3   Programming Exercises

1.   Write a program that emulates the behavior of a bus. The bus must have a schedule (a finite number of times for it to stop) and a certain capacity (number of passengers). In this program the bus has two states: stopped and going. Over time, events take place, such as stopping the bus (for which the bus must already be going), loading passengers, unloading passengers, or starting the bus. For each event, the current state of the bus must change accordingly. Each time the bus stops, it must load and unload passengers. The number of passengers that will be unloaded at every bus stop must be generated randomly. The number of passengers waiting for the bus at each stop is also generated randomly. The bus should load as many waiting passengers as possible without exceeding the bus capacity. Write a program that implements this model, with the following operations:

```
void stop_bus();    /* Stops the bus      */
void start_bus();   /* Starts the bus     */
void load_pass();   /* Load passengers    */
void unlo_pass();   /* Unload passengers  */
```

Note: These function prototypes lack parameters; add whatever parameters you feel are necessary so that the program works without global variables. The program's output should reflect the bus's actions by reporting each change in state, along with the number of passengers loaded and unloaded.

2. Determine the output of the following program.

```
#include <stdio.h>

#define   N 15
#define   FALSE 0
#define   TRUE  1

int i;
int eval(void);

main()
{
  i = N;
  i = eval();
  if (!i)
    printf("FALSE\n");
  else
    printf("TRUE\n");
  return 0;
}

int eval(void)
{
  int i = 0;

  i += N;
  return ((i / 2) == N);
}
```

3. Describe the principal use for external variables.

4. Fix the code of Exercise 2 so that it'll write TRUE. Do it by deleting only one line.

5. Consider this code:

```
int next_five_mul(void)
{
  if (!(mul % 5))
    return mul;
  else {
    mul++;
    next_five_mul();
  }
}
```

Obviously this function obtains the next multiple of five of mul, by calculating it in a pretty inefficient way. In addition, the function uses external variable mul. Make the necessary changes for the function to work with mul being a static variable.

6. Section 10.1.4 shows the main text's recommended organization of a program. Give three reasons for this particular way to organize a program.

7. Write a function delete_set(int v, int a[]) that deletes a specific element from a set, according to the set implementation shown in Section 10.2.1.

8. Use the function delete_set in Exercise 7 to implement set_difference(int a[], int b[], int c[]), which calculates the set of all elements that are in set a, but not in b.

9. Write a function sym_diff(int a[], int b[], int c[]) that calculates the symmetric difference between two sets. Symmetric difference between two sets A and B is defined as the set of all elements in either A or B, but not in both.

10. Write the same function sym_diff(int a[], int b[], int c[]) as in Exercise 9, but using only existing functions. *Hint:* you'll find set_difference and union_set useful.

11. Reimplement the program in Exercise 1 so that it uses global variables instead of static ones.

12. What is the output of the following program?

```
#include <stdio.h>

int i;
int test_func(void);

main()
{
  int j;

  i = 10;
  j = test_func();
  printf("%d\n", i);
  return 0;
}

int test_func(void)
{
  int i;

  i = 15;
  return i;
}
```

13. Suppose you need a function that prints the following message each time it is called:

I've been called n times

The function should, of course, print the actual number of times it has been called. How can you achieve this using only variables declared inside the function?

14. The following program has an error. Solve it by moving just one line.

```
#include <stdio.h>

int dummy(int q);

main()
{
  int j = 9;
  int i;

  i = 15;
  j = dummy(j);
  printf("%d\n", j);
  return 0;
}

int dummy(int q)
{
  q = q + i;
  return q;
}
```

15. Organize the following code so it matches the pattern shown in Section 10.1.4.

```
int i, j;

void function_1(void)
{
   /* ********************************** */
   /*  Here's the code for function_1    */
   /* ********************************** */
}

#include <stdio.h>

#define TRUE 1

void function_2(void);

main()
{
   /* **************************** */
   /*  Here's the code for main    */
   /* **************************** */
}

void function_2(void)
{
   /* ********************************** */
   /*  Here's the code for function_2    */
   /* ********************************** */
}
```

16. What is the output of the following program?

```
#include <stdio.h>

main()
{
   int i;
   i = 10;
   if (i > 9) {
      int i;

      i = 9;
      printf("%d\n", i);
   }
   printf("%d\n", i);
   return 0;
}
```

17. Redo Exercise 13 without using a static variable. You are not limited to declaring variables only inside the function.

18. Name three reasons to avoid using global variables.

19. In Section 10.2.1 we implemented sets of numbers. Add the function count_sets. This function should return the number of sets that have been created with create_set.

20. What's the difference between block scope and file scope?

11 Pointers

11.1 Chapter Summary

To understand pointers, we must first understand what they represent at the machine level. Computer memory is typically divided into units called *bytes*, with eight *bits* (a zero or a one) apiece. Each byte has an *address*, a sequentially numbered location. For example, an integer variable i may reside at address 4096. Since an integer occupies (typically) four bytes, the integer "lives" at bytes 4096, 4097, 4098, and 4099.

A *pointer* is variable whose value is the address of some other variable. A pointer contains not merely an integer or float value, but the address of some other location in memory that interests us. Pictorially,

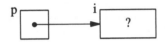

Here p is a pointer variable, which points to the address of integer variable i. We declare such a pointer variable as follows: int *p. It is possible to declare pointers to all sorts of objects, such as float *q, or char *r, including large composite objects that we will discuss in later chapters.

Like other types of variables we've seen before, merely declaring a pointer does not give it a value. So how does one obtain the address of a variable? C has two complementary operators for this, the *address* operator and the *indirection* operator. The address operator &, when placed in front of a variable name, yields that variable's address, known as its *lvalue*. Thus p = &i assigns the address of i to pointer variable p, as shown in the picture above. Note that the value of i is unaffected; it is variable p whose value is changed, so that it points to i. The declaration of the pointer variable, and its initialization, can be combined: int *p = &i. Of course, variable i must have been declared previously.

The indirection operator * is used to access a value through a pointer variable. When placed in front of a pointer variable, the indirection operator uses the value of the pointer variable (which is an address) and retrieves the value stored at that address. In the above picture, we would use the following to print the value of i: printf("%d\n",*p);. It is also possible to assign a value to i without mentioning the variable name i: *p = 3. This would store a 3 in the right box above. In a sense, * is the inverse of &, since *&i is the same as the value of i. As long as p points to i, *p is an alias for i.

The values of pointer variables can be assigned and/or copied; the effect is to create one or more additional aliases for the variable in question. For example, int i, j, *p = &i, *q;, yields the following scenario:

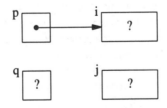

Note that the value of i is still undefined, as are the values of q and j. We can make q into another alias for i by copying the value of p into q: q = p. Then we can change the value of i by accessing it through q: *q = 3. This yields:

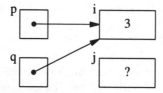

Now we can change q so it points to j with the statement q = &j. Then we can copy the value 3 from i to j, without mentioning the integer variables, only the pointer variables: *q = *p. This yields:

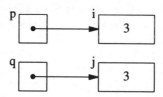

Pointers can be passed as arguments to functions; the principal advantage is that if a pointer to a variable is passed to a function, then that function can modify that variable. For example, in the following program, the function initialize receives pointers to two variables and assigns values to those variables. When calling initialize, the addresses of the variables must be used. Beware! Forgetting the & operator can have disastrous consequences.

```
#include <stdio.h>

void initialize(int *p, int *q)
{
    *p = 3;
    *q = 7;
}

main()
{
    int a, b;

    initialize(&a, &b);
    printf("%d %d\n", a, b);
    return 0;
}
```

In fact, we've been using pointers as parameters since Chapter 2: in the statement scanf("%d", &i); we allow scanf to modify variable i precisely because we supply scanf with i's address. In general, passing a pointer to a function grants the function permission to modify the corresponding variable. However, sometimes we wish to pass a pointer (perhaps for efficiency reasons, which we'll discuss later), but we still wish to prohibit the function from modifying the variable. This can be accomplished using the word const, as in the following example:

```
int *max(const int *a, const int *b)
{
    if (*a > *b)
        return a;
    else
        return b;
}
```

In this example, which also illustrates how functions can return pointers, the very purpose of the function (choosing one of two pointers and returning it) requires that it receive pointers as parameters. However, the function has no intention of modifying the variables in question. This is documented (and enforced!) using the word const.

11.2 Solved Exercises

11.2.1 Solved Exercise 1: Complex Numbers

As our first example in dealing with pointers, we're going to write a program that adds, subtracts, and multiplies complex numbers. The program will prompt the user for the choice of operation, read in the complex numbers, perform the operation, and print the results. We first develop a prototype for each of the operations, a function to read in the complex numbers and one to print them out. The main program repeatedly prints the menu, reads in the user's selection, reads in the complex numbers, performs the operation, and prints out the results. We use pointers only for those arguments that the function intends to change. For example, read_nums changes all four of its arguments. In contrast, add uses r1,i1,r2,i2 to change the values of r3,i3. The last step is to develop functions add, subtract, multiply, read_nums, and print_complex. In read_nums, we read in two complex numbers. To avoid repetitive code, we include another auxiliary function read_num, which does the actual reading. In read_num, the calls to scanf do *not* use the address operator &: r and i are already pointers to the variables in question. Here's the program.

```
#include <stdio.h>

/*-------------------------------------------------------------*/
/* This program adds, subtracts, or multiplies complex numbers. */
/* In all the functions below, r represents the real component  */
/* and i represents the imaginary component.                    */
/*-------------------------------------------------------------*/

void add(float r1, float i1, float r2, float i2,
         float *r3, float *i3);
void subtract(float r1, float i1, float r2, float i2,
              float *r3, float *i3);
void multiply(float r1, float i1, float r2, float i2,
              float *r3, float *i3);
void read_nums(float *r1, float *i1, float *r2, float *i2);
void read_num(float *r, float *i);
void print_complex(float r, float i);

main()
{
  float r1, r2, r3, i1, i2, i3;
  char c;

  printf("COMPLEX NUMBER ARITHMETIC PROGRAM:\n\n");
  while (1) {
    printf("1) Add two complex numbers\n");
    printf("2) Subtract two complex numbers\n");
    printf("3) Multiply two complex numbers\n");
    printf("4) Quit\n\n");
    printf("Choose an option (1 - 4): ");
    scanf("%c", &c);
    switch (c) {
      case '1':
        read_nums(&r1, &i1, &r2, &i2);
        add(r1, i1, r2, i2, &r3, &i3);
        print_complex(r3, i3);
        break;
      case '2':
        read_nums(&r1, &i1, &r2, &i2);
        subtract(r1, i1, r2, i2, &r3, &i3);
        print_complex(r3, i3);
        break;
      case '3':
```

```
            read_nums(&r1, &i1, &r2, &i2);
            multiply(r1, i1, r2, i2, &r3, &i3);
            print_complex(r3, i3);
            break;
          case '4':
            return 0;
      }
    }
    return 0;
  }

void add(float r1, float i1, float r2, float i2,
         float *r3, float *i3)
{
  *r3 = r1 + r2;
  *i3 = i1 + i2;
}

void subtract(float r1, float i1, float r2, float i2,
              float *r3, float *i3)
{
  *r3 = r1 - r2;
  *i3 = i1 - i2;
}

void multiply(float r1, float i1, float r2, float i2,
              float *r3, float *i3)
{
  *r3 = r1 * r2 - i1 * i2;
  *i3 = ((r1 * i2) + (r2 * i1));
}

void read_nums(float *r1, float *i1, float *r2, float *i2)
{
  printf("Reading the first number ...\n");
  read_num(r1, i1);
  printf("Reading the second number ...\n");
  read_num(r2, i2);
}

void read_num(float *r, float *i)
{
  printf("Please type the real component: ");
  /* r and i are pointers; can't use the & operator here */
  scanf("%f", r);
  printf("\n");
  printf("Please type the imaginary component: ");
  scanf("%f", i);
  printf("\n");
}

void print_complex(float r3, float i3)
{
  printf("The operation yields %6.3f + %6.3fi\n\n", r3, i3);
}
```

Here's some sample output of our complex number program.

```
COMPLEX NUMBER ARITHMETIC PROGRAM:

1) Add two complex numbers
2) Subtract two complex numbers
3) Multiply two complex numbers
4) Quit

Choose an option (1 - 4): 1
Reading the first number ...
Please type the real component: 1.5

Please type the imaginary component: 3.7

Reading the second number ...
Please type the real component: 5.4

Please type the imaginary component: 2.3

The operation yields   6.900 +   6.000i

1) Add two complex numbers
2) Subtract two complex numbers
3) Multiply two complex numbers
4) Quit

Choose an option (1 - 4): 3
Reading the first number ...
Please type the real component: 1.5

Please type the imaginary component: 3.7

Reading the second number ...
Please type the real component: 5.4

Please type the imaginary component: 2.3

The operation yields -0.410 + 23.430i

1) Add two complex numbers
2) Subtract two complex numbers
3) Multiply two complex numbers
4) Quit

Choose an option (1 - 4): 4
Bye!
```

11.3 Programming Exercises

1. Consider the following code:

    ```
    int i, *p;
    i = 5;
    p = &i;
    p = 10;
    ```

    What's the value of i after this code segment is executed?

2. What's wrong with the following code?

    ```c
    int *ticket(int n)
    {
      int i;

      i = *n * 2;
      *n += i;
      return n;
    }
    ```

3. What's wrong with the following code?

    ```c
    int *function_1(int *n, float *m)
    {
      *m += *n;
      return m;
    }
    ```

4. What will the values of p and q be after the following code segment is executed?

    ```c
    int i, *p, *q;

    i = 5;
    p = &i;
    *q = *p;
    i = 10;
    ```

5. Write the following function:

    ```c
    void read_max(int *n1, int *n2, int *max);
    ```

    The function should read two values from the input and return them in n1 and n2. It should return in max the greater of the two values.

6. Write the following function:

    ```c
    int *find_number(int vec[], int *num, int dim);
    ```

    The function should change num to the lowest index (in vec) in which the value of num can be found. If there's no matching value for num in vec, num's value should be changed to 0. The array vec has dim elements.

7. Write the function

    ```c
    int *c_zero(int vec[], int c);
    ```

    This function should return the number of zeroes in the array vec. The array vec has c elements.

8. What's wrong with this code?

    ```c
    int number(int *n)
    {
      int i;

      for (i = 0; i < n; i++)
        i += n;
      return i;
    }
    ```

9. What's the difference between `const int *p` and `int const *p`?

10. Write the function

    ```c
    void get_date(int *day, int *month, int *year);
    ```

    The function should read the date from the user (via keyboard) and return it using the function's parameters.

11. What's wrong with this code?

```
int avg(int a[], int n)
{
  int i, j = 0;

  for (i = 0; i < n; i++)
    j += a[i];
  j /= n;
  return &j;
}
```

The length of the array is n.

12. Fix the problem in the previous exercise by making a single change.

13. Write the following function:

```
void get_rational(int *num, int *den)
```

The function should read a rational number from the input. It should return the numerator in num and the denominator in den.

14. Write the following function:

```
void sub_sum(float *x1, float *i1, float *x2, float *i2)
```

This function receives two complex numbers (one in x1 and i1, the other in x2 and i2), returns their sum in x1 and i1, and returns their difference in x2 and i2.

12 Pointers and Arrays

12.1 Chapter Summary

Pointers and arrays are closely related in C. Their connection is crucial in order to understand many other uses of pointers, including strings and dynamically allocated structures, which will be discussed later.

Pointers can point to array elements, not just to isolated variables. For example, int a[10], *p = &a[0]; looks like this:

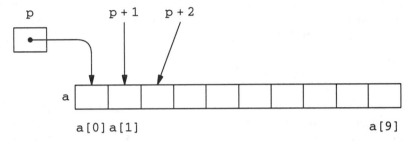

Through pointer p we can access (and modify) a[0]. More importantly, by performing *pointer arithmetic* on p, we can access the other elements of a. Three forms of pointer arithmetic are supported in C: A pointer can be added to an integer, an integer can be subtracted from a pointer, and a pointer can be subtracted from another pointer. In our example, the expressions p + 1 and p + 2 yield the addresses of the second and third element of the array; if we add the declaration int *q = p + 6;, the situation now looks like this:

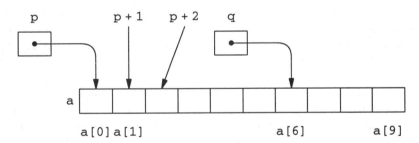

At this point, the expression q + 2 would yield the address of a[8]. The expression q - 2 yields the address of a[4], and the expression q - p yields the value 6. You must be very careful with pointer arithmetic: evaluating the expression p - 1 yields the address of *whatever happens to be next to the array in memory*. Attempting to access that location could have disastrous effects. Similarly, attempting to access a + 10 could be disastrous.

When two pointers are subtracted, the result is the distance between them, measured in array elements. For example, the value of q - p is 6. The value of p - q is -6. You can also tell which of the two pointers points "higher" in the array by comparing them. All the usual comparison operators (==, !=, <, >, <=, >=) apply to pointers.

Pointer arithmetic allows us to traverse an array by incrementing a pointer, rather than incrementing an index. For example, the following loop sets all array elements to zero:

```
for(p = &a[0]; p < &a[10]; p++) *p = 0;
```

A special note: evaluating the address of a[10] is okay, even though that array location doesn't exist. What matters is that memory location a[10] is not *accessed*, because the loop quits before p reaches that location.

C programmers often combine the indirection and increment operators. In our case, we wish to set *p to 0 before incrementing p. This can be done with the statement *p++ = 0;. Here the increment operator takes precedence over the indirection operator. Our for loop can now be expressed as follows:

```
p = &a[0];
while (p < &a[10])
   *p++ = 0;
```

Many combinations of these operators are legal, such as `(*p)++` (which increments the value pointed to), `*++p` (which increments p before accessing the location in question), and `*--p` and `*p--`, which decrement p (before or after, respectively) accessing the location in question. The latter two are typically used when the array must be traversed in reverse order.

The name of an array is in fact a pointer to the first location in that array. Thus, in the above situation, the value of a is the same as the value of `&a[0]`. Thus `*a = 0` sets the first element in the array to zero. Pointer arithmetic applies to the array name as well: `*(a + 6) = 5;` changes `a[6]` to 5. This allows us to simplify our loop:

```
p = a;
while (p < a +10)
   *p++ = 0;
```

Important: although the value of a is the address of `a[0]`, the value of a *cannot* be changed.

When an array is passed as an argument to a function, it is always treated as a pointer. Thus, unlike ordinary variables, which are copied when passed as parameters, an array is not copied. The function that receives the array parameter is allowed to change any portion of the array, unless the parameter is prefixed with word `const`. Thus, in C, there is no penalty for passing large arrays as parameters; since they are not copied, efficiency is not an issue. The array parameter can be declared either as an array or as a pointer. For example, the following two function declarations are equivalent:

```
void f(int a[], int n) { ... }
void f(int *a, int n) { ... }
```

One pleasant side effect of all this is that the argument passed into the function can be an array "slice," or a portion beginning at a location other than the start of the array. For example, if the function f above is intended to print the first n elements of its array parameter a, we may call it as follows: `f(&b[6], 4)`. This would cause the function to print the values of `b[6]` through `b[9]`.

A similar argument applies to multidimensional arrays: a function intended to process a single-dimensional array can receive, as its argument, the entry point to a specific *row* in a two-dimensional array, and would work as usual, because the elements of a row in a two-dimensional array are contiguous in memory, as is expected by the function. Consider the following function:

```
void init_array(int a[], int n)
{
   int *p;

   p = a;
   while (p < a + n)
      *p++ = 0;
}
```

This function initializes the first n elements of array a, and thus could be called as follows:

```
int a[10];
init_array(a, 10);
```

However, we could equally use `init_array` to initialize row i of a given two-dimensional array, as follows:

```
int b[12][12];
init_array(&b[i][0], 12);
```

Here we passed in the address of the zeroth element of `b[i]`, which is the first element in the row we wish to have initialized. However, the expression `&b[i][0]` is the same as `b[i]`, so we can write

```
init_array(b[i], 12);
```

Finally, it is possible to use our `init_array` function to initialize an entire two-dimensional array, although some care is required. Our first attempt looks like this:

```
int c[10][10];
init_array(c, 100);
```

Unfortunately, this won't work because c has type int **, whereas init_array expects an argument of type int *. We need to pass c[0] as the argument, because the array c is an array of arrays, and its zeroth element contains the address of element 0 in row 0. The following call works quite nicely:

```
int c[10][10];
init_array(c[0], 100);
```

12.2   Solved Exercises

12.2.1   Solved Exercise 1: Matrix Multiplication

Matrices are the mathematical equivalent of two-dimensional arrays. Adding matrices is quite straightforward: we simply add on an entry-by-entry basis. Multiplying them is quite a different matter. We'll simplify things by assuming that our matrices are square. Here's a description of the result of multiplying two 3×3 matrices, which we'll call A and B:

$$\begin{bmatrix} a & b & c \\ d & e & f \\ g & h & i \end{bmatrix} \times \begin{bmatrix} j & k & l \\ m & n & o \\ p & q & r \end{bmatrix} = \begin{bmatrix} aj+bm+cp & ak+bn+cq & al+bo+cr \\ dj+em+fp & dk+en+fq & dl+eo+fr \\ gj+hm+ip & gk+hn+iq & gl+ho+ir \end{bmatrix}$$

Each entry in the product matrix is the inner product of an entire row of matrix A and an entire column of matrix B. The inner product is obtained by multiplying the corresponding entries, and adding up the results. For example, the top-left entry in the product matrix, aj + bm + cp, is the result of traversing the top row of A (a, b, c), and the left column of B (j, m, p).

Let's develop a program that uses pointer arithmetic to multiply two matrices. The program will prompt the user for the two matrices and it will print the result. In the first version of the program, shown below, we provide a prototype for each of the operations: a function that reads a matrix, a function that fills a matrix with zeroes, a function that multiplies two matrices, and a function that prints a matrix. The main program calls these functions in the proper sequence to solve our problem.

```
#include <stdio.h>

#define N 3

void multiply(int *mat1, int *mat2, int *mat3);
void fill_zero(int *mat);
void read_matrix(int *mat);
void print_matrix(const int *mat);

main()
{
  int mat1[N][N];
  int mat2[N][N];
  int mat3[N][N];

  printf("MATRIX MULTIPLICATION PROGRAM:\n\n");

  fill_zero(mat1[0]);
  fill_zero(mat2[0]);
  fill_zero(mat3[0]);

  printf("Reading the first matrix ...\n");
  read_matrix(mat1[0]);
  printf("Reading the second matrix ...\n");
  read_matrix(mat2[0]);
```

```
    multiply(mat1[0], mat2[0], mat3[0]);

    printf("The resulting matrix is:\n");
    print_matrix(mat3[0]);
    return 0;
}
```

Note that we don't pass as argument the name of any matrix alone; we pass instead the address of the first element in that array. To complete the program, we need to write the code for the various functions. To write `fill_zero`, we need to traverse the entire array, placing zeroes everywhere. A single loop from 0 to N * N - 1 will do; in each iteration we use the current value of `mat` to access the array location, store the zero, and increment `mat`. Note that the value of `mat` itself, like any other parameter, is passed *by value*: we have a copy of the argument value, which is the address of the first element in the array. Thus we are free to modify it, with no danger to the matrix itself. However, once we modify `mat`, `put_zero` has forgotten the address where the matrix began and is unable to process the array a second time (unless we cheat a little and subtract N * N from the final value of `mat`). Fortunately, `fill_zero` needs to traverse the array only once.

To write `print_matrix`, a double `for` loop from 0 to N will do; inside the loop we access the array element, print it, and move on to the next array element. A single loop from 1 to N * N would have worked, but we need to stop every N elements and print a new-line character. With the double `for` loop, our intentions are quite clear.

To write `read_matrix`, a single loop from 0 to N * N - 1 will do; to prompt for the matrix value, we calculate the row and column values as i/N + 1, and i%N + 1. We add one because for the user, the matrix entries are numbered from 1 to N.

Finally, we reach the heart of the matter: multiplying the matrices. Let's consider an example:

$$\begin{bmatrix} 1 & 2 & 3 \\ 4 & 5 & 6 \\ 7 & 8 & 9 \end{bmatrix} \times \begin{bmatrix} 9 & 8 & 7 \\ 6 & 5 & 4 \\ 3 & 2 & 1 \end{bmatrix} = \begin{bmatrix} 30 & 24 & 18 \\ 84 & 69 & 54 \\ 138 & 114 & 90 \end{bmatrix}$$

The traditional method of multiplying the two matrices involves three nested `for` loops: one to iterate through all rows, one to iterate through all columns, and one to calculate the inner product of the current row in `mat1` and the current column in `mat2`. In array terms,

```
for (i = 0; i < N; i++)
    for (j = 0; j < N; j++)
        for (k = 0; k < N; k++)
            mat3[i][j] += mat1[i][k] * mat2[k][j];
```

This version is arguably the clearest and most understandable. However, in the final version of our program (below), we've decided to use pointers. Only two loops are necessary: one that will visit each position in `mat3`, and the other to simultaneously traverse the correct row in `mat1` and the correct column in `mat2` multiplying the corresponding values and adding them up to produce the value to be stored in the current location in `mat3`. Thus, we need three pointers, p1, p2, and p3, each pointing to a specific location in `mat1`, `mat2`, and `mat3`, respectively. The outer loop is as follows:

```
for (p3 = mat3; p3 < mat3 + N * N; p3++) {
    /* Get the current row number   */
    row1 = (p3 - mat3) / N;
    /* Get the current col number */
    col2 = (p3 - mat3) % N;
    /* Pointer to first row, current column in mat2*/
    p2 = mat2 + col2;

    /***********************************************/
    /*   Calculate the value at p3.              */
    /***********************************************/
}
```

For each location p3 visited by this loop, we first calculate a row number (row1) and a column number (col2). Our goal is to process row row1 in mat1, and column col2 in mat2, to calculate the value that belongs at p3. Using row1, we obtain p1row, a pointer to the first element in row row1 in mat1. Then, using col2, we obtain p2, a pointer to the top element in column col2 in mat2. Then the inner loop traverses the row in mat1 and the column in mat2.

```
/* Pointer to start of current row in mat1 */
p1row = mat1 +row1 * N;
/* Traverse the current row */
for (p1 = p1row; p1 < p1row + N; p1++){
   /*  Add result to position in mat3.     */
   *p3 += *p1 * *p2;
   /* Move pointer in mat2 to next row. */
   p2 += N;
}
```

Inside this loop, we multiply the values pointed to by p1 and p2 and add the result to *p3. With each iteration, p1 moves ahead by one array element, and p2 moves down to the next row by advancing N elements.

Here's the final version of the program.

```
#include <stdio.h>

#define N 3

void multiply(int *mat1, int *mat2, int *mat3);
void fill_zero(int *mat);
void read_matrix(int *mat);
void print_matrix(const int *mat);

main()
{
  int mat1[N][N];
  int mat2[N][N];
  int mat3[N][N];

  printf("MATRIX MULTIPLICATION PROGRAM:\n\n");

  fill_zero(mat1[0]);
  fill_zero(mat2[0]);
  fill_zero(mat3[0]);

  printf("Reading the first matrix ...\n");
  read_matrix(mat1[0]);
  printf("Reading the second matrix ...\n");
  read_matrix(mat2[0]);

  multiply(mat1[0], mat2[0], mat3[0]);

  printf("The resulting matrix is:\n");
  print_matrix(mat3[0]);
  return 0;
}

void multiply(int *mat1, int *mat2, int *mat3)
{
  int row1, col2;
  int *p1row, *p1, *p2, *p3;

  /* traverse all of mat3   */
  for (p3 = mat3; p3 < mat3 + N * N; p3++) {
    /* Get the current row number   */
```

```
      row1 = (p3 - mat3) / N;
      /* Get the current col number */
      col2 = (p3 - mat3) % N;
      /* Pointer to first row, current column in mat2*/
      p2 = mat2 + col2;
      /* Pointer to start of current row in mat1 */
      p1row = mat1 +row1 * N;

      /* Traverse the current row */
      for (p1 = p1row; p1 < p1row + N; p1++){
        /* Multiply values from mat1 and mat2; */
        /*  Add result to position in mat3.     */
        *p3 += *p1 * *p2;
        /* Move pointer in mat2 to next row. */
        p2 += N;
      }
    }
  }
}

void read_matrix(int *mat)
{
  int i;

  for (i = 0; i < N * N; i++) {
    printf("Please type the element in row %d, column %d: ",
           i / N + 1, i % N +1);
    scanf("%d", mat++);
  }
  printf("\n\n");
}

void print_matrix(const int *mat)
{
  int i, j;

  for (i = 0; i < N; i++) {
    for (j = 0; j < N; j++)
      printf("%3i  ", *mat++);
    printf("\n");
  }
}

void fill_zero(int *mat)
{
  int i;

  for (i = 0; i < N * N; i++)
    *mat++ = 0;
}
```

Here's some sample output of the program:

```
MATRIX MULTIPLICATION PROGRAM:

Reading the first matrix ...
Please type the element in row 1, column 1: 1
Please type the element in row 1, column 2: 2
Please type the element in row 1, column 3: 3
Please type the element in row 2, column 1: 4
Please type the element in row 2, column 2: 5
Please type the element in row 2, column 3: 6
Please type the element in row 3, column 1: 7
Please type the element in row 3, column 2: 8
Please type the element in row 3, column 3: 9
```

```
Reading the second matrix ...
Please type the element in row 1, column 1: 9
Please type the element in row 1, column 2: 8
Please type the element in row 1, column 3: 7
Please type the element in row 2, column 1: 6
Please type the element in row 2, column 2: 5
Please type the element in row 2, column 3: 4
Please type the element in row 3, column 1: 3
Please type the element in row 3, column 2: 2
Please type the element in row 3, column 3: 1


The resulting matrix is:
 30   24   18
 84   69   54
138  114   90
```

12.3   Programming Exercises

1. A vector is an ordered collection of values; the term is used by mathematicians and physicists. An array is a very straightforward way to implement a vector on a computer. Two vectors are multiplied on an entry-by-entry basis, e.g. (1,2,3) * (4,5,6) = (4,10,18). Write the function `mult_vec(int *v1, int *v2, int *v3, int n);`. This function multiplies vectors v1 and v2 and stores the result in v3. n is the length of the vectors.

2. Write the function `int comp_vec(int *v1, int *v2, int n);`. It should return 1 if vectors v1 and v2 are equal, and 0 otherwise. n is the length of the vectors.

3. Modify Solved Exercise 1 in Chapter 11 so that we use a two-cell array to represent a complex number. You'll need to change all the operations.

4. Write the function `int is_ident(int *mat, int n);`. mat is an n×n matrix. This function should return 1 if mat is the identity matrix, and 0 otherwise. (Reminder: the identity matrix has zeroes everywhere, except along its main diagonal).

5. Write the function `sort_vec(int *vec, int n);`. v is an array of length n. This function should sort its elements.

6. Rewrite the function of Exercise 2 so that it will compare matrices instead of vectors. Is there a way you can do this while leaving your function unchanged?

7. Rewrite the solved exercise of this chapter, so that instead of multiplying two N×N matrices, it multiplies an N×M matrix by an M×L matrix.

8. Extend the matrix multiplication program to add and subtract matrices.

9. The lower triangle of a 5×5 matrix is shown in the following diagram:

$$\begin{bmatrix} 0 & 0 & 0 & 0 & 0 \\ 0 & 0 & 0 & 0 & 0 \\ 0 & 0 & X & 0 & 0 \\ 0 & X & X & X & 0 \\ X & X & X & X & X \end{bmatrix}$$

Write a function that fills the lower triangle of an N×N matrix with zeroes. *Hint:* if N is even, the matrix's lower triangle doesn't have a single entry at its apex.

10. The upper triangle of a 5×5 matrix is shown in the following diagram:

$$\begin{bmatrix} X & X & X & X & X \\ 0 & X & X & X & 0 \\ 0 & 0 & X & 0 & 0 \\ 0 & 0 & 0 & 0 & 0 \\ 0 & 0 & 0 & 0 & 0 \end{bmatrix}$$

Write a function that compares the lower triangle of an n×n matrix with its own upper triangle. The function should return 1 if they're equal, and 0 otherwise. For example:

$$\begin{bmatrix} 1 & 2 & 3 & 4 & 5 \\ 6 & 1 & 2 & 3 & 9 \\ 0 & 5 & 1 & 0 & 0 \\ 0 & 1 & 2 & 3 & 0 \\ 1 & 2 & 3 & 4 & 5 \end{bmatrix} \text{ returns 1, but } \begin{bmatrix} 1 & 2 & 3 & 4 & 5 \\ 0 & 1 & 2 & 3 & 0 \\ 0 & 0 & 1 & 0 & 0 \\ 0 & 3 & 4 & 5 & 0 \\ 1 & 4 & 7 & 1 & 7 \end{bmatrix} \text{ returns 0.}$$

11. Write the function `vec_to_mat(int *v, int *mat, int n)`; v is a vector with n×n elements, stored in *column-major* representation. mat is an n×n matrix. The function should copy the elements from v to mat. For example, if v is (1 2 3 4 5 6 7 8 9), the value of mat should be

$$\begin{bmatrix} 1 & 4 & 7 \\ 2 & 5 & 8 \\ 3 & 6 & 9 \end{bmatrix}$$

12. Write a function that reverses the positions of the elements in a vector. For example, reversing the vector (1 6 3 7) yields the vector (7 3 6 1). *Note:* The goal is not merely to print the numbers in reverse order; it is to *store* them in reverse order.

13. Write the function `void transpose(int *mat, int n)`; mat is an n×n matrix. The function transposes its rows with its columns. For example,

$$\begin{bmatrix} 1 & 2 & 3 \\ 4 & 5 & 6 \\ 7 & 8 & 9 \end{bmatrix} \text{ transposed is } \begin{bmatrix} 1 & 4 & 7 \\ 2 & 5 & 8 \\ 3 & 6 & 9 \end{bmatrix}$$

14. Write a program that fills an n×n matrix in a spiral pattern. Example:

$$\begin{bmatrix} 7 & 6 & 5 \\ 8 & 1 & 4 \\ 9 & 2 & 3 \end{bmatrix}$$

15. Modify the `max_min.c` program on page 214 in the main text so that it uses pointer arithmetic.

13 Strings

13.1 Chapter Summary

13.1.1 String Basics

C has *string constants* (also known as *literals*), and *string variables*, whose value can change during the execution of a program. A string literal is a sequence of characters enclosed in double quotes, such as `"abc"`. The characters inside a string literal can contain escape sequences, such as `"abc\n"`. String literals can be continued from one line to another, by either placing a backslash at the end of the line being continued, or by splitting the string over several lines, closing the string on the current line, and reopening it on the next. In ANSI C, two such adjacent strings are interpreted as a single one, for example,

```
printf("This is a long, long, long, long, long, "
       "long, long, long, long, long string");
```

String literals are stored as arrays of characters, with the special *null character* stored at the end of the string. Thus the string `"abc"` is stored in an array of four adjacent characters: `'a'`, `'b'`, `'c'`, and `'\0'`. A string literal is of type `char *`, i.e., a pointer to a character.

A string literal can be used in an expression, and its value (which is a pointer) can be assigned, as in `char *p; p = "abc"`. Such a pointer can also be subscripted as if it were an array: `"abc"[2]` yields the character `'c'`.

String literals are very different from character constants. `"a"` is very different from `'a'`; the former is a pointer to a memory location that contains the character a (followed by `'\0'`), and the latter is the ASCII value 97. For example, the statement `printf("%d %d\n", 'a', "a")` will print something like `97 74226`. The second number is the address of `"a"`, which depends on the compiler. Using double quotes when single quotes are required, or vice versa, can cause severe problems.

Unlike other programming languages, C has no special data type for strings. Instead, an array of characters is a string, and the null character is used to terminate it. We typically declare a string variable as an array of characters: `char str[11]` will hold strings of maximum length 10. The actual length of the string, at any given point, is determined by the location of the null character.

A string variable can be initialized when declared: `char message[6] = "Hello";`. The initial value is *not* a literal; it is in fact a shorthand for the traditional manner for initializing arrays: `char message[6] = {'H','e','l','l','o','\0'}`. If not enough values are given, the compiler will fill in with zeroes (null characters), as is usual for arrays. It is often a good idea to omit the length of the string, leaving it for the compiler to calculate.

Character arrays and character pointers are very similar, but not identical. For example, `char a[] = "hi"` and `char *a = "hi"` can both be used as strings and can be passed as parameters in either form to functions, but they are quite different. In the array version, the characters can be changed. Not so in the pointer version. In the array version, the name a cannot be changed, but in the pointer version it can be changed to point to another string.

To read and write strings, we generally use the `%s` conversion specification in the `printf` and `scanf` functions. When using `scanf` to read in a string, it's not necessary to use the address operator `&`: `scanf("%s", str)` is enough because `str` is already a pointer. When reading a string with `scanf`, leading white-space characters are ignored, and then characters are read in until another white-space character appears. Thus `scanf` will not necessarily read until the end of the current input line; it will stop when it encounters, for instance, a space. To get around this we use `gets(str)`. The `gets` function reads characters until the first new-line character, allowing spaces and tabs to form part of the input string. Similarly, `puts(str)` will print string `str` and add a new-line character.

C programmers often write their own string input routines, reading in the characters one by one, to suit their own needs. To process the characters in a string, we can use the string name as an array, and repeatedly increment an index i, as in

```
for (i = 0; s[i] != '\0'; i++) /* use s[i] ...*/
```

or we can repeatedly increment a string pointer *s:

```
for (; *s != '\0'; s++) /* use *s ... */
```

C programmers traditionally prefer to use pointers to access characters in a string, rather than an array index, although either one is legal.

13.1.2   String Operations

The C language itself has very few operators that work on strings. Specifically, = (assignment), == (equality), and the relational operators do not work with strings, because the string name is merely a pointer. Fortunately, the C library provides a rich set of functions for performing operations on strings. To use them, you must add the directive #include <string.h> to your program. The four most commonly used string functions in the string library are:

1. String copy: char *strcpy(char *s1, const char *s2);.
    This copies characters from s2 to s1, up to and including the first null character in s2. Note the const modifier: strcpy will not change string s2. strcpy is used to assign values to string variables, such as strcpy(str, "abc"), and to copy strings from one variable to another, such as strcpy(str1, str2). Note that strcpy does *not* check whether the string s2 fits in s1; if it doesn't, the results will be unpredictable. The function returns the value of its first argument, which on occasion is useful.
2. String concatenation: char *strcat(char *s1, const char *s2);.
    This appends characters from s2 onto the end of s1. s2 is not modified, and the length of s1 is extended. strcat does not verify whether s1 is long enough to accommodate the new characters added on to it.
3. String comparison: int strcmp(const char *s1, const char *s2);.
    This function compares strings s1 and s2 and returns a negative value, zero, or a positive value, depending on whether s1 is less than, equal to, or greater than s2. We can then test the return value: if (strcmp(str1, str2) >= 0).... In this way any relation between strings can be tested. strcmp uses *lexicographical* ordering to compare strings, which is similar to the ordering used in dictionaries: "abc" is less than "abd", and "abc" is less than "abcd". Individual characters are compared according to their numerical values. It's useful to know where some characters lie in the ASCII code: the space character has the value 32, characters '0' through '9' have values 48 through 57, upper-case letters have values 65 through 90, and lower-case letters have values 97 through 122.
4. String length: size_t strlen(const char *s);.
    This returns the number of characters in string s without including the null character. The type size_t is defined in the C library and is usually either unsigned int or unsigned long int. Under normal circumstances, we treat the return value as an ordinary integer.

Many useful expressions in C, called *idioms*, have been developed. First, to locate the end of a string, we use while (*s) s++; or while (*s++); The first version leaves s pointing to the null character that terminates s. The second version leaves s pointing just past the null character. To copy one string to another, we use while (*s1++ = *s2++);. With each iteration, *s2 is copied to *s1, and then both pointers move ahead by one character. The loop quits when the result of the assignment is zero, which will take place is soon as the null character is copied.

13.1.3   Arrays of Strings

The first (obvious) way to store a collection of strings is to have a two-dimensional array:

```
char names[][10] = {"Joe", "Bob", "Emeterius"};
```

The first dimension can be omitted, because it's obvious from the initializer that there are three rows. In the other dimension, we're forced to specify the length of the longest string we have, i.e., 10. Each of three rows in the array has 10 columns, much of which is wasted. To prevent this waste, we instead create an array of pointers to strings:

```
char *names[] = {"Joe", "Bob", "Emeterius"};
```

We no longer have a two-dimensional array. Instead, each array element contains a pointer to the corresponding string, and each string is of exactly the correct length. Thus, names[2] points to a string with 10 characters, but names[1] and names[0] each point to a string containing 4 characters.

A very useful application of arrays of strings appears when we use ***program parameters***, sometimes known as ***command-line arguments***. Once a C program is compiled, often a command line is used to execute it, such as >myprog. Many programs allow options, or arguments, on the command line that executes the program. For example, the UNIX ls command lists the contents of the current directory. One option is to obtain the "long" format, and another is to recursively list the contents of subdirectories: ls -l -r. These command-line arguments are available to *all* C programs (including the ls program, which is written in, you guessed it, C). To use them, one must declare main as a function with two parameters, as follows:

```
main(int argc, char *argv[])
{
    ...
}
```

argc contains the number of command-line arguments, including the name of the program. argv is an array containing all the strings that form the command line. For example, assume the command ls -l -r is used. In the ls program, argc will be 3, argv[0] will be the program name, argv[1] will be the string "-l", argv[2] will be string "-r", and argv[3] will be the null pointer.

13.2   Solved Exercises

13.2.1   Solved Exercise 1: Indenting a C Program

We're often a little careless about indenting our programs. Let's write a program that will read in the source text of a program, indent it properly, and write it back out. We'll take the number of characters to indent as a program parameter. To simplify the program, we'll assume all the { and } characters are the first non-space characters in the lines in which they appear. This means deviating a little from our established program style. Specifically, left braces following keywords (e.g., if, while), which we normally place at the end of the same line, will appear by themselves on the next line. In addition, case statements in switch statements will have to be surrounded by braces; otherwise the indenting program will be unable to indent them.

The program, shown below, allows lines of maximum length 512 characters. We have two functions, remove_spaces and add_spaces, to remove leading spaces from a given line and to indent or add the proper number of spaces. The main program first ensures that a program parameter is in fact provided. The string stored in argv[1] must be converted to an int. A number of ways to do this exist and will be covered later. For now, we simply assume that the string begins with a single digit, and we extract it. Then the program repeatedly reads in a complete line using gets (quitting the loop if the string is empty, i.e., if gets returns NULL), de-spaces the line with remove_spaces, and examines the first character. If it's a '{', the line is indented before incrementing the current indentation depth. If the first character is '}', then the current indentation depth is decremented before indenting the line. Empty lines are left alone, and all other lines are indented at the current indentation depth. After processing each line, it is printed using puts. Here's the complete program. You may notice that it is poorly (in fact, pathetically) indented.

```c
#include <stdio.h>
#include <string.h>

#define LINE_SIZE 512
#define TAB '\t'

/**********************************************************/
/* This program indents the source text of a C program. */
/* It requires that every bracket ('{') be the first    */
/* non-space character in the line. Lines of maximum     */
/* length 512 can be handled. The number of characters   */
/* to indent is taken as a program parameter.            */
/**********************************************************/

void remove_spaces(char *s);
void add_spaces(char *s, int curr_indent);

main(int argc, char *argv[])
  {
    int curr_indent = 0, indent;
    char line[LINE_SIZE];

  if (argc != 2)
   {
   printf("INDENTER needs an integer value\n");
   }
   else
   {
     indent = argv[1][0] - '0';
    while (gets(line) != NULL)
     {
     remove_spaces(line);
     switch (line[0])
       {
       case '\n': break;
       case '{' :
       {
         add_spaces(line, curr_indent);
           curr_indent +=  indent;
           break;
       }
       case '}' :
       {
          curr_indent -= indent;
          add_spaces(line, curr_indent);
        break;
       }
       default  :
       {
             add_spaces(line, curr_indent);
           }
       }
     puts(line);
     }
 }
return 0;
}

void remove_spaces(char *s)
{
  int i = 0;
  char p[LINE_SIZE];
```

```
  strcpy(p, "");
    strcpy(p, s);
  while ((p[i] == ' ') || (p[i] == TAB))
    {
   i++;
  }
  strcpy(s, &p[i]);
}

void add_spaces(char *s, int curr_indent)
{
 char p[LINE_SIZE];
   int i = 0;

 strcpy(p, "");
 while (i++ < curr_indent)
  {
   strcat(p, " ");
   }
 strcat(p, s);
 strcpy(s, p);
}
```

After compiling this program, we can run it on its own source file! Since the program reads from standard input and writes to standard output, we need to use file redirection. For example, the following UNIX commands would do it:

```
cc indenter.c -o indenter
indenter 2 < indenter.c
```

The resulting program text looks much better:

```
#include <stdio.h>
#include <string.h>

#define LINE_SIZE 512
#define TAB '\t'

/**********************************************************/
/* This program indents the source text of a C program. */
/* It requires that every bracket ('{') be the first    */
/* non-space character in the line. Lines of maximum     */
/* length 512 can be handled. The number of characters   */
/* to indent is taken as a program parameter.            */
/**********************************************************/

void remove_spaces(char *s);
void add_spaces(char *s, int curr_indent);

main(int argc, char *argv[])
{
  int curr_indent = 0, indent;
  char line[LINE_SIZE];

  if (argc != 2)
  {
    printf("INDENTER needs an integer value\n");
  }
  else
  {
    indent = argv[1][0] - '0';
    while (gets(line) > 0)
    {
      remove_spaces(line);
```

```
        switch (line[0])
        {
          case '\n': break;
          case '{' :
          {
            add_spaces(line, curr_indent);
            curr_indent +=  indent;
            break;
          }
          case '}' :
          {
            curr_indent -= indent;
            add_spaces(line, curr_indent);
            break;
          }
          default   :
          {
            add_spaces(line, curr_indent);
          }
        }
        puts(line);
      }
    }
    return 0;
}

void remove_spaces(char *s)
{
  int i = 0;
  char p[LINE_SIZE];

  strcpy(p, "");
  strcpy(p, s);
  while ((p[i] == ' ') || (p[i] == TAB))
  {
    i++;
  }
  strcpy(s, &p[i]);
}

void add_spaces(char *s, int curr_indent)
{
  char p[LINE_SIZE];
  int i = 0;

  strcpy(p, "");
  while (i++ < curr_indent)
  {
    strcat(p, " ");
  }
  strcat(p, s);
  strcpy(s, p);
}
```

13.3   Programming Exercises

1.   Write a program that reads the first word on the first input line (say, w_1), the first word on the second line (say, w_2), and replaces every occurrence of w_1 with w_2 in the remaining lines of the input file. Assume that spaces and tabs are word separators.

2.   Write a program that will read in two numbers (n_1 and n_2) from the first line of the input, and then swaps lines n_1 and n_2 on the remaining lines of the input. For example, if n_1 is 3 and n_2 is 7, then lines 3 and 7 on the input are to be swapped. Generate an error message if the input file contains an insufficient number of lines to carry out this task.

3.   Write a program similar to that of the preceding exercise, except that instead of swapping lines n_1 and n_2, copy line n_1 to line n_2. Print an error message if there are not enough lines in the input.

4.   Write a program that will justify its input text. The first line of the input will determine the type of justification. The first word on the input should read `left`, `center`, or `right`. An error message should appear if none of these three appear there. The remaining input lines should be justified accordingly. Assume a maximum line length of 80 characters.

5.   Write a program that will merge two pieces of text, line by line. Both files appear on the input, one after the other, separated by a line with a single character `%`. Calculate the length of the longest line on the first portion of text. For example, consider the input

```
abc
def
%
ghi
jkl
mno
```

The output would be as follows:

```
abc ghi
def jkl
    mno
```

6.   Write a program that reads in the first word of the first line, then counts the number of occurrences of that word in the remainder of the input file.

7.   Write a program that counts the number of characters, words, and lines in its input. Assume spaces, tabs, and new-line characters separate words.

8.   Write a program that reads in and reverses the lines of its input file, so the first line will be last on the output and vice versa.

9.   Write a program that reads in a string and prints it in reverse. The program should recognize palindromes (strings that are the same whether reversed or not).

10. Combine exercises 8 and 9.

11. Make three lists of constant strings: one of nouns (N), one of verbs (V), and one of adjectives (A). Then write a program that generates all possible sentences you can write using the words on your lists, using the following formula: NVAN.

12. Write a program that eliminates duplicate lines from its input.

13. Write a function `string_replace(char *s, int c, int r)` that replaces every instance of character `c` in string `s` with character `r`.

14. Write a program that reads two strings (one on each line) and returns the number of times the first string appears in the second one.

15. Write a program that will format its input for printing purposes. Using the `argc` and `argv` program parameters, have your program accept options `-l` *n* (to print pages with *n* lines apiece), `-d` (to doublespace the output), `-t` *n* (to replace each tab with *n* spaces), `-s` *n* (to replace every *n* spaces with a tab), `-o` *n* (to offset the output by *n* characters in the left margin, and `-n` (to number the lines on the output).

16. Reimplement the plotting program (Solved Exercise of Chapter 9) using strings.

17. Write a simple address book program. Store the names of people in an array of strings. In two additional parallel arrays, store their addresses and telephone numbers. Set up a menu to insert, delete, and look up addresses and numbers in the address book.

18. Write a program that will copy its input to its output, but will eliminate any two consecutive identical lines.

19. Write a function `stoi(char *s)` that converts the digit characters stored in s into an integer. Use Horner's rule, discussed in Exercise 21 of Chapter 6.

14 The Preprocessor

14.1 Chapter Summary

The `#include` and `#define` directives aren't really processed by the C compiler. They are processed by the C *preprocessor*, a program that edits the text of the C program before passing it along to the C compiler.

The preprocessor goes through the user's program looking for *preprocessor directives*: commands that begin with the # character. The preprocessor carries out these directives and removes them, replacing them with empty lines. The # symbol need not be the first one on the line, but it must be the first non-white-space character on that line. The various tokens in a preprocessor directive can be separated by white space. To continue a preprocessor directive on the next line, you must use the backslash (\). Directives can appear anywhere, not just at the beginning of the program, and they can contain comments like any other piece of C code.

There are three principal types of directives: *macro definitions* (`#define`), *file inclusions* (`#include`), and *conditional compilation* (`#if`).

The `#include` directive tells the preprocessor to open a file and to include its contents as part of the program being compiled. For example, upon encountering `#include <stdio.h>`, the preprocessor brings in the contents of file `stdio.h`, which is in a predetermined location. The file contains (among other things) prototypes for the input/output functions. More details on the `#include` directive will be covered in Chapter 15.

14.1.1 Macro Definition

The `#define` directive defines a *macro*, a name that the user wishes to have replaced with something else. The preprocessor stores the name and the definition. Later, whenever the name occurs in the program, the preprocessor replaces the name with the definition. The general form of the `#define` directive is

$$\text{\#define } identifier \text{ } replacement\text{-}list$$

The replacement list is a sequence of tokens, including identifiers, keywords, numbers, character constants, string literals, operators, and punctuation. Simple macros are most useful for naming important values. There are several advantages. The first is readability; TRUE is more descriptive than 1. Second, the program is easier to modify, because if a value changes, we only need to change the macro definition, rather than tracking down all the places where the macro is used. Third, by typing a value only once, we avoid typographical errors, especially for complicated values such as `#define PI 3.141592`. Fourth, we can enhance the language somewhat by replacing certain keywords with others that we may find more descriptive. For example, Pascal programmers prefer begin and end to { and }. Technically, we can change the language's syntax quite a bit, but it's generally not considered a good idea, because other people might have trouble reading our programs. Fifth, we can name new types, such as `#define BOOL int`, although type definitions are a better way to do it. Finally, through a directive such as `#define DEBUG` (with no value) we can use the fact that DEBUG has been defined to control conditional compilation, as we shall see soon.

A *parameterized macro* has the following form:

$$\text{\#define } identifier(x_1, x_2, \ldots x_n) \text{ } replacement\text{-}list$$

The *x*'s are identifiers, and the idea is to use them in the replacement list. There can be no space between the identifier and the left parenthesis, otherwise the preprocessor will think we have a simple macro. The preprocessor stores the name of the macro and its parameterized definition. Later, when an *invocation* of the form $identifier(y_1, y_2, \ldots y_n)$ appears, the preprocessor replaces the invocation with the replacement list, substituting y_1 for x_1, etc. For example, consider

```
#define IS_ODD(n) ((n) % 2 != 0)
```

When it encounters the invocation IS_ODD(3 + 5), the preprocessor will replace n with the expression 3 + 5, yielding ((3 + 5) % 2 != 0), which evaluates to 0. The set of parentheses around n is a good idea, in case the invocation contains operators with a lower precedence than %. For example, you are encouraged to try the invocation IS_ODD(3 > 5) both with and without the parentheses around n in the macro definition. In general, parentheses surrounding the replacement list are recommended if the list contains any operator, and parentheses are recommended surrounding every parameter.

Parameterized macros can serve as simple functions to do a variety of tasks, such as character manipulation, input/output handling, or useful comparisons. The parameter list can be empty, but is useful so the macro will look like a function. Using parameterized macros can be slightly faster, because function calls incur overhead: the return address must be saved, arguments copied, etc. Macros incur no overhead. Macros can also be "generic": a comparison operation can work for integers, floats, characters, doubles, and so on.

Using macros also has some disadvantages. First, the code generated by the compiler can be larger, because each and every occurrence of the macro will be expanded. Second, the arguments are subjected to no type-checking whatsoever, and errors can go undetected by the compiler. Third, it's not possible to have a pointer to a macro, as is the case (which we'll see later) for functions. Fourth, the arguments of a macro can be evaluated more than once, but those of a function will only be evaluated once. This is especially problematic whenever the invocation of a macro has a side effect. For example, consider

```
#define twice(n) (n + n)
... twice(i++)
```

Here we smartly thought that adding n to itself would be more efficient than multiplying by 2, but the expression i++ is evaluated twice, causing i to be incremented twice. With a function, that would not have happened.

Two other macro operators are # and ##. # can appear only in the replacement list of a parameterized macro, and its purpose is to substitute the text of the argument in the form of a string literal, rather than the usual form of the argument's text. For example, consider

```
#define PRINT(x) printf("%s = %d\n", #x, x)
int i = 3;
PRINT(i);
PRINT(i+7);
```

This will print

```
i = 3
i+7 = 10
```

The ## macro operator glues tokens together to form a single token. Although this is not a very commonly used feature, it is useful in some cases. Consider the following program:

```
#include <stdio.h>

#define GEN_PRINT(type, letter) \
    void print_##type(type x) {printf("%" #letter "\n", x);}
GEN_PRINT(int, d)
GEN_PRINT(float, f)

main()
{
  print_int(3);
  print_float(3.4);
  return 0;
}
```

In this program the macro GEN_PRINT takes two arguments: a type name and a conversion specification letter. GEN_PRINT then generates a type-specific printing function, which will print a value of the given type with the given conversion specification letter. In the above example, two functions named print_int and print_float were generated.

Macros may invoke other macros in their replacement lists, such as

```
#define TRUE 1
#define FALSE (1-TRUE)
```

When invoking FALSE, we obtain (1-TRUE), which is then *rescanned* to look for other macros. Macros are rescanned as many times as necessary.

The preprocessor replaces only the text of entire tokens, not portions thereof. For example, after #define n 30, the text int m = n will undergo the replacement of only one n, the second one. The first n is part of a larger token, namely int. To make this problem even less likely to occur, I recommend you stick to using all capital letters in macro names. Macro definitions normally remain in effect until the end of the file, regardless of scope rules. Macro definitions are not local to functions. Macros cannot be redefined, unless the new definition is identical to the old one. However, macros can be *undefined*, using the #undef directive, which then allows a new definition for the macro.

The comma and semicolon operators can appear in the replacement list of a macro, thereby creating long macros containing entire sequences of instructions, but you must be careful with semicolons.

Several handy predefined macros exist. Type and run the following program.

```
#include <stdio.h>

main()
{
  printf("%d\n", __LINE__);
  printf("%s\n", __FILE__);
  printf("%s\n", __DATE__);
  printf("%s\n", __TIME__);
  printf("%d\n", __STDC__);
  return 0;
}
```

14.1.2   Conditional Compilation

The #if and #endif directives are used to include or exclude sections of the program text, depending on the outcome of a test performed by the preprocessor. For example, if we wish to print debugging information, we'll begin with the macro definition #define DEBUG 1. The statements that produce the debugging information can now be surrounded by an #if-#endif pair. As long as DEBUG has that nonzero value, the debugging statements will be left in the program. If we wish to turn off the printing of debugging information, we merely change the macro definition: #define DEBUG 0. When the preprocessor encounters the #if, the lines between it and the #endif directive are excluded.

The defined operator (which applies to an identifier) determines whether that identifier is currently defined as a macro. If it is, the result is the value 1 (true). If not, the resulting value is 0 (false). Thus the #if directive can include or exclude code, depending on whether a macro is currently defined: #if defined DEBUG. Another way to accomplish this is to use #ifdef and ifndef, which test whether the identifier is currently defined or not defined, respectively.

The #line directive is used to change the way the compiler keeps track of line numbers, mostly for purposes of reporting error messages. #line *n* tells the compiler to begin acting as if the current line number were *n*, i.e., it changes the __LINE__ macro. The #line *n "file"* macro changes both __LINE__ and __FILE__, to make the compiler think it is currently located at line *n* in file *"file"*. This feature is mostly used by programs that generate C code as their output, usually by taking some code from the user and appending it to some other code that provides a certain facility. The resulting file may be, say, 30 lines longer than the original. When compiling the new file, it is useful to have error messages refer not only to the line numbers in the original file, but to the original file name.

Finally, the #pragma directive is used to give special commands to the C compiler. This directive varies from compiler to compiler.

14.2   Solved Exercises

We'll use the preprocessor to solve two problems in this chapter. First, we'll implement stacks in two ways, using macros and functions, so we can compare their efficiency. Second, we'll implement stacks of three different types of values (int, float, and char) without having to write three similar pieces of code.

14.2.1   Solved Exercise 1: Macros versus Functions

Here we contrast two programs, both of which reverse a series of numbers by pushing them onto a stack and then popping them off. The first program, shown below, uses macros to push and pop values from the stack. We include the <time.h> header (see Chapter 26), because we wish to use the clock function, which returns the time elapsed (in "clock ticks") since the beginning of the program's execution. In the program, we call clock and store its value, once when we are about to begin pushing the values onto the stack, and once again when we're done, so we can subtract the second value from the first. The stack elements are stored in an array s, with s[0] reserved for storing the number of element currently in the stack. The program requests the user to enter the number of values to be reversed. Here's the first program.

```
/**************************************************************/
/* This program implements one STACK, with basic operations  */
/* push, pop, and init.                                       */
/* The operations are implemented via macros to contrast      */
/* their performance versus functions.                        */
/**************************************************************/

#include <stdio.h>
#include <time.h>          /* to access the internal clock */

#define MAX_STACK_SIZE 1024
#define count(s) s[0]
      /* s[0] contains the current number of elements  */

#define init(s) \
  do { \
    for (i = 1; i < MAX_STACK_SIZE; i++) \
      s[i] = 0; \
    count(s) = 0; \
  } while (0)

#define push(e, s) \
  do { \
    if (count(s) < stack_size) \
      s[stack_size - count(s)++] = e; \
    else \
      printf("Stack's full.\n"); \
  } while (0);

#define pop(e, s) \
  do { \
    if (count(s) == 0) \
      printf("The stack is empty.\n"); \
    else \
      e = s[stack_size - (count(s)--) + 1]; \
  } while (0)
```

```
main()
{
  int i, e, stack_size;
  int s[MAX_STACK_SIZE];
  clock_t first_tick;

  printf("Enter number of values to be reversed: ");
  scanf("%d", &stack_size);
  if (stack_size > MAX_STACK_SIZE) {
    printf("Maximum stack size allowed is %d.\n",
           MAX_STACK_SIZE - 1);
    return 1;
  }
  first_tick = clock();
  init(s);
  for (i = 1; i <= stack_size; i++)
    push(i, s);
  printf("The reversed list is:\n");
  for (i = 1; i <= stack_size; i++) {
    pop(e, s);
    printf("%d, ", e);
  }
  printf("\n");
  printf("Elapsed time: %d\n", (int)(clock() - first_tick));
  return 0;
}
```

In the second version of the program, we use functions instead of macros. You should type in and run these two programs to contrast their running times. Functions generally incur some overhead, through time spent setting up the function call, copying parameters, etc. Macros have no such cost, so generally you'll find the first program a little faster (but often not by much!) than the second one. To appreciate the difference in performance a little better, you might want to change MAX_STACK_SIZE to a larger value.

```
/**********************************************************/
/* This program implements one STACK, with basic operations */
/* push, pop, and init.                                      */
/* The operations are implemented via functions to contrast  */
/* their performance versus macros.                          */
/**********************************************************/

#include <stdio.h>
#include <stdlib.h>
#include <time.h>        /* to access the internal clock */

#define MAX_STACK_SIZE 1024
#define count(s) s[0]
       /* s[0] contains the current number of elements */

int stack_size = 0;

void init(int *s);
void push(int e, int *s);
int  pop(int *s);

main()
{
  int i, e;
  int s[MAX_STACK_SIZE];
  clock_t first_tick;

  printf("Enter number of values to be reversed: ");
  scanf("%d", &stack_size);
  if (stack_size > MAX_STACK_SIZE) {
```

```
      printf("Maximum stack size allowed is %d.\n",
             MAX_STACK_SIZE - 1);
      return 1;
    }
    first_tick = clock();
    init(s);
    for (i = 1; i <= stack_size; i++)
      push(i, s);
    printf("The reversed list is:\n");
    for (i = 1; i <= stack_size; i++) {
      e = pop(s);
      printf("%d, ", e);
    }
    printf("\n");
    printf("Elapsed time: %d.\n", (int)(clock() - first_tick));
    return 0;
  }

  void init(int *s)
  {
    int i;

    for (i = 1; i < MAX_STACK_SIZE; i++)
      s[i] = 0;
    count(s) = 0;
  }

  void push(int e, int *s)
  {
    if (count(s) < stack_size)
      s[stack_size - count(s)++] = e;
    else
      printf("Stack is full.\n");
  }

  int pop(int *s)
  {
    if (count(s) == 0) {
      printf("The stack is empty.\n");
      exit(1);
    } else
      return (s[stack_size - count(s)-- + 1]);
  }
```

14.2.2   Solved Exercise 2: Stacks of Different Types

Here we'll implement stacks of three different types of values (int, float, and char) without
having to write three entire programs. We'll share code that is common to all three types, and we'll use
the preprocessor to select the appropriate type whenever necessary. We will read the values from the
input, push them onto the stack, and print them out in reverse order.

```
/******************************************************************/
/* This program implements one STACK, with basic operations       */
/* push, pop, and init.                                            */
/* The operations are implemented via macros, using macros         */
/* to allow stack elements to be of various types.                 */
/******************************************************************/

#include <stdio.h>

#define MAX_STACK_SIZE 12
#define FALSE 0
#define TRUE  1
```

```
#define INT   TRUE
#define CHAR  FALSE
#define FLOAT FALSE
#define count(s) s[0]

#if INT
  #define TYPE int
#elif  FLOAT
  #define TYPE float
#else
  #define TYPE char
#endif

int stack_size = 0;
void init(TYPE *s);
void push(TYPE e, TYPE *s);
TYPE pop(TYPE *s);

main(int argc, char *argv[])
{
  TYPE e;
  int i;
  TYPE s[MAX_STACK_SIZE];

  printf("Enter number of values to be reversed: ");
  scanf("%d", &stack_size);
  if (stack_size > MAX_STACK_SIZE) {
    printf("Maximum stack size allowed is %d.\n",
            MAX_STACK_SIZE - 1);
    exit(1);
  }
  printf("This program reverses a list of values of type ");
#if INT
    printf("int.");
#elif  FLOAT
    printf("float.");
#else
    printf("char.");
#endif
  printf("\n\n");

  init(s);
  for (i = 0; i < stack_size; i++) {
    printf("Enter value #%1d: ", i);
    #if INT
      scanf("%d", &e);
    #elif  FLOAT
      scanf("%f", &e);
    #else
      scanf(" %c", &e);
    #endif
    push(e, s);
  }
  for (i = 1; i <= stack_size; i++) {
    e = pop(s);
    #if INT
      printf("%d,", e);
    #elif FLOAT
      printf("%6.3f,", e);
    #else
      printf("%c,", e);
    #endif
  }
```

```
      printf("\n");
      return 0;
    }

void init(TYPE *s) {
  int i;

  for (i = 1; i < MAX_STACK_SIZE; i++)
    s[i] = 0;
  count(s) = 0;
}

void push(TYPE e, TYPE *s) {
  if (count(s) < stack_size)
    s[stack_size - (int)count(s)++] = e;
  else
    printf("The Stack is full.\n");
}

TYPE pop(TYPE *s) {
  if (count(s) == 0) {
    printf("The Stack is empty.\n");
    exit(1);
  }
  else
    return (s[stack_size - (int)(count(s)--) + 1]);
}
```

Note that we begin with three #define directives, for INT, CHAR, and FLOAT. Only one should be TRUE (and the rest FALSE) each time the program is compiled. TYPE is defined with a cascade of if-elif-else directives, so the functions can manipulate values of the chosen type. The cascade of if-elif-else preprocessor directives is needed in two more places: when we need to read in a value, and when we need to print a value popped from the stack. All other functions (init, push, and pop) use TYPE directly and need no further modification.

14.3   Programming Exercises

1.   What's the difference between the source code and the preprocessor's output?

2.   Argue for or against the following statement: "There's no reason to ever check the preprocessor's output; whatever our problem is, it must be in the source code."

3.   What's the main difference between the two kinds of macros?

4.   What are the advantages of defining constants as simple macros?

5.   Consider the following code:

```
#include <stdio.h>

#define VALUE 41 /* Value to be printed */

void value_printer();

main()
{
  #undef VALUE
  #define VALUE 45
  value_printer();
  return 0;
}
```

```
    void value_printer()
    {
      #undef VALUE
      #define VALUE 12
      printf("Value = %d\n", VALUE);
    }
```

What is this program's output?

6. Consider the code of the following macro.

```
/*****************************************************/
/* This macro calculates the SIGMA function, from */
/* bottom to top, and places the result in 'sum'. */
/*****************************************************/
#define SIGMA(func, bottom, top, sum) \
do { \
    int i; \
            \
    sum = 0; \
    for (i = bottom; i <= top; i++){ \
      sum += func(i); \
    } \
} while (0)
```

Write the necessary functions and statements to calculate each of the following:

a. $\displaystyle\sum_{i=1}^{100} i$

b. $\displaystyle\sum_{i=-3}^{7} i^3$

c. $\displaystyle\sum_{i=20}^{25} \frac{i}{2}$

d. $\displaystyle\sum_{i=1}^{15} \sqrt{i}$

e. $\displaystyle\sum_{i=10}^{15} \sin(i)$

7. Rewrite the SIGMA macro so that one macro sums up values of various types.

8. Write a macro that counts the number of letters that appear more than once in a string.

9. Write a macro that returns the top element of a stack, using the definitions in the solved exercises.

10. Write a macro that copies stack A to stack B using the stack definitions of the solved exercises.

11. Write a macro named ASSERT(c) that tests the condition c and prints an error message if it is false. Such as macro can be quite useful in verifying that the program is proceeding as expected.

12. Modify your ASSERT(c) macro so that it prints a comprehensive error message, including the text of the condition that failed, the file, and the line number.

13. Revisit some of the programs you have written so far. Look for opportunities to simplify expressions using macros.

14. Write a macro NULLPTR(type), which returns the null pointer, cast to the specified type. For example, NULLPTR(int) would be (int *)NULL.

15. Write a macro GENERIC_PRINT(type) that will produce a type-specific printing function definition. For example, GENERIC_PRINT(int) would produce print_int(int n) {printf("%d\n", n)}.

16. Write a macro STR_WALK(str, func) that traverses string str and calls function func for each character. For example, STR_WALK("abc", f) calls f('a'), then f('b'), and finally f('c').

17. Write a macro error(condition, msg) that prints the string msg only if the condition is true.

18. Write a macro FOREVER that will perform an infinite loop, as follows: FOREVER {printf("young\n");}.

19. Write a macro IN_RANGE(low, high, value) that tests whether value is between low and high.

20. Write a macro PRSTR(s) that prints a string.

15 Writing Large Programs

15.1 Chapter Summary

Large programs in C (and even modest-sized ones) are best written in more than one file. The main advantage of breaking down a program into several files is that its development and debugging are easier, as well as its maintenance. Programs are commonly broken down into several *source files* and *header files*. Header files contain information (usually variable declarations and function prototypes) that is to be shared among several source files. Source files typically contain function definitions and external variables.

Each source file contains a portion of the complete program. By convention, they have names that end in .c. One of the source files must contain the definition of main. Why would we want to break down a program into several pieces? In general, programs manipulate data, and it usually makes sense to collect together all the functions that manipulate data of some kind. For example, in Chapter 10 we developed a program that manipulates sets. It would be useful to isolate the code that implements the sets from the portions of the program that use sets for the particular purpose at hand. This way, we can reuse the code later to perform some other set operations we might want.

15.1.1 Header Files

Whenever a program is divided into pieces, we wind up with situations in which a function in one file calls another in another file. One way to do this is to place the prototype of the function in a header file and use the #include directive to bring that prototype into other files. The #include directive has two forms. The first form is used for library header files:

$$\#include\ <\textit{filename}>$$

A predetermined directory (typically a library directory) is searched for *filename*. The second form is used for all other header files:

$$\#include\ \textit{"filename"}$$

Typically, the current directory is searched for *filename*.

Header files usually contain macro definitions, variable declarations, type definitions, and function prototypes. If a collection of such definitions appears in foo.h, then the directive #include "foo.h" must appear in every source file that intends to either use or define any of the items that appear in the header file. For example, consider the following header file bool.h:

```
#define TRUE 1
#define FALSE 0
typedef int Bool;
extern Bool i_exist;
int logical_and(Bool a, Bool b);
void print_bool(Bool b);
```

This header file contains two preprocessor definitions, the type definition of Bool, the declaration (but not the definition) of i_exist, and two function prototypes (their declarations, but not their definitions). Any file that uses or defines any of these should bring in the header file, using the directive #include "bool.h". We have placed the definitions of i_exist, logical_and, and print_bool in one source file called bool.c:

```
/**********************/
/*      bool.c        */
/**********************/

#include <stdio.h>
#include "bool.h"
```

```
Bool logical_and(Bool a, Bool b)
{
  return (a && b);
}

void print_bool(Bool b)
{
  printf("%s\n", (b ? "TRUE" : "FALSE"));
}

Bool i_exist = TRUE;
```

Other source files might make use of the new type `Bool`, the boolean functions, and perhaps the variable `i_exist`. One example is the following source file, which we have named `booltest.c`:

```
/***********************/
/*    booltest.c      */
/***********************/

#include <stdio.h>
#include "bool.h"

main()
{
  Bool a = TRUE;
  Bool b = FALSE;

  print_bool(logical_and(a, b));
  print_bool(i_exist);
  return 0;
}
```

Includes can be nested. For example, given this `Bool` type, any header file that declares boolean-valued functions would find `Bool` useful. Thus, that header file would contain the directive `#include "bool.h"`. In fact, let's assume that two such header files (we'll call them `a.h` and `b.h`) include `bool.h`. Then the main program, which would naturally include `a.h` and `b.h`, would have included `bool.h` twice. To protect against this, we wrap the contents of the `bool.h` file in a `#ifndef-#endif` pair, as follows:

```
/*********************/
/*    bool.h        */
/*********************/

#ifndef BOOL_H
#define BOOL_H

#define TRUE 1
#define FALSE 0

typedef int Bool;

extern Bool i_exist;

int logical_and(Bool a, Bool b);
void print_bool(Bool b);

#endif
```

The first time anyone includes this header file, BOOL_H will *not* be defined, so the the preprocessor will keep the text inside the `#ifndef-#endif` pair, thereby defining BOOL_H. In any subsequent inclusion of `bool.h`, the preprocessor will find that BOOL_H *is* defined, and it will exclude the text contained between `#ifndef` and `#endif`.

15.1.2   Building a Multiple-File Program

Generally, functions should be gathered together (and their declarations placed in a header file) according to their degree of cohesion, or their ability to be used together to solve problems. For example, a collection of functions (and some accompanying declarations) that manipulate boolean values are declared together in a header file, called `bool.h`. Then the corresponding definitions of these functions appear in a file called `bool.c`. Finally, any program that intends to manipulate boolean values should begin with `#include "bool.h"`.

To compile such fragments of programs that span over several files, each `.c` file must be compiled separately, and the resulting *object files* linked together to form a single executable program. An object file typically has the same name as the source file from which it was compiled, but a different extension, such as `.o` under UNIX, or `.obj` under DOS.

A flag is typically used to indicate to the compiler that the source file being compiled is only a fragment and not the entire program. Under UNIX, the `-c` option is used. In the example above, the following UNIX commands would compile the two source files and link together the resulting object files:

```
cc -c bool.c
cc -c booltest.c
cc -o bool booltest.o bool.o
```

Under other operating systems, the name of the compiler might be different, as well as some of the file naming conventions. For example, under DOS, the executable file above would be named `bool.exe`.

Large programs usually require many source files, each providing a certain facility that is useful for some other part(s) of the program. Since not all source files depend on each other, keeping track of the dependencies can be a daunting problem. If we change a given file, we should recompile all source files that depend on it, and all others that depend on those, etc. A useful tool, developed under UNIX but now available in different forms on different systems, is the *makefile*. Here's the makefile for our boolean example:

```
bool:   booltest.o bool.o
    cc -o bool booltest.o bool.o

bool.o: bool.c
    cc -c bool.c

booltest.o: booltest.c
    cc -c booltest.c
```

The first line states that `bool` depends on `booltest.o` and on `bool.o`. The second line (which is indented by a tab character) gives the command necessary to satisfy the preceding dependency. The other two groups of lines state that each `.o` file depends on its corresponding `.c` file, and that a `cc -c` command should be used to satisfy the dependency.

The `make` utility program reads the above makefile and examines the dates on the various files. Any file that is out of date is updated using the information from the makefile, and any file that depends on it (directly or indirectly) is updated as well. For example, if we made a single change in `bool.c` (thereby changing its date of last modification), the `make` utility would recompile `bool.c`, but not `booltest.c`, and would link the old `booltest.o` with the new `bool.o` to form a new `bool`.

Not everyone uses makefiles. On some systems, "project files" or some other mechanism form part of the programming environment and allow facilities similar to those described here. Check your system documentation.

C compilers usually allow the specification of a macro at compilation time. For example,

```
cc -DDEBUG booltest.c
```

will act as if there were a `#define DEBUG 1` directive at the beginning of the program. Similarly,

```
cc -UDEBUG booltest.c
```

will act as if we had the directive #define DEBUG 0. The specific value of the macro can also be specified, as in -DDEBUG = 3.

15.2   Solved Exercises

15.2.1   Solved Exercise 1: Sets of Numbers

Let's reimplement the sets program from Chapter 10. Our main program, which we call test-set.c, is as follows:

```
/*********************************/
/*        File: testset.c        */
/*********************************/
#include <stdio.h>
#include "bool.h"
#include "commandline.h"
#include "set.h"
#include "menu.h"

main(int argc, char *argv[])
{
  commandline(argc, argv);
  main_menu_loop();
  return 0;
}
```

Notice that we have included four header files. bool.h handles booleans (as seen in earlier chapters). commandline.h provides a facility for examining the command line string, looking for options to the program, as explained later. set.h implements the sets themselves, and menu.h defines function main_menu_loop(). It is important to note the different nature of the various program components: set.h provides a facility for manipulating sets, whereas menu.h simply accomplishes the task of repeatedly printing the menu, accepting the user's choice, and carrying out the corresponding action. File bool.h is quite simple. Note that there's no need for a corresponding bool.c file.

```
/*****************************/
/*       File: bool.h        */
/*****************************/
#ifndef BOOL_H
#define BOOL_H

#define TRUE 1
#define FALSE 0

typedef int Bool;

#endif
```

Header file commandline.h declares three functions, as shown below.

```
/*********************************/
/*      File: commandline.h      */
/*********************************/
#ifndef COMMAND_LINE_H
#define COMMAND_LINE_H

char *program_argument(char *flag, char *name, int argc, char *argv[]);
int program_flag(char *flag, int argc, char *argv[]);
void commandline(int argc, char *argv[]);

#endif
```

program_argument is useful for finding user-specified flags on the command line. It takes two strings flag and name, and the values of argc and argv. The intent is to search for flag on the command line. If found, we'll return the word that appears after it. If not, we'll return the "default" string name. For example, assume the command line is `testset -p 10`. The statement

```
program_argument("-p", "20", argc, argv);
```

will return the string `"10"` because it appears after −p on the command line. If the command line does not contain −p, we return the given default value, `"20"`. Function `program_argument` uses `program_flag`, which does the actual searching through the command line. Function `commandline` brings it all together, by calling `program_argument`, converting the resulting string to an integer, and using the integer to set `elements_per_line`, which is used for formatting purposes by the `print_set` function in `set.c`. Here's the actual code in file `commandline.c`.

```c
/**********************************/
/*      File: commandline.c       */
/**********************************/

#include "commandline.h"
#include "set.h"

char *program_argument(char *flag, char *name, int argc, char *argv[])
{
  int position = program_flag(flag, argc, argv);

  if (position)
    return (argv[position + 1]);
  else
    return name;
}

int program_flag(char *flag, int argc, char *argv[])
{
  int index = 0;
  char *base;
  char *fl;

  while (index < argc) {
    base = argv[index];
    fl = flag;
    while ((*base == *fl) & (*fl != '\0')) {
      base++;
      fl++;
    }
    if (*base == *fl)
      return index;
    else
      index++;
  }
  return 0;
}

int str_to_int(char *s)
{
  int i = 0;
  char c;

  while ((c = *s++) != '\0')
    i = i * 10 + c - '0';
  return i;
}
```

```
void commandline(int argc, char *argv[])
{
  elements_per_line =
    str_to_int(program_argument("-p", "20", argc, argv));
}
```

File `set.h` contains the declaration of `elements_per_line`, the definition of `MAX_SET_SIZE`, and the prototypes of the various functions for manipulating sets:

```
/*****************************/
/*        File: set.h        */
/*****************************/

#ifndef SET_H
#define SET_H

#include "bool.h"
#define MAX_SET_SIZE 50

int elements_per_line;
void create_set(int a[]);
void read_set(int a[]);
void read_sets(int a[], int b[]);
void print_set(int a[]);
void union_set(int a[], int b[], int c[]);
void intersect_set(int a[], int b[], int c[]);
void difference_set(int a[], int b[], int c[]);
void enter_set(int v, int a[]);
Bool element_of(int v, int a[]);

#endif
```

The actual code for these set-manipulating functions appears in `set.c`:

```
/*****************************/
/*        File: set.c        */
/*****************************/

#include <stdio.h>
#include "bool.h"
#include "set.h"

void create_set(int a[])
{
  a[0] = 0;
}

void read_set(int a[])
{
  int value;

  create_set(a);
  printf("Enter set values, end with -1.\n");
  scanf("%d", &value);
  while (value != -1) {
    enter_set(value, a);
    scanf("%d", &value);
  }
}

void read_sets(int a[], int b[])
{
  read_set(a);
  read_set(b);
  printf("Set A:\n");
```

```
    print_set(a);
    printf("Set B:\n");
    print_set(b);
}

void print_set(int a[])
{
  int i;

  printf("{");
  for (i = 1; i <= a[0]; i++) {
    printf("%d", a[i]);
    if (i < a[0]) printf(", ");
    if (i % elements_per_line == 0)
      printf("\n");
  }
  printf("}\n");
}

void union_set(int a[], int b[], int c[])
{
  int i;

  create_set(c);
  for (i = 1; i <= a[0]; i++)
    enter_set(a[i], c);
  for (i = 1; i <= b[0]; i++)
    enter_set(b[i], c);
}

void intersect_set(int a[], int b[], int c[])
{
  int i;

  create_set(c);
  for (i = 1; i <= a[0]; i++)
    if (element_of(a[i], b))
      enter_set(a[i], c);
}

void difference_set(int a[], int b[], int c[])
{
  int i;

  create_set(c);
  for (i = 1; i <= a[0]; i++)
    if (!element_of(a[i], b))
      enter_set(a[i], c);
}

void enter_set(int v, int a[])
{
  if (a[0] == MAX_SET_SIZE)
    printf("MAX SET SIZE EXCEEDED\n");
  else if (!element_of(v, a)) {
    a[0]++;
    a[a[0]] = v;
  }
}
```

```
Bool element_of(int v, int a[])
{
  int i;

  for (i = 1; i <= a[0]; i++)
    if (a[i] == v) return TRUE;
  return FALSE;
}
```

The menu function is declared in menu.h:

```
/******************************/
/*      File: menu.h          */
/******************************/

#ifndef MENU_H
#define MENU_H

void main_menu_loop();

#endif
```

The actual menu code declares the three sets to be used and performs the main menu loop. It appears in menu.c, as follows:

```
/******************************/
/*      File: menu.c          */
/******************************/

#include <stdio.h>
#include "bool.h"
#include "set.h"
#include "menu.h"

void main_menu_loop()
{
  int done, user_choice;
  int a[MAX_SET_SIZE];
  int b[MAX_SET_SIZE];
  int c[MAX_SET_SIZE];

  done = FALSE;
  while (!done) {
    printf("SET MANIPULATION PROGRAM:\n\n");
    printf("Main Menu:\n");
    printf("1. Union of sets.\n");
    printf("2. Intersection of sets.\n");
    printf("3. Difference between sets.\n");
    printf("4. Quit this program.\n\n");
    printf("Your selection (by number): ");
    scanf("%d", &user_choice);
    switch (user_choice) {
      case 1:
        read_sets(a, b);
        union_set(a, b, c);
        printf("Set C: Union of A and B:\n");
        print_set(c);
        break;
      case 2:
        read_sets(a, b);
        intersect_set(a, b, c);
        printf("Set C: Intersection of A and B:\n");
        print_set(c);
        break;
      case 3:
```

```
            read_sets(a, b);
            difference_set(a, b, c);
            printf("Set C: Difference between A and B:\n");
            print_set(c);
            break;
          case 4:
            done = TRUE;
            printf("Bye!\n");
            break;
          default:
            printf("INVALID MENU SELECTION\n\n");
        }
      }
    }
```

Finally, a makefile puts it all together:

```
    testset: testset.o set.o commandline.o menu.o
          cc -o testset menu.o testset.o set.o commandline.o
    testset.o:   testset.c commandline.h set.h bool.h
          cc -c testset.c
    commandline.o: commandline.c commandline.h
          cc -c commandline.c
    set.o: set.c set.h
          cc -c set.c
    menu.o: menu.c menu.h
          cc -c menu.c
    clean:
          rm -f *.o testset
```

Here's some sample output from this program:

```
    SET MANIPULATION PROGRAM:

    Main Menu:
    1. Union of sets.
    2. Intersection of sets.
    3. Difference between sets.
    4. Quit this program.

    Your selection (by number): 3
    Enter set values, end with -1.
    1
    2
    3
    -1
    Enter set values, end with -1.
    2
    3
    4
    -1
    Set A:
    {1, 2, 3}
    Set B:
    {2, 3, 4}
    Set C: Difference between A and B:
    {1}
    SET MANIPULATION PROGRAM:

    Main Menu:
    1. Union of sets.
    2. Intersection of sets.
    3. Difference between sets.
    4. Quit this program.
```

```
Your selection (by number): 4
Bye!
```

15.3   Programming Exercises

1. It is recommended that header files have a sentinel definition to avoid multiple inclusion, as shown here:

    ```
    /* maxmin.h ==> define max() && min() macros */

    #ifndef  MAXMIN_H
    #define  MAXMIN_H  /* include sentinel */

    #define  max(x, y) ((x) > (y) ? (x) : (y))
    #define  min(x, y) ((x) < (y) ? (x) : (y))

    #endif
    /* maxmin.h ==> end of file */
    ```

    Write three examples of header files that need no sentinel definitions.

2. Write three examples of header files that when implemented without include sentinels will cause compilation errors with every program module that includes them more than once.

3. Suppose a computer virus invades your system and changes the header file shown below, from the definitions shown on the left to the definitions shown on the right.

    ```
    /* boolean.h ==> define boolean values */

    /* broken values */            /* correct values */
    #ifndef  BOOL_H                #ifndef BOOL_H
    #define  BOOL_H                #define BOOL_H

    #define  TRUE  0               #define  TRUE  1
    #define  FALSE 1               #define  FALSE 0
    #define  and   ||              #define  and   &&
    #define  or    &&              #define  or    ||

    #endif
    /* boolean.h ==> end of file */
    ```

    Here the implementor thought that it might be better to use the and and or idioms in boolean expressions, instead of the C operators && and ||. Write a program that includes the boolean.h header and uses the and and or idioms in boolean expressions. Write your program so that it behaves correctly with the correct values shown on the left above, but behaves incorrectly with the incorrect values shown on the right.

4. Redo the preceding exercise, writing your program so that it behaves incorrectly with the correct values, but behaves correctly with the incorrect values. Can you categorize the programs that can withstand the "boolean virus"?

5. When an angry programmer at the HAL Corporation foresaw his own dismissal, he decided to write an include header file to break current programs as payback. The following are the three header files that were left in the C library by this person:

    ```
    /* void.h */
    #ifndef BOOL_H
    #define BOOL_H
    #define void int
    #endif

    /* include.h */
    #ifndef INCLUDE_H
    #define INCLUDE_H
    ```

```
#define include define
#endif

/* define.h */
#ifndef DEFINE_H
#define DEFINE_H
#define define include
#endif
```

Explain the consequences of including each of these three header files in an otherwise correct C program. Explain what happens if they are included in a header file instead. Then consider what happens if any two (or all three) header files are included in a program, like so:

```
/* main.c */
#include "include.h"
#include "define.h"
/* etc ... */
```

6. The external variable array is declared in module main.c as an integer array, and in the header file array.h it is exported to other modules:

```
/* main.c */
#define SIZE 10000          /* array.h */
#include "structs.h"        extern int array[SIZE];

int array[SIZE];
/* etc ... */
```

As shown above, the macro SIZE is not defined in the array.h header file, probably for security reasons. Write another version of these two files so that the same objective is accomplished, but without requiring the programmer to define the SIZE macro in module main.c. Is there a way for a third module, say third.c, to see array[] as a shorter array than it actually is?

7. What happens if the same variable is declared in two different program modules?

```
/* main.c */              /* second.c */
#define SIZE 100          #define SIZE 100
int array[SIZE];          int array[SIZE];
```

What happens when the same array is declared in different modules but with different sizes?

```
/* main.c */              /* second.c */
#define SIZE 100          #define SIZE 100000
int array[SIZE];          int array[SIZE];
```

When will the programmer discover the multiple declaration of array[]? Show how these problems can be avoided using header files and macros.

8. A programmer needs to round up floating-point values because they represent money quantities, which need to be adjusted after divisions and multiplications. The idea is to use a ROUND function in this fashion:

```
float a, b, res;
res := ROUND( (a + b) / ((a - b) * 135.0) );
```

Here ROUND would add the remaining fractions of a cent into an external variable called Cent_Fixes. Implement ROUND both as a macro and as a function and compare the advantages and drawbacks of each approach. If you were a bank, which version of ROUND would you use?

9. Usually makefiles don't have circular references, like the one below does:

```
fmt: fmt.o
        cc -o fmt fmt.o
fmt.o: fmt
        cc -c fmt.c
```

Explain what the `make` program will do when run against this makefile. Then run it on your computer system and explain the results you obtain.

10. The object files in a makefile usually have file name extensions `.o` or `.obj` and are placed on the left side (before the colon) in each dependency rule in the makefile. On the right side appear both program module names and header files:

    ```
    fmt.o: fmt.c word.h line.h
           cc -c fmt.c
    ```

    Explain why it is never necessary to put either a `.c` or `.h` filename on the left side of a dependency rule.

11. Write a header file that can be used to obtain an object module:

    ```
    what.o: what.h
            cc -c what.h
    ```

    Would you say that it is possible for header file `what.h` to be included multiple times in other program modules? Would you consider it good programming practice to write a program using such a header file? Explain carefully.

12. Portability has always been a great concern to C programmers, who struggle to have their programs run on different computing systems. One problem programmers face is the difference in size of integer and pointer values. Write a header file named `portable.h` that defines the following C objects for different implementations:

    $$
    \begin{aligned}
    &\texttt{INT2} \implies \text{2-byte integer} \\
    &\texttt{INT4} \implies \text{4-byte integer} \\
    &\texttt{UNS2} \implies \text{2-byte unsigned integer} \\
    &\texttt{UNS4} \implies \text{4-byte unsigned integer}
    \end{aligned}
    $$

    Modify some of your programs (you should have quite a collection by now!) to use this `portable.h` header file, and try to compile and run it in different computer systems. Then try to extend this file with other definitions (floats, characters, etc.), and look into your own C system's header files to see if a header file similar to `portable.h` is being used.

13. Modify the sentinel include technique so that multiple inclusions of a header file will result in an error produced with the `#error` directive. Can you think of a real-world application where such a scheme can be put to good use?

14. Decompose the `plot` program in Chapter 9 into modules. Perhaps one module for input and another for plotting would be appropriate.

15. The grading program in Chapter 5 is a good example of a long program that would probably benefit from being broken down into modules. Rewrite that program using arrays and separate modules, one for the menu selection and another for the grade calculation itself.

16. Extend and rewrite the very large numbers program in Chapter 8. You should have a module that provides a facility for handling large numbers. Initially, limit the module to the multiplication of a large number by an ordinary integer, as was done in the calculation of the factorial of 1000. Develop a makefile early on; you'll find it useful. Then add the addition and subtraction of two large numbers, and finally, add the multiplication of large numbers. Important: develop the program incrementally.

17. Develop a simple statistical package, a menu-based program that will allow the user to enter a collection of floating-point data, calculate various statistics such as mean, mode, and median, and percentages. Break the program down into various modules and compile them separately.

18. Reorganize the complex numbers program in Chapter 11 so the various program modules can compile separately.

19. Develop a vector and matrix manipulation program. Use the matrix multiplication program in Chapter 12 as a starting point. First, separate the various components, using header files and a makefile. Then extend the program's capabilities by multiplying nonsquare matrices, recognizing the identity matrix, transposing matrices, and recognizing symmetric matrices. Then add vector manipulation, such as vector addition, subtraction, and inner product.

20. Develop a simple calendar program. It should be capable of storing appointment dates and times, as well as a description of each appointment (a string). Your program should be capable of printing a list of appointments for the day. Develop the program incrementally, and then add some advanced features, such as producing reminders, handling the current date, counting down to a vacation date, and printing a nicely formatted calendar for the month.

16 Structures, Unions, and Enumerations

16.1 Chapter Summary

A *structure* is a collection of *members*, possibly of different types. A *union* is like a structure, but its members share storage; only one member at a time can be used to store data. An *enumeration* is an integer type, whose values are named by the programmer.

16.1.1 Structures

Arrays are *homogeneous*—all elements in an array are of the same type. To access an array element, we specify the element's position. In contrast, a structure is *heterogeneous*: its members can all be of different types, and to access a structure element, we specify its name, not its position. In some programming languages, structures are known as *records*, and their members are known as *fields*. A structure declaration is merely a collection of declarations surrounded by braces, preceded by the word `struct`, and followed by the name we wish for the structure variable(s), if any. Suppose we wish to store information about a bank account: we might have the owner's name (a string), the type of account (say, 1 for savings, 2 for checking), and the balance (a float). The structure declaration would look like this:

```
struct {
  char name[20];
  int type;
  float balance;
} account1, account2;
```

Here we declared two structures, named `account1` and `account2`. Each structure variable has all three members: `name`, `type`, and `balance`, all of which are stored consecutively in the order in which they appear in the structure declaration. Each structure has its own *scope*: as is usual for most sets of braces, the variables declared within them do not conflict with those declared outside.

To initialize a structure variable, we use a notation similar to that used to initialize arrays:

```
struct {
  char name[20];
  int type;
  float balance;
} account1 = {"John Smith", 1, 34.12},
  account2 = {"Mary Jones", 2, 213.55};
```

The constant values must appear in the same order as they do in the structure declaration. The most common operation on structures is accessing a member. This is done with the "." operator:

struct_name . member_name

For example, the following statements are all valid:

```
printf("%s", account1.name);
account2.type = 1;
account1.balance += 23.50;
scanf("%f", &account2.balance);
account1 = account2;
```

Here we print the name of `account1`, change the type of `account2` to 1 (representing "savings"), credit `account1`'s balance with $23.50, read in `account2`'s balance, and then copy all of `account2` into `account1`. The "." operator has the same precedence as the postfix `++` and `--` operators; in the call of `scanf`, the `&` operator has lower precedence than ".," so the address of `balance` is used, not the address of the entire structure. As illustrated, the assignment operator works on entire structures (unlike arrays), as long as the structures are compatible.

Often we wish to name a particular kind of structure so that we may later declare more variables of the same structure type and ensure compatibility among them. This is done with a structure *tag*:

```
struct bank_account {
   char name[20];
   int type;
   float balance;
} account1 = {"John Smith", 1, 34.12};
```

The semicolon at the end is important, because it terminates the declaration. As illustrated, the structure tag name can be given, and variables can be initialized, in the same declaration. However, the purpose of the structure type name is to be able to declare structure variables separately:

```
struct bank_account account1, account2;
```

The word `struct` is required and can't be dropped. Another way to attach a name to the particular kind of structure we're using is `typedef`:

```
typedef struct {
   char name[20];
   int type;
   float balance;
} Bank_account;
Bank_account account1, account2;
```

Once the type name `Bank_account` is defined, variables of that type can be declared. Structures can be passed as parameters to functions and can be returned from functions. For example, consider the following complete program:

```
#include <stdio.h>
#include <string.h>

typedef struct {
  char name[20];
  int type;
  float balance;
} Bank_account;

Bank_account make_account(const char *name, int type, float balance);
void print_account(Bank_account b);

main()
{
  Bank_account account1, account2;

  account1 = make_account("John Smith", 1, 23.50);
  account2 = make_account("Mary Jones", 2, 18.23);
  print_account(account1);
  print_account(account2);
  return 0;
}

Bank_account make_account(const char *name, int type, float balance)
{
  Bank_account b;

  strcpy(b.name, name);
  b.type = type;
  b.balance = balance;
  return b;
}
```

```
void print_account(Bank_account b)
{
  printf("%s: ", b.name);
  printf("%s account has a balance of ",
         (b.type == 1) ? "savings" : "checking");
  printf("%5.2f\n", b.balance);
}
```

Arrays and structures can be nested without restriction. In our example, we might replace name with a structure containing three strings instead of only one:

```
typedef struct {
    struct name {
        char first[20];
        char middle[20];
        char last[20];
    } name;
    int type;
    float balance;
} Bank_account;
```

Then we would access a given account's last name as follows:

```
printf("%s", account1.name.last);
```

This is better than merely having three strings inside the Bank_account structure; as a single structure, all three pieces can be manipulated simultaneously. For example, a new and improved version of print_name, which would take a struct name as a parameter, could be used as follows:

```
print_name(account1.name).
```

A very common combination is an array of structures. In our example, we'd like to have an array of Bank_accounts, a very simple banking database:

```
Bank_account accounts[100];
```

To print one particular bank account:

```
print_account(accounts[i]);
```

To change the type of a certain account:

```
accounts[i].type = 2;
```

To change the last name of a certain account holder:

```
strcpy(accounts[i].name.last, "newname");
```

16.1.2   Unions and Enumerations

Unions are similar to structures, but with one major difference. The compiler allocates space for every member of a structure, but only enough space for the largest member of a union. Thus the members of a union are *overlaid*: changing one of them changes them all. More specifically, in a structure, every member has a different address; in a union, every member has the same address, even if they all have different types. In our example, we might have an interest rate for savings accounts, but an overdraft limit for checking accounts. Neither type of account has both items, so storing them both is wasteful. Below we have named the union item. To access it, we must use the usual "." operator. It is customary to have one of the structure members indicate which of the union members is currently "there." We have encoded (using macros) the two possible values for the type of banking account: 1 for savings, 2 for checking. Now, declaring an account, assigning a value to its type, and printing out some information about the account, is quite straightforward:

```
#define ACCOUNT_TYPE int
#define SAVINGS 1
#define CHECKING 2
```

```
        typedef struct {
          char name[20];
          float balance;
          ACCOUNT_TYPE type;
          union {
            int overdraft_limit;
            float interest_rate;
          } item;
        } Bank_account;

        Bank_account account;
         ...
        account.type = SAVINGS;
         ...
        if (account.type == SAVINGS)
          printf("Savings account interest rate is %5.2f.",
                 account.item.interest_rate);
        else
          printf("Checking account overdraft limit is %5d.",
                 account.item.overdraft_limit);
```

The `type` member is being used as a ***tag field*** in this case, to indicate whether the `item` is an interest rate or an overdraft limit. It is the responsibility of the programmer to maintain the accuracy of `type` by changing it anytime the `item` changes. Otherwise unpredictable results can occur.

Still, there is a better solution to the problem of needing to encode values such as CHECKING and SAVINGS. C provides the ***enumeration*** type, a type whose values are listed by the programmer. For example:

```
        enum {SAVINGS, CHECKING} type;
```

An enumeration does *not* define a new scope: the names of the enumeration constants must be different from those of all other identifiers declared in the enclosing scope. Unlike macro names, the enumeration constants are subject to the usual scope rules—they are local to the function in which they are declared. An enumeration can have a tag name or can be declared using `typedef` to create a type name. In our banking example,

```
        typedef enum {SAVINGS, CHECKING} Account_type;
        typedef struct {
          char name[20];
          float balance;
          Account_type type;
          union {
            int overdraft_limit;
            float interest_rate;
          } item;
        } Bank_account;
```

Enumeration constants actually have integer values and are numbered, by default, from zero on. We can specify these values if we so desire. For example, if we simply *must* use 1 for SAVINGS and 2 for CHECKING (perhaps for reasons of compatibility with previously written software), we would declare the enumerated type as follows:

```
        typedef enum {SAVINGS = 1, CHECKING} Account_type;
```

We could have used completely unrelated values, such as 23 and 78. Each of the constants can be assigned a value (which does not have to differ from all the others). If none is assigned, the value will be one greater than that of the predecessor.

16.2   Solved Exercises

16.2.1   Solved Exercise 1: A Bank Simulation

In this example, we'll develop a program that simulates a very simple version of a bank. The program prints a menu that asks whether you have an account already, or whether you wish to create a new account. There are two types of accounts. In a savings account, money earns interest, but there's a limit on withdrawals. The interest rate and the maximum withdrawal are determined by the initial deposit. A checking account pays no interest but can be overdrawn. The maximum overdraft is determined by the amount of the initial deposit. However, interest must be paid on the overdrawn amount. The interest to be paid is also determined by the amount of the initial deposit.

We first design our data structures and the operations upon them. We have a `struct` for savings accounts, and another for checking accounts. The new type `Account` contains the account number and balance, along with a `union` holding either a savings or checking structure. Three operations are provided by the `account.h` header file: `clear_accounts`, `insert_account`, and `transactions`. Other operations will become necessary soon enough, but they need not be made available through the header file.

```
/*******************************/
/*          account.h          */
/*******************************/

#ifndef ACCOUNT_H
#define ACCOUNT_H

#include <stdio.h>

typedef enum {SAVINGS, CHECKING} Account_type;

/* savings account */
struct saving {
  int interest;         /* Interest paid        */
  float max_withdraw;   /* Maximum withdrawal */
};

/* checking account */
struct check {
  float max_overdraw;   /* Maximum overdraft permitted */
  float overdraw;       /* Current overdraft */
  float interest;       /* Interest charged on overdrawn amount   */
};

typedef struct {
  int number;           /* Account number */
  Account_type type;    /* Savings or checking */
  float balance;        /* Account balance */
  union {
    struct saving s;    /* savings account, or */
    struct check c;     /* checking account    */
  } item;
} Account;

void clear_accounts(Account bank[], int max_accounts);
void insert_account(Account bank[], int max_accounts);
void transactions(Account bank[], int max_accounts);

#endif
```

The design of the header file goes hand-in-hand with the design of the main program, called bank.c. In the main program, we declare the array of bank accounts, clear it, and then repeatedly elicit a choice from the user: insert a new account, work on an existing one, or quit. Here's the main program, called bank.c:

```
/*******************************/
/*            bank.c           */
/*******************************/
#include <stdio.h>
#include "account.h"

#define MAX_ACCOUNTS 25

main()
{
  int choice;
  Account bank[MAX_ACCOUNTS];

  clear_accounts(bank, MAX_ACCOUNTS);

  printf("        ALMOST A BANK!\n\n");
  printf("We'll keep your money safe\n");
  printf("  (at least for a while)");
  do {
    printf("\n\n1. Create a new account.\n");
    printf("2. Transact on an existing account.\n");
    printf("3. Exit.\n\n");
    printf("Please choose an option: ");
    scanf("%d", &choice);
    switch (choice) {
      case 1:
        insert_account(bank, MAX_ACCOUNTS);
        break;
      case 2:
        transactions(bank, MAX_ACCOUNTS);
        break;
      case 3:
        printf("It has been a pleasure serving you!\n");
        break;
      default :
        printf("Sorry. That's not an option\n");
    }
  } while (choice != 3);
  return 0;
}
```

Now we get to the heart of the matter, the account.c file. The clear_accounts and display_account operations are fairly straightforward. The transactions operation consists of obtaining the user's choice (deposit or withdrawal), and calling an appropriate function in each case (deposit and withdraw, respectively). The insert_account operation obtains the user's choice of account type (checking or savings) and calls the appropriate function in either case (functions open_savings and open_checking). The latter two functions both require an extra function to obtain the initial deposit from the user when opening an account (function get_initial_deposit). Here's the rather lengthy file account.c:

```
/*******************************/
/*           account.c         */
/*******************************/
#include "account.h"

void clear_accounts(Account bank[], int max_accounts)
{
  int i;

  for (i = 0; i < max_accounts; i++)
    bank[i].number = -1;
    /* -1 indicates an available cell */
}

void display_account(Account bank[], int account)
{
  if (bank[account].type == SAVINGS)
    printf("SAVINGS ACCOUNT #%d\n", bank[account].number);
  else
    printf("CHECKING ACCOUNT #%d\n", bank[account].number);

  printf("Balance: $%5.2f\n", bank[account].balance);

  if (bank[account].type == SAVINGS) {
    printf("Maximum daily withdrawal: $%5.2f\n",
            bank[account].item.s.max_withdraw);
    printf("Interest earned: %d\n", bank[account].item.s.interest);

  } else {     /* CHECKING */
    printf("Amount currently overdrawn: $%5.2f\n",
            bank[account].item.c.overdraw);
    if (bank[account].item.c.overdraw !=
        bank[account].item.c.max_overdraw)
      printf("You can overdraw yourself by $%5.2f\n",
              bank[account].item.c.max_overdraw -
              bank[account].item.c.overdraw);
    printf("Interest paid by overdrawing: $%5.2f\n",
            bank[account].item.c.interest);
  }
}

void deposit(Account bank[], int account)
{
  float amount;

  printf("Deposit Amount? ");
  scanf("%f", &amount);
  if (bank[account].type == SAVINGS)
    bank[account].balance += amount;
  else if (bank[account].item.c.overdraw == 0)
    bank[account].balance += amount;
  else if (amount > bank[account].item.c.overdraw) {
    bank[account].balance = amount - bank[account].item.c.overdraw;
    bank[account].item.c.overdraw = 0;
  } else
    bank[account].item.c.overdraw -= amount;
}
```

```
void withdraw(Account bank[], int account)
{
  float amount;

  printf("Withdrawal amount ? ");
  scanf("%f", &amount);
  if (bank[account].type == SAVINGS)
    if ((bank[account].balance >= amount) &&
          (bank[account].item.s.max_withdraw >= amount))
      bank[account].balance -= amount;
    else
      printf("We cannot satisfy your request. "
             "Please check your balance.\n");

  else                   /* CHECKING  */
    if (bank[account].item.c.overdraw == 0 && bank[account].balance > 0)
      if (amount <= bank[account].balance)
        bank[account].balance -= amount;
      else      /* withdrawal will cause overdraw */
        if (amount <= (bank[account].balance +
                      (bank[account].item.c.max_overdraw -
                       bank[account].item.c.overdraw))) {
          bank[account].item.c.overdraw = amount -
                bank[account].balance + bank[account].item.c.overdraw;
          bank[account].balance = 0;
        } else   /* withdrawal exceeds max_overdraw */
          printf("We cannot satisfy your request. "
                 "Please check your balance\n");
    else         /* account already overdrawn  */
      if (amount <= (bank[account].item.c.max_overdraw -
                    bank[account].item.c.overdraw))
        /* withdrawal still covered under max_overdraw */
        bank[account].item.c.overdraw += amount;
      else  /* withdrawal exceeds max_overdraw */
        printf("We cannot satisfy your request. "
               "Please check your balance\n");
}

void transactions(Account bank[], int max_accounts)
{
  int account, choice = 1;

  printf("Account number: ");
  scanf("%d", &account);
  if (account >= 0 && account < max_accounts)
    if (bank[account].number != -1)
      do {
        display_account(bank, account);
        printf("\n\n1. Make a deposit\n");
        printf("2. Make a withdrawal\n");
        printf("3. Close your account\n");
        printf("4. Exit\n\n");
        printf("Please choose an option: ");
        scanf("%d", &choice);
        switch (choice) {
          case 1:
            deposit(bank, account);
            break;
          case 2:
            withdraw(bank, account);
            break;
          case 3:
            bank[account].number = -1;
```

```
                    printf("Your account has been terminated.\n");
                    printf(" We'll keep your balance as a fee "
                            "for services rendered\n");
                    choice = 4;
                    break;
                 case 4:
                    printf("Thanks for preferring us!\n\n");
                    break;
                 default:
                    printf("Sorry. That's not an option.\n\n");
            }
        } while (choice != 4);
      else
        printf("Account not open.\n");
    else
      printf("Invalid account number\n");
}

void get_initial_deposit(Account bank[], int account)
{
   float amount;

   printf("Initial deposit? ");
   scanf("%f", &amount);
   bank[account].balance = amount;
}

void open_savings(Account bank[], int account)
{
   bank[account].type = SAVINGS;
   get_initial_deposit(bank, account);
   /* The initial deposit determines the interest */
   if (bank[account].balance > 100000) {
     bank[account].item.s.interest = 30;
     bank[account].item.s.max_withdraw = bank[account].balance / 15;
   } else if (bank[account].balance > 50000) {
     bank[account].item.s.interest = 20;
     bank[account].item.s.max_withdraw = bank[account].balance / 10;
   } else {
     bank[account].item.s.interest = 10;
     bank[account].item.s.max_withdraw = bank[account].balance / 5;
   }
}

void open_checking(Account bank[], int account)
{
   bank[account].type = CHECKING;
   bank[account].item.c.overdraw = 0;
   get_initial_deposit(bank, account);
   if (bank[account].balance > 100000) {
     bank[account].item.c.max_overdraw = bank[account].balance / 15;
     bank[account].item.c.interest = 23.5;
   } else if (bank[account].balance > 50000) {
     bank[account].item.c.max_overdraw = bank[account].balance / 10;
     bank[account].item.c.interest = 17.5;
   } else {
     bank[account].item.c.max_overdraw = bank[account].balance / 5;
     bank[account].item.c.interest = 8.5;
   }
}
```

```
void insert_account(Account bank[], int max_accounts)
{
  int account, choice;

  /*  Find first unoccupied account */
  for (account = 0; bank[account].number != -1 &&
       account < max_accounts; account++);

  if (account == max_accounts)
    printf("Sorry, we have our hands full at the moment!\n");
  else {
    bank[account].number = account;
    printf("Your account number is: %d\n\n", account);
    printf("What kind of account do you wish?\n\n");
    printf("1. Savings account\n");
    printf("2. Checking account\n\n");
    printf("Please choose an option: ");
    scanf("%d", &choice);
    switch (choice) {
      case 1:
        open_savings(bank, account);
        break;
      case 2:
        open_checking(bank, account);
        break;
      default:
         printf("Sorry. That's not a option\n");
    }
  }
}
```

Here's some sample output:

```
        ALMOST A BANK!

    We'll keep your money safe
      (at least for a while)

    1. Create a new account.
    2. Transact on an existing account.
    3. Exit.

    Please choose an option: 1
    Your account number is: 0

    What kind of account do you wish?

    1. Savings account
    2. Checking account

    Please choose an option: 2
    Initial deposit? 100


    1. Create a new account.
    2. Transact on an existing account.
    3. Exit.

    Please choose an option: 2
    Account number: 0
    CHECKING ACCOUNT #0
    Balance: $100.00
    Amount currently overdrawn: $ 0.00
```

```
      You can overdraw yourself by $20.00
      Interest charged for overdrawing: $ 8.50


      1. Make a deposit
      2. Make a withdrawal
      3. Close your account
      4. Exit

      Please choose an option: 2
      Withdrawal amount ? 110
      CHECKING ACCOUNT #0
      Balance: $ 0.00
      Amount currently overdrawn: $10.00
      You can overdraw yourself by $10.00
      Interest charged for overdrawing: $ 8.50


      1. Make a deposit
      2. Make a withdrawal
      3. Close your account
      4. Exit

      Please choose an option: 1
      Deposit Amount? 30
      CHECKING ACCOUNT #0
      Balance: $20.00
      Amount currently overdrawn: $ 0.00
      You can overdraw yourself by $20.00
      Interest charged for overdrawing: $ 8.50


      1. Make a deposit
      2. Make a withdrawal
      3. Close your account
      4. Exit

      Please choose an option: 4
      Thanks for preferring us!


      1. Create a new account.
      2. Transact on an existing account.
      3. Exit.

      Please choose an option: 3
      It has been a pleasure serving you!
```

16.3 Programming Exercises

1. Your local college just decided to keep students' records in their new HAL mainframe computer. C is the chosen language for the job, and you get commissioned to define a structure to store the name (last, first, initial), date of birth, date of admission, number of credits already earned, and expected graduation date. Write the C struct declarations needed for this application, and also implement a function Age that takes a student structure and returns that student's age in years, up to today's date. Have your program prompt for the current date.

2. The local telephone company needs to keep track of its clients' information. The computer system needs to track the client name (last and first, with initial), the rate group they belong to (1 = Normal, 2 = Preferential, 3 = Bulk), and the hours when they can use the phone system for free (either

zero, one, or two time ranges). A sample table of information to keep track of this is the following:

Name	Group	Free
John Doe	Normal	() none
Bill Gates	Preferential	(12:00 P.M. --> 1:00 P.M.)
		(9:00 P.M. --> 6:00 A.M.)
Roddy Piper	Bulk	(9:00 P.M. --> 6:00 A.M.)

Write the C structure declarations needed to keep track of this type of information. Include in your code a function called `telco_init` to assign values to the `telco` structure you declared. Then write a small program to read in and display this data.

3. Consider the following sales table, which gathers data for a local drugstore in a small town:

	Jan	Feb	Mar	Apr	May	Jun	Jul	Aug
Aspirin	3/2		5/2				7	
Contac				0/4		4		8
Tylenol	2		1		0/4	1		
Pepto		0/3		4	3			2

The numbers represent sales, in units of 1000. When there is stock left, the remaining amount appears after a slash, as in 5/2, which means that 5000 units were sold, but 2000 are still left. Not all entries are filled. Write a program that can read in the sales data and print the above table. Represent the data as a two-dimensional array of structures.

4. Consider the following structure declaration:

```
struct something {
   char* f1;
   char  f2[25];
   float f3;
   int   f4;
};
```

(a) Write this same structure as a `typedef` declaration.
(b) Write two functions, `clear` and `print`, that use the structure to give it initial values and to print it.
(c) Rewrite the two functions, but now use the `typedef` version of the declaration.
(d) Compare both styles of programming and decide which one you like better.

5. Repeat Exercise 4, but now use an array and its pointer:

```
struct the_thing {
   char* f1;
   char  f2[25];
   float f3;
   int   f4;
} TH[200], *p;
```

Did you foresee any problems with not using `typedef`? Are there any occasions when you would not recommend using `typedef`, but merely `struct`?

6. The following data lists the telephone numbers of a group of students, all of whom are roommates, and some of whom share telephone numbers.

Joe Legalia	407-1532	408-1521
Frank Hans	402-1313	407-1532
Lila Quiros	408-1521	412-1122
June Myers	407-1532	402-1313
Joe Jin Jan	408-1521	402-1313

As you can tell by looking at the numbers, these guys repeat their numbers and there's no way to tell whose is which. You could represent this as either an array of students with two phone numbers, or as an array of phone numbers with the names of the students they locate. Write both versions of the structure required.

7.   In the previous question, decide which representation results in storing the least amount of redundant data. Calculate how much space will be used in each representation. Would you use the less space-expensive alternative? Can you think of a situation in which you would use the more space-expensive alternative?

8.   Consider the following function, and use it to deduce the structure declaration that corresponds to the function's argument. If there is more than one possibility, list them all.

```
void func(struct me bango)
{
  bango.nail = 13;
  strcpy(bango.list, "none");
  bango.go = ( bango.first == bango.last );
  bango.digital = '2';
  bango.i++;
};
```

9.   Your university initially only offers undergraduate courses, but due to your success as a professor, it decides to teach extension courses also. Soon afterwards, both graduate and undergraduate courses are taught. At first, you kept track of student records with a simple C structure containing the student's name, age, graduation date, courses, and grades. For extension courses, you had to add a single member to store the enrollment fee. In contrast, for graduate courses you added two members to the student structure: the first to store the lab grade, and a second one to keep track of field hours used for the course. Write the necessary declarations for the initial student structure and build upon it to construct the other two. Suppose you had already written a number of functions to manipulate the first student structure; explain whether these functions could be used with the graduate and extension structures. Try to measure the impact of using these new structures on the software you had already written.

10. In the same scenario depicted for the preceding question, try to solve the problem using unions. Will the impact on the software you already have be less when you use this other technique to implement your programs? Write the actual code for input and output routines for each of the three structures, and compare both approaches.

11. Declare an employee structure, including members for employee number, name, phone number, salary, and position (an enumerated type). Write a program that can read and create new employee records, delete them, change any information item for a given employee, and print a personnel roster.

12. Write a declaration for a `struct point` type, which will hold two `float` values (*x,y* coordinates in a two-dimensional space). Write a function called `distance` that calculates the distance in a straight line between two `point`s. Write another function called `manhattan_distance` which calculates the distance between two points in Manhattan style, as if each point were an office location in a high-rise building in Manhattan: to get from one to the other, one must first descend to street level in one's own building, travel the necessary horizontal distance, and then ride an elevator up to the destination point. In our case we drop down to the *x*-axis, travel along the *y*-axis, and then up (or down) to our destination. The Manhattan distance is the sum of those three distances, as illustrated in the following diagram.

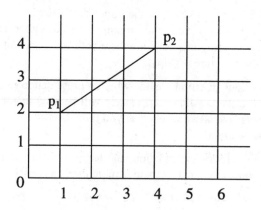

The distance between p_1 and p_2 is calculated using Pythagoras' theorem: $c = \sqrt{a^2 + b^2}$. In this case, the distance is $\sqrt{3^2 + 2^2} = \sqrt{9 + 4} = 3.6055513$. The Manhattan distance between p_1 and p_2 is $2 + 3 + 4 = 9$.

13. Define an enumerated type `weekday` with a value for each day of the week. Write functions `next(weekday d)` and `previous(weekday d)`.

14. Define a structure type `complex` (consisting of two floats, `real` and `imaginary`). Write functions to carry out operations on complex numbers, such as `add` and `multiply`.

15. Write a program that manipulates fractions, such as 2/7. Store the numerator and denominator of a fraction in a structure and write functions to add, subtract, multiply, and divide rational numbers. Reduce the result of each of these operations to its simplest form, using a GCD (greatest common divisor) function.

17 Advanced Uses of Pointers

17.1 Chapter Summary

Using *dynamic storage allocation*, a C program can obtain and use a block of memory as it is needed during program execution. These blocks can be used for arrays, strings, and structures. Dynamically allocated structures are particularly useful, since they can be linked together to form chains called *linked lists*. When handling linked lists, pointers to pointers come in quite handy. Pointers to functions are also very useful.

17.1.1 Dynamic Storage

Arrays and structures in C are of a fixed size, which cannot change once the program has been compiled. In the real world, however, we often need data structures that can grow (and shrink) upon demand, or when the program needs it. C supports *dynamic memory allocation* through a number of library functions that allocate blocks of memory whenever they are called.

There are three memory allocation functions declared in <stdlib.h>: malloc, calloc, and realloc. All three return a pointer of type (void *). The most commonly used function is malloc, which allocates a block of memory but leaves it uninitialized. calloc fills the block it allocates with zeroes, and realloc resizes a previously allocated block. All three return the null pointer (known as NULL) if they are unable to allocate the desired amount of memory. This condition can be tested:

```
if ((p = malloc(10000)) == NULL) error("NO MEMORY !");
```

The value of NULL can be tested like a number, and any valid pointer value (such as those returned by malloc) will be non-NULL, so the same pointer p above can be tested with if (!p) error(...);. Here's malloc's prototype:

```
void *malloc(size_t size);
```

The function allocates a block of size consecutive bytes and returns the address of the first byte. size_t is an unsigned integer type; except for very large memory blocks, we think of it as the ordinary integer type. The statement

```
p = malloc(n + 1);
```

allocates enough bytes for a string of length n (plus one for the null character) and assigns that address to p. The memory is left uninitialized; it's up to the programmer to fill in the string with data, perhaps with a call such as strcpy(p, "abc");.

With the allocation functions, you can define a function that returns a pointer to a brand-new string. For example, the following function takes two strings and merges them into a new string, which it returns. The original two strings are left untouched.

```
char *strmerge(const char *s1, const char *s2)
{
  int n, i;
  char *result, *p, c;

  n = strlen(s1) + strlen(s2);
  result = malloc(n + 1);
  if (result == NULL) {
    printf("Memory allocation failed.\n");
    exit(1);
  }
  p = result;
  for (i = 1; i <= n; i++) {
    if (i % 2)
      if (*s1)
        c = *s1++;
```

```
        else
            c = *s2++;
    else
      if (*s2)
        c = *s2++;
      else
        c = *s1++;
    *p++ = c;
  }
  *p = '\0';
  return result;
}
```

The function first calculates the number of characters n and allocates enough space for the result-ing string (n + 1). Then a loop to process n characters is carried out. Odd-numbered characters are taken from s1, and even-numbered ones from s2, unless the character to be taken is null, in which case we've reached the end of that string, and we take the character from the other (longer) string. The char-acter in question, c, is placed in *p++. When we're done processing n characters, we place the null character in the last slot and return the pointer to the new string.

Dynamically allocated strings are very useful when they are stored in arrays; instead of storing a two-dimensional array, we have a one-dimensional array of pointers to strings. Manipulating the collec-tion of strings is easier: moving entire strings around in the array can be accomplished by moving the pointers, rather than the entire strings. For example, the following code swaps strings 10 and 15:

```
char *A[20], *t;
    ...
t = A[10];
A[10] = A[15];
A[15] = t;
```

In general, space for an array can be allocated in the same way as for strings, except that the num-ber of bytes required (one byte per character in a string) will have to be calculated. Below we allocate storage for an array a of n floats.

```
float *a;
a = malloc (n * sizeof(float));
```

The calloc(size_t nmemb, size_t size) function allocates space for an array of nmemb members, each of which occupies size bytes. Thus, calloc is convenient for allocating space for structures and arrays that we wish to have initialized.

The realloc(void *ptr, size_t size) function resizes (to size bytes) a block of memory previously allocated. Either ptr should be NULL (in which case realloc behaves like mal-loc), or ptr should point to a previously allocated memory block (and strange things will happen if it doesn't). Resizing the memory block can make it shrink or expand. When expanding, the new bytes are uninitialized, and realloc normally will attempt to do it in the old memory location; if it can't, a new block will be allocated elsewhere, and all the old data copied over. When shrinking, realloc does so without moving the data. If size is zero, the memory block is freed up.

You must be careful with programs that allocate memory. It is easy to allocate a block of memory and lose or change the pointer to it, making it impossible to access those memory locations and leaving them as garbage. Unlike some other languages, C has no garbage collection. Garbage should be freed up by the programmer, so that space can be used for some other purpose, using the following function.

```
void free(void *ptr);
```

Calling free releases the block of memory pointed to by ptr, but doesn't change p itself. Thus p becomes a ***dangling pointer*** that points to a memory location that can no longer be used. If you attempt to use it, bad things can happen.

17.1.2   Linked Lists

Linked lists are chains of structures called **nodes** in which each node contains a pointer to the next node in the list:

Nodes are usually structures containing at least one "information" member and a pointer member, as follows:

```
struct node {
  int value;
  struct node *next;
};
```

To allocate a new node, we would use `malloc`, as shown below. After creating the new node, we can access the `value` member through the `new_node` pointer, using the `->` operator, which is a shorthand for a combination of the indirection operator `*` and the member selection operator `.`:

```
struct node *new_node;
new_node = malloc(sizeof(struct node));
new_node->value = 10;
/* equivalent to (*new_node).value = 10;  */
```

To create an additional node (and link it to `new_node`), we would first allocate it and then modify its `next` member so the new one will point to the old one. More generally, let's insert a new node (with value n) at the beginning of an old list. We'll assume the list begins at `list`, and it doesn't even matter whether `list` is NULL:

```
new_node = malloc(sizeof(struct node));
new_node->value = n;
new_node->next = list;
```

The advantage of a linked list is that its size is variable, unlike an array whose size must be known at compile time. On the other hand, you may not directly access the nth element in a linked list; instead you must traverse the list to find the element desired. Here's a function that searches through linked list `list` and returns a pointer to the first element whose value is n. If the value n appears nowhere in the list, the function returns NULL.

```
struct node *search_list(struct node *list, int n)
{
  while (list != NULL && list->value != n)
    list = list->next;
  return list;
}
```

To delete a node from a linked list, we first locate the element we wish to delete by traversing the list, then change the previous node so it will bypass the node we wish to delete, and finally deallocate the memory used by the node we're deleting. A modified version of our previous `search_list` function will find the predecessor of the first node containing n:

```
struct node *find_pred(struct node *list, int n)
{
  struct node *pred;
  pred = NULL;
  while (list != NULL && list->value != n) {
    pred = list;
    list = list->next;
  }
  return pred;
}
```

After calling `find_pred`, its successor (perhaps NULL) is the node where the value n is stored. To delete it, we consider several cases. First, if `list` is empty, nothing can be deleted. If `previous = find_pred` is NULL, then the node to be deleted is at the beginning of the list. Otherwise, the successor of `previous` is deleted, unless that successor is NULL. Here's the code to do it:

```
previous = find_pred(list, n);
if (list == NULL) ;   /* do nothing */
else if (previous == NULL)
  list = list->next;
            /* bypass first node */
else {
  current = previous->next;
  if (current == NULL) ;   /* do nothing */
  else {
    previous->next = current->next;
    free(current);
  }
}
```

If we were to package this code in a function, there might be two ways to design it. Below are the two most likely prototypes.

```
struct node *delete(struct node *list, int n);
void delete(struct node **list, int n);
```

In the first option, the function would return `list`, the (possibly modified) pointer to the first element in the list from which the first n has been deleted. To call that function, we would have to assign the return value to `list`:

```
list = delete(list, n);
```

In the second option, the call would be simpler:

```
delete(&list, n);
```

However, we do need the address of `list`, because its value has to be modified by the function. The function itself would return nothing. The complete function would be as follows:

```
void delete(struct node **list, int n)
{
  struct node *previous;
  struct node *current;

  previous = find_pred(*list, n);
  if (*list == NULL) ;   /* do nothing */
  else
    if (previous == NULL)
      *list = (*list)->next;
              /* bypass first node */
  else {
    current = previous->next;
    if (current == NULL) ;   /* do nothing */
    else {
      previous->next = current->next;
      free(current);
    }
  }
}
```

17.1.3   Pointers to Functions

We normally think of pointers as pointing to data, but they can point to functions as well. For example, we might wish to extend the sine-plotting program in Chapter 9 so we can plot any function at all. The plotting function could receive, as an argument, the function that the user wishes to have plotted. For example, the plot function's prototype could look like this:

```
float plot(float (*f)(float), float lower, float upper, float interval);
```

The function call needed to plot, say, the sine function between 0 and $\pi/2$ with intervals of 0.01 would look like this:

```
plot(sin, 0, PI/2, 0.01);
```

Within `plot`, we can call the function to which f points: `(*f)(x)`.

Function pointers can be used in a variety of ways. For example, we can store pointers to functions in an array, and select the nth function for some task, such as plotting that function, or integrating it, or simply calling it. This is done as easily as retrieving any other type of array element. For example, if an array is declared with `float (*a[N])(float)` (an array of N pointers to functions that take a `float` argument and return `float`), then we use (*a[n])(x) to call the nth function.

17.2 Solved Exercises

17.2.1 Solved Exercise 1: Sets (Revisited)

Let's rewrite our sets program from chapters 10 and 15, this time using linked lists. We'll work with sets of integers. The program will read two sets from the user and then allow her to add or delete elements from either set. The program can also calculate the union, the intersection, and the cardinality (number of elements) of the sets. When the program runs, it reads two sets from the user, and then it displays a menu like this:

```
1.  Add an element to set 1.
2.  Add an element to set 2.
3.  Delete an element from set 1.
4.  Delete an element from set 2.
5.  View the cardinality of the sets.
6.  View the union of the sets.
7.  View the intersection of the sets.
8.  Exit.
```

The first order of business is to design the prototypes of the various functions to be used. We place the prototypes in a header file called `node.h`, along with the definition of `struct node`.

```
/************************/
/*        node.h        */
/************************/
#ifndef NODE_H
#define NODE_H

struct node {
  int elem;
  struct node *next;
};
typedef struct node Node;

void insert_prompt(Node **set, int n);
void insert(Node **set, int elem);
void delete(Node **set, int elem);
void done(Node **set);
void print(Node *set);
int cardinality(Node *set);
int locate(Node *set, int elem);
Node *sunion(Node *set1, Node *set2);
Node *intersection(Node *set1, Node *set2);
Node *get_set(int n);

#endif
```

Functions `insert`, `delete`, and `done` are capable of modifying the entry point to the linked list and therefore need the address of the pointer variable that points to the first node in the list. Thus the parameter they receive is of type `node **`. In those cases, to access the value we must dereference the pointer's address, and then dereference the pointer itself, to arrive at the node. This is accomplished with the expression `(*set) -> elem`. The parentheses are required; without them, the meaning would be `*(set -> elem)`, which would cause compilation errors, because `set` is not of type `(Node *)`.

Next comes our main module, called `sets.c`. We first read in the two sets, using `get_set`. Then we repeatedly print the main menu, get the user's choice, and call the appropriate function defined in `node.c` to carry out the work. Here's the main program.

```c
/****************************************************************/
/* This program will implement sets, with the following operations:*/
/* union, intersection, and cardinality. Operations for         */
/* creating, destroying, and printing the sets are also available. */
/* The sets are implemented as linked lists.                    */
/****************************************************************/

#include <stdio.h>
#include "node.h"

main()
{
  int choice;
  Node *set1, *set2;

  printf("SET MANIPULATION PROGRAM:\n");
  printf("Insert, Delete, Union and Intersect two sets\n\n");
  set1 = get_set(1);
  set2 = get_set(2);
  choice = 0;
  while (choice != 8) {
    printf("\nMENU:\n-----\n");
    printf("1. Add an element to Set 1\n");
    printf("2. Add an element to Set 2\n");
    printf("3. Delete an element from Set 1\n");
    printf("4. Delete an element form Set 2\n");
    printf("5. View the cardinality of the sets\n");
    printf("6. View the union of the sets\n");
    printf("7. View the intersection of the sets\n");
    printf("8. Exit\n\n");
    printf("Please choose an option: ");
    scanf("%d", &choice);
    switch (choice) {
      case 1:
        insert_prompt(&set1, 1);
        break;
      case 2:
        insert_prompt(&set2, 2);
        break;
      case 3:
        delete(&set1, 1);
        break;
      case 4:
        delete(&set2, 2);
        break;
      case 5:
        printf("\nThe cardinality of Set 1 is %d.", cardinality(set1));
        printf("\nThe cardinality of Set 2 is %d.\n", cardinality(set2));
        break;
      case 6:
        printf("\nThe union of the sets is:\n");
```

```
                print(sunion(set1, set2));
                break;
            case 7:
                printf("\nThe intersection of the sets is:\n");
                print(intersection(set1, set2));
                break;
            case 8:
                printf("\nBye!\n\n");
                break;
            default:
                printf("I'm sorry. That's not a valid option\n");
                choice = 0;
        }
    }
    done(&set1);
    done(&set2);
    return 0;
}
```

Finally, file `node.c` contains the definitions of the functions that do all the work. Developing each one of them individually is relatively straightforward; when they are combined and used together, they provide a powerful collection of facilities for manipulating linked lists. Here's the `node.c` file.

```
/**************************/
/*        node.c          */
/**************************/
#include <stdio.h>
#include <stdlib.h>
#include "node.h"

void insert(Node **set, int elem)
{
    Node *new_node;

    if ((*set) == NULL)    /* the set is empty */
        if (((*set) = malloc(sizeof(Node))) != NULL) {
            (*set)->elem = elem;
            (*set)->next = NULL;
        }
        else {
            printf("Error in malloc - Function insert\n");
            exit(0);
        }
    else {     /* The set's not empty */
        new_node = *set;

        /* First we search for elem in the set */
        while ((new_node->next != NULL) && (new_node->elem != elem))
            new_node = new_node->next;

        if (new_node->elem != elem) { /* elem isn't in the set: add it */
            if ((new_node->next = malloc(sizeof(Node))) != NULL) {
                /* New element successfully created */
                new_node->next->elem = elem;
                new_node->next->next = NULL;
            }
            else {
                /* New element couldn't be created */
                printf("Error in malloc - Function insert\n");
                exit(0);
            }
        }
    }
}
```

```
void insert_prompt(Node **set, int n)
{
  int elem;

  printf("\nElement you wish to add to set %d: ", n);
  scanf("%d", &elem);
  insert(set, elem);
  printf("\nSet %d is now:\n", n);
  print(*set);
}

void delete(Node **set, int n)
{
  Node *previous, *current;
  int elem;

  printf("\nSet %d is:\n", n);
  print(*set);
  printf("\nElement you wish to delete from set %d: ", n);
  scanf("%d", &elem);

  if ((*set)->elem == elem) {
    /* The first element is being deleted */
    current = *set;
    *set = (*set)->next;
    free(current);
  }
  else {
    /* Search the list */
    previous = *set;
    current = previous->next;
    while (current != NULL && current->elem != elem) {
      /* Search for elem, or end of list */
      previous = current;
      current = current->next;
    }

    if (current == NULL) return;  /* never found it */
    if (current->elem == elem) {
      /* found elem in current, so bypass it */
      previous->next = current->next;
      free(current);
    }
  }
  printf("\nSet %d now is:\n", n);
  print(*set);
}

void done(Node **set)
{
  Node *current, *previous;

  current = *set;
  while (current != NULL) {
    /* Haven't reached the end of the list */
    previous = current;
    current = current->next;
    free(previous);
  }
  *set = NULL;
}
```

```c
Node *sunion(Node *set1, Node *set2)
{
  Node *result, *current;

  result = NULL;
  current = set1;
  /* Insert all elements of set 1 */
  while (current != NULL) {
    insert(&result, current->elem);
    current = current->next;
  }

  /* Insert all elements of set 2 */
  current = set2;
  while (current != NULL) {
    insert(&result, current->elem);
    current = current->next;
  }
  return result;
}

void print(Node *set)
{
  Node *current;

  if (set == NULL)
    printf("The set is empty.\n");
  else {
    current = set;
    while (current != NULL) {
      printf("%d", current->elem);
      if (current->next != NULL)
        printf(", ");
      current = current->next;
    }
   printf("\n");
  }
}

int cardinality(Node *set)
{
  Node *current;
  int i;

  i = 0;
  current = set;
  while (current != NULL) {
    i++;
    current = current->next;
  }
  return i;
}

int locate(Node *set, int elem)
{
  Node *current;

  current = set;
  while (current != NULL && current->elem != elem)
    current = current->next;
  return (current != NULL);
}
```

```
Node *intersection(Node *set1, Node *set2)
{
  Node *result, *current;

  result = NULL;
  current = set1;
  while (current != NULL) {
    if (locate(set2, current->elem))
      insert(&result, current->elem);
    current = current->next;
  }
  return result;
}

Node *get_set(int n)
{
  int i, nelems;
  Node * set;

  printf("Reading Set %d\n", n);
  set = NULL;
  printf("How many elements will the set have? ");
  scanf("%d", &nelems);
  for (i = 1; i <= nelems; i++)
    insert_prompt(&set, n);
  printf("\n");
  return set;
}
```

17.2.2 Solved Exercise 2: Numeric Integration

Let's develop a program to perform numeric integration. Don't panic! It's actually quite straight-forward, and you don't need a Ph.D. in mathematics. The idea is to calculate an approximation of the area under the function's curve between a low point and a high point, as in the following diagram.

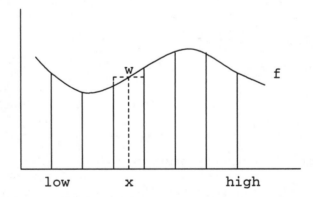

The technique consists of splitting the interval between low and high into n intervals of equal length. Each interval is of width $w = (high - low) / n$. The height of that interval varies, so we choose the mid-point x of the interval and calculate the height as $h = f(x)$ (the vertical dashed line). If we multiply the height h and the width w, we obtain the area of a rectangle that comes fairly close to the actual area under the function f in that interval. Doing this repeatedly, once for each interval, will yield a pretty good approximation of the entire area under the curve, especially if we have a large number of intervals, i.e., if n is large. The following code will do it:

```
sum = 0;
w = (high - low) / n;
x = low + w / 2;
```

```
for (i = 0; i < n; i++) {
  h = f(x);
  sum += h * w;
  x += w;
}
```

Now we need to be able to do this for several different functions. We'll use an array of pointers to the functions that we're going to integrate. When the user chooses a function, we call the `integrate` function, using the pointer to the chosen function as a parameter. Thus our `integrate` function is quite powerful: it is capable, in principle, of integrating *any* function. The complete program is shown below:

```
#include <stdio.h>
#include <stdlib.h>
#include <math.h>

float integrate(float (*func)(float x),
                float low, float high, int n);

float func0(float x); /* sine (x)   */
float func1(float x); /* cosine x)  */
float func2(float x); /* tan (x)    */
float func3(float x); /* x*x        */
float func4(float x); /* sqrt (x)   */

main()
{
  float high, low;
  int choice, npoints;
  float (*vec[5])(float);

  vec[0] = func0;
  vec[1] = func1;
  vec[2] = func2;
  vec[3] = func3;
  vec[4] = func4;

  printf("NUMERIC INTEGRATION PROGRAM\n\n");
  choice = 0;
  while (choice != 6) {
    printf("1. Sine.\n");
    printf("2. Cosine.\n");
    printf("3. Tangent.\n");
    printf("4. Square.\n");
    printf("5. Square root.\n");
    printf("6. Exit.\n\n");
    printf("Please choose one: ");
    scanf("%d", &choice);
    if ((choice > 6) || (choice <= 0))
      printf("\nSorry, that's not an option.\n");
    else if (choice != 6) {
      printf("\nPlease enter the interval's lower limit: ");
      scanf("%f", &low);
      printf("\nPlease enter the interval's upper limit: ");
      scanf("%f", &high);
      npoints = -1;
      while (npoints < 0) {
        printf("\n\nHow many subintervals ? ");
        scanf("%d", &npoints);
        if (npoints < 0)
          printf("\nMust have a positive number !\n\n");
      }
      printf("The result is : %f.\n\n",
```

```
                        integrate(vec[choice-1], low, high, npoints));
        }
    }
    printf("Bye!\n\n");
    return 0;
}

float integrate (float (*func)(float x),
                 float low, float high, int n)
{
    int i;
    float x, width, sum;

    sum = 0;
    width = (high - low) / n;
    x = low + width / 2;
    for (i = 0; i < n; i++) {
        sum += func(x) * width;
        x += width;
    }
    return sum;
}

float func0(float x) { return sin(x); }
float func1(float x) { return cos(x); }
float func2(float x) { return tan(x); }
float func3(float x) { return x * x; }
float func4(float x) { return sqrt(x); }
```

17.3   Programming Exercises

The first eight exercises all apply to Solved Exercise 1, in which we implemented sets using linked lists.

1. Implement the function `Node *difference(Node *set1, Node *set2);`. This function should calculate the difference between `set1` and `set2`.

2. Rewrite the `insert` function so that it will insert the new element in ascending order.

3. Suppose that the elements of the linked list appear in ascending order as the list is traversed. Rewrite the `locate` function so that it will take advantage of the order.

4. Write the function `int compare(Node *set1, Node *set2);`. This function should return 1 if `set1` and `set2` are equal, and 0 otherwise.

5. Write the function `Node *copy(Node *set);`. This function should return a (separately allocated) copy of `set`.

6. Rewrite the `insert` and `delete` functions so that instead of changing the set, they'll return a pointer to a new set in which the modifications have been made. Their prototypes should be:

    ```
    Node *insert(Node *set, int elem);
    Node *delete(Node *set, int elem);
    ```

7. The lists in our example aren't ordered. Write a `sort` function for a given set.

8. Write a `reverse_print` function. This function should print the list backwards, from last to first. *Hint:* there is a wonderfully simple recursive solution.

9. Consider the following structure.

    ```
    struct node {
      struct node *prev;
      int elem;
      struct node *next;
    };
    ```

    This is called a ***doubly linked list***. Each node has two pointers: one points to its predecessor (node->prev) and the other to its successor (node->next), as follows.

    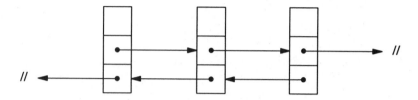

    Doubly linked lists often have two entry points, stored in a structure as follows.

    ```
    struct double_list {
      struct node *front;
      struct node *rear;
    };
    ```

    Write an ordered `insert` function for a doubly linked list.

10. Write a `delete` function for a doubly linked list.

11. Write a `reverse_print` function for a doubly linked list (it will be easier this time!)

12. Consider a *circular* linked list:

    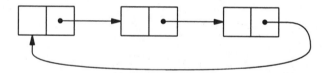

    Write an `insert` function that inserts at the beginning of a circular linked list.

13. Write an `insert` function that inserts at the end of a circular linked list.

14. Write a `delete` function that deletes at the beginning of a circular linked list.

15. Write a `delete` function that deletes at the end of a circular linked list.

16. Write a `locate` function for a circular linked list.

17. Consider the following declaration.

    ```
                        float (*p)(int);
    ```

    We know that p points to a function. What type of return value must this function have, and what are the number and types of its parameters?

18. There are three principal errors in the following code. Find them.

    ```
    struct node {
      int elem;
        struct node *next;
    }
    struct node **set;
    *set -> elem = 5;
    ```

18 Declarations

18.1 Chapter Summary

Declarations in C are more complex than in many other languages. In C, declarations can provide much information about identifiers, including their *storage class*, *qualifiers* such as `const` and `volatile`, and *initializers* for various types of variables. The general form of declarations in C is

declaration-specifiers declarators ;

There are three types of declaration specifiers:

- *storage classes*: `auto`, `static`, `extern`, and `register`. If present, these must appear first.
- *type qualifiers*: `const` and `volatile`.
- *type specifiers*: `void`, `char`, `short`, `int`, `long`, `float`, `double`, `signed`, and `unsigned`, as well as specifications of structures, unions, and enumerations.

A declarator declares a name, and uses `*` (pointer), `[]` (array) and `()` (function) to indicate the type of object being declared. The declarators must appear in a list separated by commas.

18.1.1 Storage Classes and Type Qualifiers

Every variable in C has *storage duration* (the period of time during which the variable is allocated), *scope* (the portion of program text in which the variable is visible), and *linkage* (the degree to which the variable is shared with other parts of the program). A variable with *automatic storage duration* is allocated upon entry to the block in which it is declared, and deallocated upon exit. A variable with *static storage duration* is allocated upon entry to the block in which it is declared, but remains allocated for the duration of the program. Variables can have either *block scope* (visible from its declaration to the end of that block), or *file scope* (visible from its declaration to the end of that file). Variables can have *external linkage* (they can be shared with other files), *internal linkage* (they are restricted to the current file, but can be shared by functions in that file), or *no linkage* (they belong to a single function and can't be shared). Variables have default duration, scope, and linkage, that depend on where they are declared. The defaults are:

Placed where variable is declared	duration	scope	linkage
Inside a function	automatic	block	none
Outside all blocks	static	file	external

Whenever the defaults don't suit our needs, we can modify them with the storage class specifiers `auto`, `static`, `extern`, or `register`. The following table summarizes the effect of each storage class specifier.

Storage Class Specifier	Variable Declared Inside a Block			Variable Declared Outside a Block		
	duration	scope	linkage	duration	scope	linkage
`auto`	automatic	block	none	X	X	X
`static`	static	block	none	static	file	internal
`extern`	static	block	?	static	file	?
`register`	automatic	block	none	X	X	X

In the above table, the "X" means it is illegal to have an automatic or register variable declared outside a block. The "?" means the linkage depends on where the variable is declared elsewhere. If the variable is declared `static` earlier in the same file, the linkage is internal. Otherwise, the variable normally has external linkage. A variable declared with `register` storage class behaves like an automatic variable, but the compiler is instructed to store it, if it can, in one of the computer's hardware registers rather than in main memory. This speeds up the use of this variable considerably (for example, for loop control variables), but disallows the & operator.

There are two type qualifiers: const and volatile. The latter will be discussed in Chapter 20. const is used to make read-only variables (a contradiction in terms, actually). The value of a const object cannot be changed. const is useful for documentation and verification purposes: the code will more clearly state the programmer's intent of not modifying the value, and the compiler will enforce it. At first glance it would seem that const supersedes the #define preprocessor directive, but there are differences: const applies to objects of any type, including arrays, structures, unions, and pointers. const objects obey scope rules, while preprocessor definitions don't. Finally, const object names, unlike macro names, can be viewed in a debugger. Generally, we recommend using macros for number or character constants, and const objects for everything else.

18.1.2 Declarators and Initializers

A declarator consists of an identifier, optionally preceded by * (pointer), or followed by [] (array), or by () (function). These can be combined in innumerable ways, often making the task of unraveling a declaration a daunting one. The following are all declarations:

```
int *p;
int a[];
float b[30];
int max(int a, int b);
void f(int, float *);
float read_values();
float g(void);
```

As illustrated, function declarations need not mention the name of the parameter, and in fact don't need to mention the parameters at all. In the last example above, void indicates that there are no arguments, unlike read_values;, where the empty set of parentheses indicates that no information is given about the number and/or types of the arguments.

Unraveling complex declarations is one of C's most criticized aspects, but there's help:

1. Declarators are read from the inside out, not from left to right.
2. Favor [] and () over *.

For example, consider float *(*a[5])(int). We start at a and work our way out, encountering [5], then *, then (int), and finally *. Thus the declaration is of a, an array of pointers to functions that take one integer argument and return a pointer to float (whew!!). All this can be simplified with typedef definitions:

```
typedef float *Fcn(int);
    /* Fcn is function taking int and returning (float *) */
typedef Fcn *Fcn_ptr;
    /* Fcn_ptr is pointer to Fcn   */
typedef Fcn_ptr Fcn_ptrs[5];
    /* Fcn_ptrs is an array of 5 Fcn_ptrs   */
typedef Fcn_ptrs A;
    /* A is a 'Fcn_ptrs'          */
```

Initial values can be specified when declaring variables in C. The following are all initializers:

```
int a = 65;
float x = 2.3;
int *p = &a;
int a[4] = {1,2,3,4};
int s[] = "abcd";
```

The initial value for a static variable must be a constant, not a variable. The initial value for an auto variable need not be constant. The values enclosed in braces in the initializer for a structure, union, or array must contain constant expressions, not variables or function calls. The initializer for an automatic structure or union can be another structure or union.

Uninitialized variables don't always have undefined values. Those with automatic duration have no default initial value. Those with static duration have the value zero by default. The zero is cast to the appropriate type, so `static float x` will have the value `0.0`. Still, it is best to explicitly initialize every variable used.

18.2   Solved Exercises

18.2.1   Solved Exercise 1: Arrays of Pointers to Functions

Let's develop a program that uses two arrays of pointers to functions. We first define a few functions that take a `float` argument and return a `float`. Then, to make things interesting, let's define a few functions that take two arguments: an `int` and one of the functions we just mentioned. The program looks like this:

```
#include <stdio.h>

float func0(float p) { return p; }
float func1(float p) { return p * 2.0; }
float func2(float p) { return p * p; }
float f_func0(int i, float (*func)(float));
float f_func1(int i, float (*func)(float));
float f_func2(int i, float (*func)(float));

main()
{
  float (*vec[3])(float) = {func0, func1, func2};
  float (*f_vec[3])(int, float (*func)(float)) =
         {f_func0, f_func1, f_func2};

  printf("%5.2f\n", vec[0](3.0));
  printf("%5.2f\n", f_vec[2](4, func1));
  printf("%5.2f\n", f_vec[2](4, func2));
  return 0;
}

float f_func0(int i, float (*func)(float))
{
  return func(i);
}

float f_func1(int i, float (*func)(float))
{
  return func(func(i));
}

float f_func2(int i, float (*func)(float))
{
  return func(func(func(i)));
}
```

We declare two arrays of pointers to functions, `vec` and `f_vec`. The first array is initialized to contain the three functions `func0`, `func1`, and `func2`. The other array is initialized to contain `f_func0`, `f_func1`, and `f_func2`. We then make a few sample calls to these functions. The declarations are fairly messy; we can do better using `typedef` and function prototypes.

```
#include <stdio.h>

typedef float Func(float);
typedef Func *Func_ptr;
typedef Func_ptr Vec_func[3];
```

```
Func func0, func1, func2;

typedef float F_func(int, Func_ptr);
typedef F_func *F_func_ptr;
typedef F_func_ptr Vec_f_func[3];

F_func f_func0, f_func1, f_func2;

main()
{
  Vec_func vec = {func0, func1, func2};
  Vec_f_func f_vec = {f_func0, f_func1, f_func2};

  printf("%5.2f\n", vec[0](3.0));
  printf("%5.2f\n", f_vec[2](4, func1));
  printf("%5.2f\n", f_vec[2](4, func2));
  return 0;
}

float func0(float p) { return p; }
float func1(float p) { return p * 2.0; }
float func2(float p) { return p * p; }

float f_func0(int i, float (*func)(float))
{
  return func(i);
}

float f_func1(int i, float (*func)(float))
{
  return func(func(i));
}

float f_func2(int i, float (*func)(float))
{
  return func(func(func(i)));
}
```

The new types are Func (a function that takes float and returns float), Func_ptr (a pointer to a Func), Vec_func (a vector of 3 Func_ptrs). We also have F_func (a function that takes int and Func and returns float), F_func_ptr (a pointer to F_func), and Vec_f_func (a vector of 3 F_func_ptrs). Notice that these new types can be used in the declaration (the prototypes) of functions, but not in their definitions.

As yet another twist to all this, let's try an array of functions, each of which receives as its argument an array of pointers to a second set of functions. Declaring functions like these in the conventional manner would be quite complex, and the declarations would be barely readable. Using typedef, the declarations become manageable.

```
#include <stdio.h>

typedef void Func(void);
typedef Func *Func_ptr;
typedef Func_ptr Vec_func[3];

Func func0, func1, func2;

typedef void F_func(Vec_func v_func);
typedef F_func *F_func_ptr;
typedef F_func_ptr V_f_func[3];

F_func f_func0, f_func1, f_func2;
```

```
main()
{
  Vec_func vec = {func0, func1, func2};
  V_f_func vec2 = {f_func0, f_func1, f_func2};

  vec[0]();
  vec2[1](vec);
  return 0;
}

void func0() { printf("func0\n"); }
void func1() { printf("func1\n"); }
void func2() { printf("func2\n"); }

void f_func0(Vec_func v_func)
{
  v_func[0]();
}

void f_func1(Vec_func v_func)
{
  v_func[0]();
  v_func[1]();
}

void f_func2(Vec_func v_func)
{
  v_func[0]();
  v_func[1]();
  v_func[2]();
}
```

I encourage you to study the above three programs, predict their output, and then run them.

18.3   Programming Exercises

1. Determine what's wrong with the following code.

    ```
    int i;
    char j = 1432;

    for (i = 0; i < j; i++)
    {
      /* some code here */
    }
    ```

2. Describe (in English) each of the following declarations.

    ```
    a) int *p;
    b) char vec[];
    c) extern float j;
    d) static int q;
    e) void sort(int *);
    ```

3. What are the advantages of using `const`?

4. Describe the difference between the following two declarations.

    ```
    void sort(int *);
    extern void sort(int *);
    ```

5. Under what circumstances should a function be declared `static`?

6. Write a declaration for each of the following variables and functions.

(a)   t is a pointer to a pointer to the field elem of a structure named node.

(b)   p is an integer variable with external linkage. *Hint:* there may be more than one answer.

(c)   vec is an array of pointers to a structure tag named node.

(d)   d is a function with two integer parameters that returns a pointer to a float.

7.   What's the difference between linkage and scope?

8.   Determine what's wrong with the following code.

```
int vec[5] = {3, 5, rand(), 4, 10 + 1};
```

9.   How may times are static variables initialized?

10.   How do static variables aid in information hiding?

11.   Determine the storage duration, the scope, and the linkage of each of the variables in the following code.

```
extern float a;
int b;

void dummy( int c)
{
  static float d;
  extern char e;
}
```

12.   Consider the following declarations.

```
typedef struct node *T1;
typedef T1 T2[10];

T2 *x;
```

Describe the type of x in words.

13.   Find the variables with file scope in the following code segment.

```
int a;

void dummy()
{
  static int b;
  int i;

  b = 0;
  for (i = 0; i < 10; i++)
    b = a + i;
}
```

14.   Which kinds of variables have a default initial value? What is that initial value for each of them?

15.   How can you determine the linkage of a variable? Is it always possible to find out?

19 Program Design

19.1 Chapter Summary

In real life, C programs are often very large. Writing a large program poses a different set of challenges from writing a small one. C was not designed specifically for writing very large programs, but it can be done. Here we discuss some of the most important concepts in program design and how they are handled in C++.

19.1.1 Modules, Information Hiding, and Abstract Data Types

A *module* is a collection of services that are made available to other parts of the program. Every module has an *interface*, which describes the services available, and an *implementation*, which performs the services. In C, services are provided through functions. The interface is usually a header file, containing prototypes of the functions that other other files will use. The implementation is a source file, containing the definitions of the functions. The advantages of this approach are *abstraction*, *reusability*, and *maintainability*. Abstraction occurs when we think of the various services provided in an abstract way—when we think of what the module does, rather than the details of how it does it. This allows each module to be implemented quite independently, perhaps by different people. Independent modules tend to be reusable, as when a general-purpose facility that manipulates sets is used in several different programs. Modular programs are more maintainable: bugs can usually be isolated inside specific modules. When a bug is found, or whenever an enhancement is needed, only the affected module need be recompiled and the entire program relinked. This last aspect is especially important: large programs tend to be used (and modified) over a period of years, requiring extensive maintenance.

How should one design a module? Two very desirable properties are *high cohesion* and *low coupling*. Highly cohesive modules have functions that are closely related, designed to work toward a common goal. Low coupling among modules takes place when the modules are as independent as possible, having little or no influence upon each other.

Modules come in several flavors. A *data pool* is a collection of related data items such as constants and variables, usually in the form of a header file. A *library* is a collection of functions, such as the string functions provided in <string.h>. An *abstract object* is usually a collection of functions that manipulate a hidden object, such as operations push and pop on a stack whose actual data structure remains hidden, and is thus called "abstract." Finally, an *abstract data type (ADT)* is a type of data item whose representation is hidden. For example, consider the header file point.h:

```
/****************/
/*    point.h    */
/****************/

#ifndef POINT_H
#define POINT_H

typedef struct {
  float x;
  float y;
} Pointstruct;

typedef Pointstruct *Point;
Point create_point();
void set_x(Point p, float x);
void set_y(Point p, float y);
void print_point(Point p);

#endif
```

Here's the corresponding implementation, `point.c`:

```
/**************/
/*   point.c   */
/**************/

#include <stdio.h>
#include <stdlib.h>
#include "point.h"

Point create_point()
{
   return malloc(sizeof(Pointstruct));
}

void set_x(Point p, float x)
{
   p->x = x;
}

void set_y(Point p, float y)
{
   p->y = y;
}

void print_point(Point p)
{
   printf("Point p = (%f,%f)\n", p->x, p->y);
}
```

In the main program, shown below, we can declare and manipulate variables of type `Point` without knowing what kind of object it is. We choose to implement `Point` as a pointer to a structure, rather than as a structure. When passing a `Point` as an argument to a function, only a pointer is copied, rather than an entire structure. For large objects, this can be significantly more efficient. As shown above, functions are provided to manipulate the object of the abstract data type, so the client module never needs to know the implementation details of `Point`.

```
#include "point.h"

main()
{
   Point p;

   p = create_point();
   set_x(p, 3.4);
   set_y(p, 5.6);
   print_point(p);
   return 0;
}
```

This manner of designing modules leads to another important concept in program design: *information hiding*. In the above example, we could have used an array to represent the two components of a `Point`. In a well-designed module, such details are expressly hidden from the client module. This offers two advantages: *security*, as the client module will be unable to tamper with the inner workings of the module, and *flexibility*, since we can decide to reimplement type `Point` using some other representation, without affecting the rest of the entire program at all. In C, the principal mechanism for enforcing information hiding is the `static` storage class. A `static` function has internal linkage and is only visible to functions in the same file. Similarly, a `static` variable with file scope can be used only by functions in the same file.

Unfortunately, `Point` is not really an abstract data type, because although individual functions and variables can be hidden, data types cannot. Nothing prevents a client module from dealing with a `Point` as what it really is, a pointer to a structure. For example, the client could try the following:

`p->x` = `6.7`. Preventing this kind of mayhem is called *encapsulation* of the data type. C does not support encapsulation, but C++ does.

19.1.2   C++

C++ was designed by Bjarne Stroustrup of Bell Laboratories in the 1980s as an extended version of C. Its most significant feature is the *class*, which allows encapsulation, as well as other features that support the definition and implementation of abstract data types. In addition, C++ provides a number of useful new features, such as support for *object-oriented programming*, *operator overloading*, *templates*, and *exception handling*. C++ was designed for compatibility with C: every feature in standard C appears in C++. Nevertheless, some minor incompatibilities remain. Here are some of the new features.

- Single-line comments begin with `//` and continue until the end of the current line.
- Tag names are automatically type names. `struct name { ... }` is sufficient to define `name` as a type name, without using `typedef`.
- The word `void` is not necessary to specify a function with no arguments.
- Arguments can have default values. The following function prints a message if given one as a parameter, and prints the default message `Hello` if none is given.

```
void prmsg(const char * message = "Hello")
{
  printf("%s\n", message);
}
```

- C++ allows arguments to be *passed by reference*, without having to handle the pointers explicitly. A function that decomposes a `float` monetary value into two integers would look like this in C:

```
void decomp(float amount, int *dollars, int *cents)
{
  *dollars = amount;
  *cents = (amount - *dollars) * 100;
} ...
decomp(34.67, &d, &c);
```

In C++, the indirection operator is not necessary, and we no longer need the `&` operator in the function call:

```
void decomp(float amount, int& dollars, int& cents)
{
  dollars = amount;
  cents = (amount - dollars) * 100;
} ...
decomp(34.67, d, c);
```

- In C, we allocate and free memory using `malloc` and `free`. In C++, it is better to use operators `new` and `delete`.

```
char *message;
message = new char[10];
  ...
delete message;
```

The operand for `new` is a type specifier; the operand for `delete` is a pointer.

C++ was originally named "C with Classes." A class is an abstract data type, a collection of data objects together with the operations (functions) that can manipulate them. C++ allows us to create any data type that we want, in effect allowing us to extend the language itself. For example, suppose we wanted integers with an unlimited number of digits (recall Chapter 8, when we calculated the factorial of 1000). In C++, we can create a new data type `large_int`, and using operator overloading, we can even use C++'s own operators on those objects:

```
large_int a, b, c;
a = b * c;
```

The result is objects that look natural and can be manipulated in a natural way. Since this can be done for any data type, the activity of programming can be viewed as extending C++ to include the data types we need for the situation at hand, and then using those data types to solve our problem. Those data types could include, in increasing order of importance,

1. Variations on existing data types, such as "smart" arrays that perform range checks on their subscripts, or strings that shrink and grow as needed.
2. Data structures that programmers find useful, such as stacks, queues, trees, sets, etc.
3. Types that model real-world objects, such as bank accounts, jet engines, credit bureau databases, store inventories, personnel files, etc.

Class definitions in C++ are like structure definitions in C, except that both function and data definitions are allowed. For example, the following declares a class `Complex`.

```
class Complex {
private:
  float real;
  float imag;
public:
  Complex(float x, float y);
  void print();
  Complex operator+(Complex c);
};
```

`real` and `imag` are *private data members* of class `Complex`. If we declare `Complex a;`, member `real` of a cannot be accessed with the expression `a.real`. Instead, we provide *public member functions*, which are declared inside the class. We also have a *constructor* `Complex`, a member function `print`, and an overloaded operator `operator+`. We use `Complex::` to inform the compiler that we are defining a class member function, not just an ordinary function. The definitions, and a sample main program, appear below.

```
Complex::Complex(float x=0.0, float y=0.0)
{
    real = x; imag = y;
}

void Complex::print()
{
    cout << "(" << real << "+" << imag << "i)" << "\n";
}

Complex Complex::operator+(Complex c)
{
  Complex result;

  result.real = real + c.real;
  result.imag = imag + c.imag;
  return result;
}

main()
{
  Complex a(1.2, 3.4), b(5.6), c;

  a.print();
  b.print();
  c = a + b;
  c.print();
  return 0;
}
```

Member functions are accessed the same way as data members, using the "." operator. `Complex` is a constructor; it is invoked automatically whenever a `Complex` variable is declared. It stores the values given (if any) and assumes default values of zero. `print` is a member function, which sends the two components of the complex number to the ***output stream*** `cout`. `operator+` is an overloaded operator, which makes the built-in + operator work on `Complex` variables. It takes a `Complex` argument `c` and adds `c`'s `real` and `imag` members to its own `real` and `imag`, storing the results in a new `Complex` number, which it returns. These definitions could have appeared inside the class definition (typically in a header file), but generally they are placed in the corresponding implementation source file. In the main program, `a`, `b`, and `c` are ***instances*** of class `Complex`. The code in the main program looks and feels as if `Complex` numbers were built into the language. It's even possible to send a complex number to the output stream with a statement like `cout << c;`, but we won't go into details here.

C++ is object-oriented: it supports encapsulation (the ability to hide implementation details of an abstract data type), ***inheritance*** (the ability to derive new types and their various properties from old types), and ***polymorphism*** (the ability of objects of different classes to respond to the same operation).

Inheritance can be used to establish a class hierarchy:

```
class employee { ... };
class manager:
  public employee { ... };
class director:
  public manager { ... };
class temporary { ... };
class secretary:
  public employee { ... };
class tsec:
  public temporary, // Multiple Inheritance
  public secretary { ... };
class consultant:
  public temporary,
  public manager { ... };
```

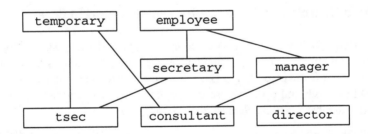

Here data members in each class are inherited from the base class. For example, if every employee has a name, then every class derived from `employee` (`secretary`, `tsec`, `manager`, `director`, and `consultant`) also has a name. Each derived class can contain additional members, so `manager` is a particular case of `employee` (with a name, Social Security number, etc.), but also, say, with a department name and an annual management bonus. Thus, class hierarchies are very useful in modeling real-world situations.

Member functions in C++ can be ***virtual***. In the above example, we could define a `print_employee` function as `virtual` in the `employee` class and then define it again differently in the `manager` class. When invoked through a pointer, the "correct" print function (the one to which the pointer points) will be invoked. For example, if we have a linked list of `employee`s, each element in the list can be of a different type (some are `secretary`, some are `manager`, but all are `employee`). We can traverse the linked list, applying the virtual printing function to each element in the list. Each element in the linked list will respond differently to the printing request, depending on its class.

In C++, we can define a template, a pattern from which a class can be generated. Suppose we needed sets of `float` numbers and sets of `Complex` numbers. A `set` template would help:

```
template <class T>
class set {
 private: ...
 public :
    void add_element(T elem);
    ...
};

template <class T>
void set<T>::add_element(T elem)
{
    // code to add element to set
}
```

Later we *instantiate* the type-specific set classes. In the code below, `s1` is a set of integers and `s2` is a set of `Complex` numbers.

```
set<int> s1;
set<Complex> s2;
s1.add_element(3);
s2.add_element(c);
```

C++ also has a facility for handling *exceptions*, special conditions that arise during the execution of a program. In C++, we use the `throw` statement to activate an *exception handler*. The handler is a `catch` block (attached to a `try` block) in which the appropriate action to handle the special situation is taken. If there's no handler for the exception at hand, C++ tries any enclosing `try`. If that fails, the function is terminated and the search for a handler continues, aborting all functions if necessary, all the way back to `main`. This makes for a good error recovery strategy: no error will be ignored by accident.

19.2   Solved Exercises

19.2.1   Solved Exercise 1: A Stack Program in C and in C++

Below we show a side-by-side comparison between C and C++. Both programs implement a simple stack of numbers. The C version defines the type `Stack` and provides four named operations: `initialize`, `push`, `pop`, and `print`. In the C++ version, we use overloaded operators `<<` and `>>` instead of `push` and `pop`. We use the `Stack` constructor instead of `initialize`, and we provide a `print` member function. Here are the two programs.

```
#include <stdio.h>                    #include <iostream.h>
#define STACK_SIZE 10                 const int STACK_SIZE = 10;

struct stack {                        class Stack {
                                      private:
 int items[STACK_SIZE];                int items[STACK_SIZE];
 int sp;                               int sp;
};                                    public:
typedef struct stack Stack;
                                       void print(void);

void initialize(Stack* s)             Stack()
{                                     {
 s->sp=-1;                             sp=-1;
}                                     }

void push(Stack* s, int i)            void Stack::operator<<(int i)
{                                     {
 s->items[++s->sp]=i;                  items[++sp]=i;
}                                     }
```

```
int pop(Stack *s)                    void Stack::operator>>(int& i)
{                                    {
 return s->items[s->sp--];             i=items[sp--];
}                                     }
                                    };

void print(const Stack* s)           void Stack::print(void)
{                                    {
 int i;                               int i;

 printf("Stack:\n");                  cout << "Stack:\n";
 for (i=0;i<=s->sp;i++)               for (i=0;i<=sp;i++)
  printf("%d ",s->items[i]);           cout << items[i] << " ";
 printf("\n");                        cout << "\n";
}                                     };

main()                               main()
{                                    {
 Stack s;                             Stack s;
 int i;                               int i;

 initialize(&s);
 push(&s, 1);                         s << 1;
 push(&s, 2);                         s << 2;
 print(&s);                           s.print();
 i=pop(&s);                           s >> i;
 print(&s);                           s.print();
 return 0;                            return 0;
}                                    }
```

C++ programmers generally prefer to use the <iostream.h> library over the <stdio.h> library, for a number of reasons. One of them is that the <iostream.h> library already contains an overloaded << operator, which we can overload further. C++ programmers also prefer to use the const qualifier on declared variables, rather than using the #define directive to define simple macros. In C++, we declare the class Stack with private members items and sp. No typedef is needed. The public operations are the constructor Stack, the print function to print a stack, the overloaded << operator to push values on to the stack, and an overloaded >> operator to pop items from the stack. The C++ programmer is allowed to declare these operations within the class definition, or to define them there as well. In this case, we've chosen to define the printing operator<< outside the class definition, and to define Stack, operator<<, and operator>> within the class definition. The constructor Stack simply sets sp to -1. The "push" operation operator<< takes an integer i, and stores it in the items array. Conversely, the "pop" operation operator>> takes a reference to an integer i, because it must modify that integer.

It is worth noting how convenient the declaration and handling of a variable of type Stack becomes in the main program. The code looks and feels as if the data type Stack had been part of the C++ language from the beginning. Pushing and popping values from the Stack is done in a manner consistent with the C++ language, using the << and >> operators, as if we were sending values to and from a data stream.

19.2.2 Solved Exercise 2: The ADT Car

Here we'll develop a program that simulates the behavior of a car. We first design the car itself: a structure, containing the car's current direction (a char), and whether the ignition is on (an int). Then we develop prototypes of the car's operations. The result is the header file car.h, as follows:

```
/*********************/
/*        car.h      */
/*********************/
```

```
#ifndef CAR_H
#define CAR_H

typedef struct {
  char direction;  /* 'N', 'S', 'E', 'W'  */
  int ignition_on;
} Car;

void start_car(Car *c);
void forward(Car c);
void uturn(Car *c);
void left(Car *c);
void right(Car *c);
int running(Car c);
void stop(Car *c);

#endif
```

We then implement the operations of ADT Car and place the function definitions in an implementation file called car.c: We decide that the car's ignition will initially be on, and that it will be facing north.

```
/********************/
/*      car.c       */
/********************/
#include <stdio.h>
#include "car.h"

void start_car(Car *c)
{
  c->direction = 'N';
  c->ignition_on = 1;
}

void forward(Car c)
{
  printf("Going Forward. Heading %c.\n", c.direction);
}

void uturn(Car *c)
{
  switch (c->direction) {
    case 'N':
      c->direction = 'S';
      break;
    case 'S':
      c->direction = 'N';
      break;
    case 'E':
      c->direction = 'W';
      break;
    case 'W':
      c->direction = 'E';
      break;
  }
  printf("Making U turn. Now heading %c.\n", c->direction);
}

void left(Car *c)
{
  switch (c->direction) {
    case 'N':
      c->direction = 'W';
      break;
```

```
      case 'S':
        c->direction = 'E';
        break;
      case 'E':
        c->direction = 'N';
        break;
      case 'W':
        c->direction = 'S';
        break;
    }
    printf("Turning Left. Now heading %c.\n", c->direction);
}

void right(Car *c)
{
    switch (c->direction) {
      case 'N':
        c->direction = 'E';
        break;
      case 'S':
        c->direction = 'W';
        break;
      case 'E':
        c->direction = 'S';
        break;
      case 'W':
        c->direction = 'N';
        break;
    }
    printf("Turning Right. Now heading %c.\n", c->direction);
}

int running(Car c)
{
    return c.ignition_on;
}

void stop(Car *c)
{
    printf("Car stopped.\n");
    c->ignition_on = 0;
}
```

Finally, we implement an application for the ADT Car. This main program prompts the user for a letter to indicate a change in direction. The main program calls the appropriate operations to obtain the desired effect, and turns off the car's ignition when done.

```
#include <stdio.h>
#include "car.h"

main()
{
    char choice;
    Car c;

    start_car(&c);
    printf("Please type the correct key for each operation:\n");
    printf("(f)orward, (u)turn, (l)eft, (r)ight, (s)top\n");
    forward(c);
    while (running(c)){
      scanf(" %c", &choice);
      switch (choice){
        case 'r':
          right(&c);
```

```
        break;
      case 'l':
        left(&c);
        break;
      case 'f':
        forward(c);
        break;
      case 'u':
        uturn(&c);
        break;
      case 's':
        stop(&c);
        break;
      default :
        printf("Not an allowed operation.\n");
        break;
    }
  }
  return 0;
}
```

Here's some of this program's output:

```
Please type the correct key for each operation:
(f)orward, (u)turn, (l)eft, (r)ight, (s)top
Going Forward. Heading N.
l
Turning Left. Now heading W.
r
Turning Right. Now heading N.
u
Making U turn. Now heading S.
l
Turning Left. Now heading E.
r
Turning Right. Now heading S.
u
Making U turn. Now heading N.
s
Car stopped.
```

This last solved exercise shows how to systematically organize a program so that it has good characteristics: extensibility, maintainability, readability, etc. The car module has high cohesion: the various functions are all related to providing a facility for manipulating Cars. It should also have low coupling, although in this case there are no other modules with which coupling could occur. Information hiding is quite limited in this example: there are no variables to hide, and the one variable of type Car is local to main. In the main program, a statement such as

```
            c.direction = 'W';
```

would invade the ADT Car, violating encapsulation by effecting a change in the state of the Car variable c without going through the interface (one of the operations).

19.3   Programming Exercises

1.   What does a constructor do?

2.   What does a destructor do?

3.   What advantages do virtual member functions have over those that are not virtual?

4. Modify the ADT `Car` program, adding a field called `door_status` to the `Car` structure. `door_status` should be an enumerated type with values `open` and `closed`. Add corresponding operations to open the door and close it, only while the car is stopped.

5. Modify the ADT `Car` program, adding a field called `engine_status`, of an enumerated type with values `on` and `off`. Also, change the `ignition_on` field so it belongs to an enumerated type. As in real life, the ignition can be on (usually necessary to listen to the car's radio), and the engine off at the same time. Add operations to turn the engine on and off and to turn the ignition on and off. Some combinations are not allowed: it's impossible to turn the ignition off without also turning off the engine.

6. Modify both the C and C++ versions of the `stack` program to add the `top` operation, which returns the top element of the stack without removing it.

7. Suppose we have a need to store the information for a `Car` structure very efficiently. Change the implementation in `car.c` and the header in `car.h`, so that a car occupies only one byte. You should be able to do this without changing the application in `carmain.c` at all.

8. Use templates to extend the C++ `stack` program so that the stack can hold elements of any type.

9. Extend the ADT `Car` so that the car has a speedometer, a mileage count, and a gas tank. Design operations that will keep track of these objects as the car travels.

10. Design and implement an ADT `list`, which can contain an ordered list of integers. Implement it in two ways, using arrays and using linked lists. Design the interface so that it doesn't matter which implementation is used.

11. Design and implement an ADT `binary_tree`. Structures and pointers are useful for this: each tree node has two "child" tree node pointers, `left` and `right`.

12. Design and implement an ADT `employee`, which stores information about an employee, such as name, Social Security number, age, salary, marital status, number of years with the company, etc. Develop an employee database program, which uses operations on ADT `employee` to maintain a database of employees.

13. Design an ADT `Compact_Disc` to be used in a database program for someone's collection of CDs. The information in each CD entry should be the name of the artist/group, the date purchased, the price paid, the number of recorded pieces, and the total duration.

14. Complete (as much as you can) the C++ implementation of ADT `complex`.

15. One common use of stacks is in a postfix or "Reverse Polish" calculator. The values come first, and then the operator. Instead of the usual keystroke sequence (e.g., 3 + 5 =), we enter the following sequence: 3 <ENTER> 5 <ENTER> +. The <ENTER> key pushes the value just keyed onto a stack of values; the + key pops the two most recent values from the stack, adds them, pushes the result onto the stack, and displays the result. Using an ADT stack, implement a simple postfix calculator capable of addition, subtraction, multiplication, and division.

16. Design and implement an ADT `String_Table`. Implement the table as an ordered array of strings. Provide a constructor function that allows the user to specify the size of the table by allocating the array dynamically. Design and implement operations to insert, delete, replace, and search for strings in the table.

17. Redesign the ADT `String_Table` so its implementation is based on a linked list of strings, instead of an array.

18. The ADT `String_Table` in the previous exercise can be used in a variety of settings. Use it to create another ADT `phone_book_entry`, to be used in a program that maintains a database of friends' names and telephone numbers. Try this application with both of the string table implementations in the previous two exercises.

20 Low-Level Programming

20.1 Chapter Summary

20.1.1 Bitwise Operators

There are six *bitwise* operators in C: *left shift*, *right shift*, *complement*, *and*, *exclusive or*, and *inclusive or*. The left shift operator i << j shifts the bits in i to the left by j places. For each such place, a zero bit is entered from the right. The right shift operator i >> j shifts the bits in i to the right by j places. Zero bits are entered from the left, as long as i is an unsigned type, or its value is nonnegative. If i is negative, the result is implementation-defined—zeroes or nonzeroes could be inserted from the left. It's best not to use the shift operators on signed values. For unsigned values, shifting to the left means multiplying by a power of 2: i << 3 will yield 8 times the value of i. Shifting to the right, correspondingly, means integral division by a power of 2. The shift operators have lower precedence than the arithmetic operators: in the expression i << j + k, the addition is performed first.

The bitwise complement operator ~ is unary: it replaces ones with zeroes and vice versa. The bitwise & operator performs a boolean *and* on its two operands (the result is 1 if both operand bits are 1). The bitwise | operator performs a boolean inclusive *or* on its operands (the result will be 1 if either operand bit is 1). The bitwise ^ operator performs a boolean exclusive *or*, commonly called XOR, on its two operands (the result is 1 if the two operand bits are different). The six operators occupy five operator precedence levels: ~ has the highest precedence, followed by << and >>, then &, then ^, and finally | has the lowest precedence. Also, the precedence of &, ^, and | is lower than that of the relational and equality operators: in the expression i & j == 0, the equality comparison will take place first. C provides five corresponding compound assignment operators: <<=, >>=, &=, |=, and ^=.

When doing bit-level programming, it's best to avoid making assumptions about the sizes of words and integers whenever possible. For example, to create an integer with all bits set to 1, we write ~0, which will be of the appropriate size. Some common single-bit and multiple-bit operations are:

set bit i in word	word |= 1 << i;
set bits i and j in word	word |= 1 << i | 1 << j;
clear bit i in word	word &= ~(1 << i);
clear bits i and j in word	word &= ~(1 << i | 1 << j);
test bit i in word	if (word & 1 << i) ...;
test bits i and j in word	if (word & (1 << i | 1 << j)) ...;
set v to i bits ending at position j in word	v = (word & (~ (~0 << i) << j)) >> j;
replace i bits ending at position j in word, with the value v	word = (word & ~(~(~0 << i) << j)) | (v << j);

20.1.2 Bit-Fields in Stuctures

C allows bit-fields in structures. For example, consider the following employee structure:

```
struct employee {
  char *name;
  float salary;
  unsigned int age:7;
  unsigned int sex:1;
  unsigned int years:6;
  unsigned int mstatus:2
};
```

The first two members of this structure occupy (on many machines) four bytes each. The last four could have occupied 16 bytes if they had been declared in the usual way, as `int`s. We indicate instead the number of bits each will occupy: `age` takes seven bits (the largest value is therefore 127); `sex` takes one bit (0 for female, 1 for male), `years` takes six bits (for a maximum of 63 years of employment!), and `mstatus` takes two bits (four different values: single, married, divorced, separated). The storage savings are significant: a structure that on many machines would occupy perhaps 24 bytes now takes up 10. C allows us to access the bit-fields individually in the usual way. For example:

```
struct employee e;
e.name = "howdy";
e.salary = 1234.56;
e.age = 98;
e.sex = MALE;
e.years = 32;
e.mstatus = SINGLE;
```

There's only one major restriction on bit-fields: you cannot use the address operator &, so reading bit-fields directly using `scanf` is impossible. Of course, you can read a full-blown integer value and then assign it to the bit-field.

It is often a good idea to define machine-dependent types, such as `typedef unsigned char BYTE;`. Unions can be used to provide multiple views of a data segment. For example, a single byte can be viewed as a character, or as a collection of several bit-fields, if the two different views are placed inside a union:

```
union char_fields {
  char c;
  struct empl_byte {
    unsigned int : 1;
    unsigned int mstatus:2;
    unsigned int sex:1;
    unsigned int department:4;
  } b;
};
```

Note that the first bit-field is anonymous; we don't use it because ASCII characters occupy only 7 bits. An array of the above unions can be treated (and printed or read in) as a string, which can be quite convenient for storing information efficiently, both in memory and on disk.

The `volatile` type qualifier tells the compiler that the variable in question can be changed in ways the compiler cannot predict. For example, a certain memory segment may be connected to an external device. The effect of the `volatile` qualifier is to prevent the compiler optimizing references to that variable.

20.2   Solved Exercises

20.2.1   Solved Exercise 1: Hamming Codes

Hamming codes are commonly used to detect and correct errors in data transmission. We assume that information is transmitted from one place to another in n-bit words. During transmission, there is a certain risk that a single bit may be lost, or flipped. There are many causes of transmission dropout, such as static interference on a telephone line. The receiving end of the transmission needs to determine whether the message was transmitted accurately or whether an error occurred. We'll assume that in an 8-bit word, single-bit errors are frequent enough to warrant our attention, but that two errors in a single 8-bit word are infrequent enough to be considered negligible. The strategy is to pad each word with additional bits, which carry sufficient information about the word itself so that any single error can be detected and corrected. Hamming codes add $k = \log_2 n + 1$ bits, in this case 4 extra bits. We locate those bits in positions 1, 2, 4, and 8 in what will now be a 12-bit word.

Consider the 8-bit word `01100100`. After adding the four bits, we have

1	2	3	4	5	6	7	8	9	10	11	12
p_1	p_2	0	p_4	1	1	0	p_8	0	1	0	0
1	0	1	0	1	0	1	0	1	0	1	0
0	1	1	0	0	1	1	0	0	1	1	0
0	0	0	1	1	1	1	0	0	0	0	1
0	0	0	0	0	0	0	1	1	1	1	1

Each p_i is called a ***parity check bit***. The pattern of 1s and 0s displayed under the word is used to mask the bits of the word itself and to select those bits upon which the parity check is to be performed. For example, the first row in the pattern masks bits 1, 3, 5, 7, 9, and 11. The role of p_1 is to serve as a parity check bit for bits 3, 5, 7, 9, and 11. To calculate p_1, we XOR the other bits. Thus,

$$p_1 = \text{XOR of bits } 3,5,7,9,11 \quad = 0\hat{}1\hat{}0\hat{}0\hat{}0 = 1$$
$$p_2 = \text{XOR of bits } 3,6,7,10,11 \quad = 0\hat{}1\hat{}0\hat{}1\hat{}0 = 0$$
$$p_4 = \text{XOR of bits } 5,6,7,12 \quad = 1\hat{}1\hat{}0\hat{}0 \quad = 0$$
$$p_8 = \text{XOR of bits } 9,10,11,12 \quad = 0\hat{}1\hat{}0\hat{}0 \quad = 1$$

The resulting word is `100011010100`. This 12-bit word is transmitted across the communication channel. Let's suppose bit 6 is flipped during transmission. The message received is `100010010100`. When this arrives at its destination, we can perform the four parity checks in accordance with the same masks to determine whether an error occurred.

$$c_1 = \text{XOR of bits } 1,3,5,7,9,11 \quad = 1\hat{}0\hat{}1\hat{}0\hat{}0\hat{}0 = 0$$
$$c_2 = \text{XOR of bits } 2,3,6,7,10,11 \quad = 0\hat{}0\hat{}0\hat{}0\hat{}1\hat{}0 = 1$$
$$c_4 = \text{XOR of bits } 4,5,6,7,12 \quad = 0\hat{}1\hat{}0\hat{}0\hat{}0 \quad = 1$$
$$c_8 = \text{XOR of bits } 8,9,10,11,12 \quad = 1\hat{}0\hat{}1\hat{}0\hat{}0 \quad = 0$$

If the parity check bits are all zero, no error is detected. If not, the parity check bits can be read as a binary number, as follows: $c_8 c_4 c_2 c_1$. In our case, the number is $0110 = 6$, the column where the error is located!

As another example, let's assume bit 3 was flipped during transmission. The word received is `101011010100`. We calculate the parity check bits:

$$c_1 = \text{XOR of bits } 1,3,5,7,9,11 \quad = 1\hat{}1\hat{}1\hat{}0\hat{}0\hat{}0 = 1$$
$$c_2 = \text{XOR of bits } 2,3,6,7,10,11 = 0\hat{}1\hat{}1\hat{}0\hat{}1\hat{}0 = 1$$
$$c_4 = \text{XOR of bits } 4,5,6,7,12 \quad = 0\hat{}1\hat{}1\hat{}0\hat{}0 \quad = 0$$
$$c_8 = \text{XOR of bits } 8,9,10,11,12 = 1\hat{}0\hat{}1\hat{}0\hat{}0 \quad = 0$$

Once again, not all check bits are zero. An error is detected, and its location is indicated by the parity bits: $0011 = 3$.

A program to simulate the use of Hamming codes is shown below. We will store the 12 encoded bits in a single integer. In the program, we establish a bit position by counting from zero from the right. Also, the information bits will occupy positions 0 through 7, and the parity bits will occupy positions 8, 9, 10, and 11. Since this differs a little from the scheme explained earlier, we need a mechanism for converting from one scheme to the other. The ***permutation*** vector `permute` accomplishes this: it maps 1 to 11, 2 to 10, 3 to 7, 4 to 9, 5 to 6, 6 to 5, 7 to 4, 8 to 8, 9 to 3, 10 to 2, 11 to 1, and 12 to 0. It also maps 0 to 0 whenever no error is detected.

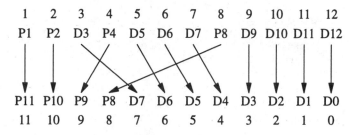

In order to isolate individual bits, we define the BIT macro, which returns the ith bit in the given word. The program repeatedly processes one word at a time, checking beforehand with the user each time. In each iteration, we generate an 8-bit number using the expression rand()%FF. The random number generator rand (from <stdlib.h>) generates a pseudo-random number (see Chapter 26). We use the % operator to reduce that number to a maximum of eight bits.

Once the word is generated, it's time to perform the Hamming encoding on it. The first parity bit (position 11) is the result of an XOR among the bits in positions 7, 6, 4, 3, and 1. The resulting value, checkbit, is |'ed into word (so to speak) after shifting it over by 11 positions. Similarly, the second parity bit results from XOR'ing bits 7, 5, 4, 2 and 1, and is placed in position 10. You should be able to verify the last two parity bits.

Once the word has been encoded, we introduce a random error. As in real life, this means there might be no error at all. We first use rand()%2 to generate the error bit (0 or 1), and then shift that bit to the left by rand()%12 positions (by up to 11 positions). Here's the program.

```c
/******************************************************/
/* Implementation of Hamming codes: single error    */
/* detection and correction in a transmitted word   */
/******************************************************/
#include <stdio.h>
#include <stdlib.h>

#define BIT(word, i) (((word) & 1 << (i)) >> (i))

void gen_error(unsigned int *word);
void encode(unsigned int *word);
unsigned int decode(unsigned int *word);
void print_bits(unsigned int word);

main()
{
  unsigned int word, error;
  char c;

  printf("HAMMING CODES PROGRAM\n");
  while (1) {
    printf("Enter to continue, 'q' to quit:");
    scanf("%c", &c);
    if (c == 'q')
      break;
    word = rand() & 0x00ff;  /* An 8-bit word */
    printf("Data Word:              ");
    print_bits(word);
    encode(&word);
    printf("Hamming encoded word:     ");
    print_bits(word);
    gen_error(&word);
    printf("Word with random error:   ");
    print_bits(word);
    error = decode(&word);
    if (!error)
      printf("No error!\n");
    else {
      printf("Error at bit %u!\n", error);
      printf("          Corrected word:    ");
      print_bits(word);
    }
  }
  return 0;
}
```

```
void gen_error(unsigned int *word)
{
/*****************************/
/*  produce the error        */
/*****************************/
  unsigned int err, loc;

  err = rand() % 2;        /* error bit */
  loc = rand() % 12;
  err <<= loc;     /* in random location */
  *word ^=  err;
}

void encode(unsigned int *word)
{
/*********************/
/* Hamming encoding  */
/*********************/
  unsigned int checkbit;

  checkbit = BIT(*word, 7) ^ BIT(*word, 6) ^ BIT(*word, 4) ^
             BIT(*word, 3) ^ BIT(*word, 1);
  *word |= checkbit << 11;
  checkbit = BIT(*word, 7) ^ BIT(*word, 5) ^ BIT(*word, 4) ^
             BIT(*word, 2) ^ BIT(*word, 1);
  *word |= checkbit << 10;
  checkbit = BIT(*word, 6) ^ BIT(*word, 5) ^ BIT(*word, 4) ^
             BIT(*word, 0);
  *word |= checkbit << 9;
  checkbit = BIT(*word, 3) ^ BIT(*word, 2) ^ BIT(*word, 1) ^
             BIT(*word, 0);
  *word |= checkbit << 8;
}

unsigned int decode(unsigned int *word)
{
  unsigned int checkbit, error = 0;
  unsigned int permute[13] = {0,11,10,7,9,6,5,4,8,3,2,1,0};

  checkbit = BIT(*word, 11) ^ BIT(*word, 7) ^ BIT(*word, 6) ^
             BIT(*word, 4)  ^ BIT(*word, 3) ^ BIT(*word, 1);
  error |= checkbit << 0;
  checkbit = BIT(*word, 10) ^ BIT(*word, 7) ^ BIT(*word, 5) ^
             BIT(*word, 4)  ^ BIT(*word, 2) ^ BIT(*word, 1);
  error |= checkbit << 1;
  checkbit = BIT(*word, 9) ^ BIT(*word, 6) ^ BIT(*word, 5) ^
             BIT(*word, 4) ^ BIT(*word, 0);
  error |= checkbit << 2;
  checkbit = BIT(*word, 8) ^ BIT(*word, 3) ^ BIT(*word, 2) ^
             BIT(*word, 1) ^ BIT(*word, 0);
  error |= checkbit << 3;

  error = permute[error];
  if (error)
    *word ^= 1 << error;
  return error;
}
```

```
void print_bits(unsigned int word)
{
  int j;

  printf("%4u: ", word);
  for (j = 11; j >= 0; j--)
    printf("%u", (word >> j) & 1 );
  printf("\n");
}
```

Finally, we decode the word by extracting the values of the parity bits in a manner very similar to the way they were calculated. This time, the parity bits are shifted by 0, 1, 2, and 3 positions respectively, so they can form (in binary) the number of the column in which the error is located. That column number (error) is permuted to find the position in the word. The permutation array has 13 elements, to allow its subscripts to range from 1 to 12. To correct the error (if there is one), we shift a 1 to the left by error positions and XOR the result with word to flip the corresponding bit. Here's some sample output:

```
HAMMING CODES PROGRAM
Enter to continue, 'q' to quit:
Data Word:                 59: 0000000000111011
Hamming encoded word:    3899: 0000111100111011
Word with random error:  3899: 0000111100111011
No error!
Enter to continue, 'q' to quit:
Data Word:                 43: 0000000000101011
Hamming encoded word:     299: 0000000100101011
Word with random error:   267: 0000000100001011
Error at bit   5!
        Corrected word:   299: 0000000100101011
Enter to continue, 'q' to quit:
Data Word:                 47: 0000000000101111
Hamming encoded word:    1071: 0000010000101111
Word with random error:  1199: 0000010010101111
Error at bit   7!
        Corrected word:  1071: 0000010000101111
Enter to continue, 'q' to quit:
Data Word:                133: 0000000010000101
Hamming encoded word:    2693: 0000101010000101
Word with random error:  2695: 0000101010000111
Error at bit   1!
        Corrected word:  2693: 0000101010000101
Enter to continue, 'q' to quit:
Data Word:                 62: 0000000000111110
Hamming encoded word:    2366: 0000100100111110
Word with random error:  2366: 0000100100111110
No error!
Enter to continue, 'q' to quit:
Data Word:                120: 0000000001111000
Hamming encoded word:    2936: 0000101101111000
Word with random error:  2920: 0000101101101000
Error at bit   4!
        Corrected word:  2936: 0000101101111000
Enter to continue, 'q' to quit:q
```

20.3   Programming Exercises

1. Write a bitwise XOR (exclusive or) function using only the & and | operators.

2. Binary Coded Decimal (BCD) notation is used to represent numbers in decimal form, one decimal digit at a time, with each decimal digit encoded in binary and occupying four bits. 1 is represented

as 0001, 2 as 0010, 3 as 0011, and so on. It's easy to see that in a 2-byte word, the maximum value that can be represented with this notation is 9999, and the minimum is 0:

```
9    9    9    9
1001|1001|1001|1001
and
0    0    0    0
0000|0000|0000|0000
```

Write a program that converts from `int` to BCD, and BCD to `int`.

3. Write the code for the four basic arithmetic operations, +, −, *, and / in BCD notation.

4. Write a program that reads a string, counts the number of characters in the string that have bit `i` equal to 1, and the number that have bit `i` equal to 0, for each bit `i` between 1 and 8.

5. Write a function `exp2(int x, int n)` that returns the value of x multiplied by 2^n. *Hint:* use bitwise operators.

6. Rewrite the error detection/correction program using bit-fields.

7. Write a program that displays the sign, exponent, and mantissa of a `float` variable, without using bit-fields. Use the representation of floating-point numbers on your particular system.

8. Repeat Exercise 7, but using bit-fields.

9. Write a function that returns a value that is one larger than its argument, using bitwise operators.

10. Write a function that returns the reversed bits of a byte, using bitwise operators.

11. Repeat Exercise 10, this time using bit-fields.

12. Write functions `divide_2(int i)` (returns its argument divided by 2) and `remainder_2(int i)` (returns the remainder of dividing its argument by 2) using bitwise operators.

13. The program on page 463 of the main text turns on and off the NumLock toggle on an IBM PC or compatible, using the `far` keyword and `MK_FP` macro. Write a program called `reportlock.c`, which prints a message indicating whether the NumLock toggle is currently on or off.

14. Write a function that prints a `char` or `int` variable in hexadecimal format.

15. Write a function that receives as parameter an array of `1`s and `0`s and prints the corresponding integer value and character value.

16. Write a program that converts decimal numbers to binary using the shift operators.

17. Write a function called `bits_0`, which counts the number of bits that are `0` in an integer argument.

18. Write a program that reads an input file one character at a time and verifies that every character is an ASCII character. *Hint:* store the result of `getchar` in an `int`, and then test the eighth bit from the right.

21 The Standard Library

21.1 Chapter Summary

The standard library is divided into fifteen parts represented by headers. Additional nonstandard headers are often supplied by the compiler vendor. The extra headers often depend on a specific computer or operating system, such as those that provide support for graphics or window-based interfaces.

Standard headers primarily contain function prototypes, type definitions, and macro definitions. We use the #include directive to include a standard header. If more than one is needed, the order in which they are included is unimportant. Whenever we include a standard header, we must obey a few rules. First, macro names defined in a header can't be used for any other purpose. Second, names with file scope (such as type names) can't be redefined at the file level. Third, you should never use identifiers that begin with two underscores, or with an underscore and an upper-case letter: these are reserved for use within the library. Fourth, identifiers that begin with an underscore should not be redefined, except inside a function. Fifth, no identifier with external linkage in the standard library (such as printf) should be redefined with external linkage, even in a file that doesn't include the corresponding header.

Function declarations in the standard library are occasionally hidden by macro definitions of the same name; the macro is usually more efficient. Since the preprocessor replaces the macro invocation with the corresponding text, the function is never called. Most of the time, this arrangement is perfectly acceptable to the programmer. Sometimes, however, we need the actual function, perhaps because we wish to have a pointer to it. In those cases, we must undefine the macro, with the #undef directive. For example, to use the isalpha function, but not the macro:

```
#include <ctype.h>
#undef isalpha
```

The fifteen headers in the standard library are as follows:

- <assert.h>. Provides the assert macro for program self-checking.
- <ctype.h>. Provides functions for character handling.
- <errno.h>. Provides errno, used to determine whether errors occurred during certain library function calls.
- <float.h>. Provides macros that describe the characteristics of floating types.
- <limits.h>. Provides macros that describe the characteristics of integer and character types.
- <locale.h>. Provides functions useful for adapting programs to other countries. Adaptations include currency symbols, the character set, and the format of the date and time.
- <math.h>. Provides a variety of mathematical functions.
- <setjmp.h>. Provides setjmp and longjmp, which can be used to bypass the normal function-return mechanism.
- <signal.h>. Provides signal handling functions to handle exceptions and run-time errors.
- <stdarg.h>. Provides functions for writing functions that can have a variable number of arguments, such as printf.
- <stddef.h>. Provides definitions of frequently used types and macros.
- <stdio.h>. Provides functions for input and output, for sequential and random-access files.
- <stdlib.h>. Provides general utilities, such as string and number conversion, memory management, interfacing with the operating system, sorting and searching, etc.
- <string.h>. Provides functions that manipulate strings (copy, concatenate, compare, and search).
- <time.h>. Provides functions for accessing and displaying the current time and date.

The <stddef.h> header provides the definitions of many frequently used types, including ptrdiff_t (the type that results from subtracting two pointers), size_t (the type returned by sizeof), and wchar_t (a character type discussed in Chapter 25). Also provided are the null pointer NULL and the macro offsetof, which is used to determine the distance (in bytes) between the beginning of a structure and a given member of that structure.

21.2   Solved Exercises

21.2.1   Solved Exercise 1: Holes in a Structure

Below is a simple program that can help us determine whether our particular compiler leaves holes in structures. We declare a structure s, which contains a char, an array of pointers to char, and a float. The program prints the size and the offset of each member, and then prints the overall size of the structure. To ensure this program works with all compilers, we cast the values returned by sizeof and offsetof to type unsigned long and print them with the %lu conversion specification.

```
#include <stdio.h>
#include <stddef.h>

main()
{
  struct s {
    char a;
    char *b[4];
    float c;
  };

  printf("Size of a: %lu. Offset of a: %lu.\n",
         (unsigned long) sizeof(char),
         (unsigned long) offsetof(struct s, a));
  printf("Size of b: %lu. Offset of b: %lu.\n",
         (unsigned long) sizeof(char *[4]),
         (unsigned long) offsetof(struct s, b));
  printf("Size of c: %lu. Offset of c: %lu.\n",
         (unsigned long) sizeof(float),
         (unsigned long) offsetof(struct s, c));

  printf("Size of s: %lu.\n",
         (unsigned long) sizeof(struct s));
  return 0;
}
```

The output on my 486 computer, running the GNU gcc compiler under the Linux operating system, is:

```
Size of a:  1. Offset of a: 0.
Size of b: 16. Offset of b: 4.
Size of c:  4. Offset of c: 20.
Size of s: 24.
```

On my particular system, it is clear that the compiler leaves a 3-byte hole after a. Although a occupies only 1 byte, the next member, b, has an offset of 4 bytes. To confirm this, the sizes of a, b, and c add up to 21 bytes, while the size of the entire structure is 24 bytes. The compiler leaves a gap by "shifting" b down by 3 bytes, either for its own convenience or to improve execution speed.

21.3   Programming Exercises

1. Determine whether your system finds errors or warnings in the following program, due to the absence of the #include <stdio.h> directive.

```
main()
{
  char name[25];

  printf("What's your name: ");
  scanf("%s", name);
  printf("Hello %s\n", name);
  return 0;
}
```

2. Expand the sample program in Section 21.2. Make it determine automatically whether there are any holes, where they are, and their size.

3. Run the following program:

```
#include <stdio.h>

main()
{
  char __name[25];

  printf("What's your name: ");
  scanf("%s", __name);
  printf("Hello %s\n", __name);
  return 0;
}
```

Does the program work? Should it work? Is this program portable?

4. Compile each of the following programs. Explain what happens.

```
#include <stddef.h>        #include <stddef.h>
int size_t;
                           main()
main()                     {
{                            int size_t;
  size_t = 2;                size_t = 2;
  return 0;                  return 0;
}                          }
```

5. In which standard header do you expect to find trigonometric functions?

6. Consult your system documentation and find a way to run only the preprocessor of your C compiler. Run the preprocessor on a few programs and analyze the preprocessor's output. Find the actual prototypes for the library functions you use, for example `printf` and `scanf`.

7. What's wrong with the following line: #include <myheader.h>?

8. In which standard header do you expect to find functions to access a file on a disk?

22 Input/Output

22.1 Chapter Summary

The `<stdio.h>` header is the largest and perhaps the most important in the C standard library. In addition to `printf` and `scanf`, the `<stdio.h>` header contains functions for performing input and output to or from *streams* and files (both text and binary), as well as reading and writing characters, strings, and blocks of data.

22.1.1 Streams

A stream is any source of input or destination for output. These are usually associated with *devices*, such as the keyboard, the computer screen, disks, printers, modems, etc. A stream is accessed through a *file pointer* of type `FILE *`. Three streams are predefined in `<stdio.h>`: `stdin`, `stdout`, and `stderr`. Most functions in `<stdio.h>` read from `stdin` and write to `stdout`, which the operating system usually associates with the keyboard and the screen. Many operating systems allow streams to be *redirected* to or from disk files or other devices, like so: `prog < data.in > data.out`.

Two types of files are supported by `<stdio.h>`: text and binary files. Text files are written in human-readable form, i.e., as characters. Binary files are stored in machine-readable form and usually look like gibberish if the user attempts to display the file's contents. On the other hand, storage is usually more efficient in binary files. We distinguish between text and binary files because different operating systems store them in different ways and have different conventions for storing (or not storing) newline and end-of-file characters. To open a file, we use the `fopen` function:

```
FILE *fopen(const char *filename, const char *mode);
```

The filename string may contain information about the file's location, such as a drive specification or directory path. If `fopen` cannot open the file, it returns the null pointer. The mode specifies the intended use of the file. For text files, we have `"r"` (for reading), `"w"` (for writing), `"a"` (for appending), `"r+"` (for reading and writing without initially truncating the file), `"w+"` (for reading and writing, initially truncating the file), and `"a+"` (for updating at the end of a file). For binary files, we have, correspondingly, `"rb"`, `"wb"`, `"ab"`, `"rb+"`, `"wb+"`, and `"ab+"`. To close a file, we use `fclose`:

```
int fclose(FILE *stream)
```

The argument to `fclose` must be a pointer to a file obtained previously from `fopen` or `freopen`. The function returns zero if it is successful, and `EOF` otherwise. Sometimes we wish to attach a new file name to a stream that's already open. This is done with `freopen`:

```
FILE *freopen(const char *name, const char *mode, FILE *stream);
```

This attaches the new file name `name` to `stream`, after closing the file previously attached to that stream. If the new file can't be opened, `freopen` returns `NULL`. One convenient way to supply the file name to the program is through the command-line arguments `argc` and `argv`, which were discussed in Chapter 13.

Temporary files, which exist only during the execution of the program, are often useful. C provides two functions for manipulating temporary files:

```
FILE *tmpfile(void);
char *tmpnam(char *s);
```

`tmpfile` returns a pointer to the temporary file it creates, and returns `NULL` if it can't create it. `tmpnam` takes a pointer argument, generates a name for a temporary file, and returns a pointer to that name. The name is stored into the character array provided as argument `s`, which should be of length `L_tmpnam; ;` if `s` is `NULL`, the name is stored in a static variable.

Files on disk are usually ***buffered***: instead of physically accessing the disk with each operation, a segment of the file called the ***buffer*** is stored in memory, and I/O operations operate upon the buffer, with a great gain in efficiency, since entire blocks of the file are read or written at once, instead of individual items. Most of the time, buffering takes place automatically. Sometimes, we wish to handle the buffering ourselves. `fflush(fp)` flushes (writes out the buffer for) file `fp`. `fflush(NULL)` flushes buffers for all output streams. `setvbuf` is used to control the type of buffering (flush when full, flush with each line, or perhaps no buffering), and the size and location of the buffer. `setbuf` assumes certain default values for parameters of `setvbuf`; its use is no longer recommended.

Some basic file manipulations can be performed, with functions `remove` and `rename`.

22.1.2 Formatted I/O

The `printf` and `fprintf` functions differ only in that `printf` always writes to `stdout`, whereas `fprintf` writes to the stream indicated by its first argument. One useful application of `fprintf` is to write error messages: `fprintf(stderr, "You goofed\n");` writes the error message to the screen, even if the program's output is redirected. As seen earlier, `printf` and `fprintf` format their output using conversion specifications. In general, a conversion specification consists of the `%` character, followed by up to five items:

1. Flags (optional). More than one is permitted. Legal flags are: − (left justify), + (begin positive-signed numbers with +), *space* (begin positive-signed numbers with a space), # (begin octal numbers with 0, begin hexadecimal numbers with 0x or 0X, include the decimal point in all floating-point numbers, and include trailing zeroes in numbers printed with g or G), and 0 (pad numbers with leading zeros).
2. Minimum field width (optional). Specifies the number of spaces the item will occupy. An item that is too small will be padded. An item that is too large will be displayed in its entirety.
3. Precision (optional). The meaning depends on the conversion. For conversions d, i, o, u, x, and X, the precision is the minimum number of digits. For conversions e, E, and f, the precision is the number of digits after the decimal point. For conversions g and G, the precision is the maximum number of significant digits. For conversion s, the precision is the maximum number of characters.
4. Size modifier (optional). This is one of the letters h, l, or L. For integers, h indicates `short` and l indicates `long`. For conversions e, E, f, g, and G, size modifier l indicates `long double`.
5. Conversion specifier. One of the characters d, i (signed integer), u (unsigned integer), o (unsigned octal integer), x, X (unsigned hexadecimal integer), f (fixed decimal), e, E (scientific notation), g, G (either f, e or E), c (character), s (string), p (printable form for `void *`), n (stores the number of characters written so far), and % (the character %).

Both the field width and the precision can be replaced with * to specify the item as an argument after the format string. For example, `printf("%*.*f\n", 3, 1, 5.17);` displays 5.2. The width and precision can also be macros or expressions. The `%p` conversion specification allows us to print the value of a pointer, although the C standard doesn't specify its appearance.

Functions `scanf` and `fscanf` read data from an input stream. `scanf` always reads from `stdin`, while `fscanf` reads from the stream indicated by its first argument. They can return prematurely if an ***input failure*** or a ***matching failure*** occur. Both return the number of items that were read and assigned to arguments, and EOF if no items could be read at all. The format string represents a pattern that the function attempts to match against the input, with the following types of items:

1. Conversion specifications. These resemble those of `printf`, although in most cases leading white-space characters are skipped.
2. White-space characters. Any one of these is matched against any number of white-space characters that appear in the input stream.
3. Non-white-space characters. These are matched, one for one, against characters in the input stream.

The `scanf` conversion specification consists of the `%` character, followed by:

1. * (optional). This causes ***assignment suppression***: the item is read but not assigned to a variable.
2. Maximum field width (optional). This limits the number of characters in the input item.

3. Size modifier (optional): one of the letters h, l, or L. When reading an integer, h indicates a short and l indicates a long. When reading with e, E, f, g, or G, l indicates a pointer to double and L indicates a pointer to long double.

4. Conversion specifier. One of the characters d (decimal integer), i (decimal, octal, or hex integer), o (unsigned octal integer), u (unsigned integer), x, X (hexadecimal unsigned integer), e, E, f, g, G (float), s (string of non-white-space characters), [(nonempty string of characters from a certain scanset), c (one or more characters), p (pointer), n (store the number of characters read so far), and % (the character %). The scanset is of the form % [*set*] (match any character in the set), or % [^*set*] (match any character not in the set).

Some of the scanf conversions are equivalent to the string conversion functions in <stdlib.h>. For example, strtol("-316", NULL, 10) produces the same value as reading −316 from the input using scanf and the %d conversion specifier.

The scanf function can terminate prematurely due to encountering the end of file, an error beyond its control, or a matching failure. Every input stream has an ***error indicator*** (set whenever there's a stream operation failure) and an ***end-of-file indicator*** (set whenever an end of file is encountered). The clearerr(fp) function clears both error indicators. We can examine the values of these indicators using feof(fp) and ferror(fp). If scanf returns a value smaller than expected, and both feof and ferror return zero, then a matching failure must have occurred.

22.1.3 Character, Line, Block, and String I/O

To print single characters, the C standard library provides functions putchar(c), which writes the character to stdout, and functions fputc and putc, which write the character to the output stream of our choice. putc is generally implemented as a macro, and fputc is generally implemented as a function. These functions return the character that was written. To read single characters, the C library provides functions getchar (read from stdin), getc(fp) and fgetc(fp) (read from stream fp), and ungetc(c, fp) ("unread" a character). An idiom for reading characters until we encounter the end-of-file character is

```
while ((ch = getc(fp)) != EOF) { ... }
```

It's important to note that ch should be an int, not a char, because of the comparison with EOF, which is a negative value. The ungetc(ch, fp) function is used to put back a character, which is useful for looking ahead. For example,

```
while (isalpha(c = getchar())) {
    ...
}
ungetc(ch, stdin);
```

reads characters until it encounters the first nonletter; the nonletter character, which had to be read so it could be tested, is then pushed back onto the input stream.

The C library provides four functions for reading and writing lines. puts(s) writes string s (plus a new-line character) to stdout, and fputs(s, fp) writes s (with no added new-line character) to stream fp. For input, gets(s) reads in characters and stores them in s, until the new-line character is encountered. fgets(s, n, fp) reads in at most n characters (stopping earlier if a new-line is found), and stores them in s. gets doesn't store the new-line character; fgets does, if that character is actually read. Both return a pointer to the string read, and both store the required null character to terminate the string.

Two functions are provided to read and write large blocks of data to streams. fwrite(a, n, m, fp) writes a portion of an array that begins at address a. n is the size of each array element (in bytes), m is the number of array elements to be written, and fp is the output stream. fread(a, n, m, fp) reads a block of m elements (at n bytes each) from stream fp, storing the elements in array a. Both functions return the number of elements actually written or read. If this value is less than the third argument, usually it's due to encountering the end-of-file character. The data to be written or read need not be in array form; structures, strings, etc., can be processed.

Random access to files is supported by the C library. Every stream has a ***file position***, which is initially set when the file is opened. `fseek(fp, offset, SEEK_SET)` changes the file position of stream `fp` to the beginning of the file, plus `offset`. The `offset` is in bytes and can be negative. Macro `SEEK_SET` is provided by the library, along with `SEEK_CUR` (current file position) and `SEEK_END` (end of the file). For example, `fseek(fp, -25L, SEEK_END)` places the file position 25 bytes before the end of the file. The current file position can be obtained using `ftell(fp)`. The `rewind(fp)` function sets the file position at the beginning of the file and clears the error indicator for `fp`. Two other functions are provided for handling very large files, in which file positions are very large numbers. `fgetpos(fp, &fpos)` stores the current file position in `fpos`, which should be of type `fpos_t`. To return to that file position later, we might use `fsetpos(fp, &fpos)`.

The C library provides two functions to read and write data from a string as if it were a stream. `sprintf` and `sscanf` work in the same way as `printf` and `scanf` do, except that their first argument is the string to or from which the I/O operation is to be performed. `sprintf(s, f, ...)` formats items in accordance with format string `f` and places the resulting output string in `s`. `sscanf(s, f, ...)` reads from string `s` as if it were a stream, matches according to format string `f`, and stores values in the items listed. Both are handy in special situations where you do not wish to produce input or output immediately. `sscanf` is especially useful for error recovery, or if there are several different ways in which we can attempt to parse the input.

22.2   Solved Exercises

22.2.1   Solved Exercise 1: A Bank Simulation (Revisited)

In Chapter 16, we wrote a simple program that simulates a bank. However, it had one serious shortcoming: as soon as the program is finished, the data is lost. Here we'll develop a new version, which will store the account information in a file in text form. First, we'll modify the main program:

```
/*******************************/
/*           bank.c            */
/*******************************/
#include <stdio.h>
#include "account.h"

#define MAX_ACCOUNTS 25
#define FILE_NAME "bank.dat"

main()
{
  int choice;
  Account bank[MAX_ACCOUNTS];

  load_bank(FILE_NAME, bank, MAX_ACCOUNTS);

  printf("      ALMOST A BANK!\n\n");
  printf("We'll keep your money safe\n");
  printf("  (at least for a while)");
  do {
    printf("\n\n1. Create a new account.\n");
    printf("2. Transact on an existing account.\n");
    printf("3. Exit.\n\n");
    printf("Please choose an option: ");
    scanf("%d", &choice);
    switch (choice) {
      case 1:
        insert_account(bank, MAX_ACCOUNTS);
        break;
      case 2:
        transactions(bank, MAX_ACCOUNTS);
        break;
```

```
                case 3:
                  printf("It has been a pleasure serving you!\n");
                  break;
                default:
                  printf("Sorry. That's not an option\n");
          }
        } while (choice != 3);
        save_bank(FILE_NAME, bank, MAX_ACCOUNTS);
        return 0;
      }
```

There are some differences between this and the main program in Chapter 16. First, instead of clearing the array at the beginning, we now call load_bank. Second, we now call save_bank before exiting the program. Third, we now have a macro specifying the file name. Clearly, the interesting functions are load_bank and save_bank. Here they are:

```
void load_bank(const char *f_name, Account bank[], int max_accounts)
{
  FILE *fp;
  int i;

  if ((fp = fopen(f_name, "r")) == NULL)
    /* If null, just clear the array */
    for (i = 0; i < max_accounts; i++)
      bank[i].number = -1;
      /* -1 indicates an available cell */
  else {
    /* Read the array from the file */
    i = 0;
    while (1) {
      if (fscanf(fp, "%d", &bank[i].number)!=1)
        break;
      if (bank[i].number == -1) continue;
      if (fscanf(fp, "%d%f", &bank[i].type, &bank[i].balance)!=2)
        break;
      if (bank[i].type == SAVINGS) {
        if (fscanf(fp, "%d%f", &bank[i].item.s.interest,
          &bank[i].item.s.max_withdraw)!=2)
          break;
      }
      else {
        if (fscanf(fp, "%f%f%f", &bank[i].item.c.max_overdraw,
          &bank[i].item.c.overdraw, &bank[i].item.c.interest)!=3)
          break;
      }
      i++;
    }
    for (; i < max_accounts; i++)
      bank[i].number = -1;
    fclose(fp);
  }
}

void save_bank(const char *f_name, Account bank[], int max_accounts)
{
  FILE *fp;
  int i = 0;

  if ((fp = fopen(f_name, "w")) == NULL)
    printf("Unable to open file for saving\n\n");
  else {
    /* Write the array to the file */
    while (i < max_accounts) {
      fprintf(fp, "%d\n", bank[i].number);
```

```
          if (bank[i].number != -1) {
            fprintf(fp, "%d %f ", bank[i].type,
                                    bank[i].balance);
            if (bank[i].type == SAVINGS)
               fprintf(fp, "%d %f\n", bank[i].item.s.interest,
                                       bank[i].item.s.max_withdraw);
            else
               /* checking account */
               fprintf(fp, "%f %f %f\n", bank[i].item.c.max_overdraw,
                                          bank[i].item.c.overdraw,
                                          bank[i].item.c.interest);
          }
          i++;
       }
       fclose(fp);
    }
}
```

I'll leave you to complete the program with the code in Chapter 16.

22.2.2   Solved Exercise 2: A Parts Database Program

Here we'll rewrite the program in Chapter 16 of the main text (page 341), modifying it to handle binary files and to allow random updates. The first major difference is that there is no array of structures to hold the data; we'll read and update directly from the file as needed. Instead of the MAX_PARTS macro that used to limit our number of parts, now we need a macro FILE_NAME.

The heart of the program is the find_part function, which searches the file for a given part number, and returns the current file position immediately after reading the structure for that part number, or returns zero if the part number is not found. Either way, find_part closes the file after it's done. This is a healthy practice; files should not be left open for too long.

The insert function takes a part number from the user, uses find_part to ensure that the part is not already in the database, obtains the name and quantity from the user, and appends the information to the end of the file. The file is kept open as little as possible. The search function is similar: after taking a part number from the user and ensuring that the part is in the database, that part's information is printed.

The update function is a little more involved. After obtaining the part number from the user, find_part is used to ensure that the part is in the database. The part's position is saved. In reality its successor's position is saved, since reading the part structure caused the file position to be moved beyond it. Then the change in the quantity on hand is obtained from the user, the file (previously closed by find_part) is reopened, the file position is set to the predecessor of the position saved earlier, and the new information written.

Finally, printing the contents of the database is fairly straightforward. The complete parts database program, except for readline.h and readline.c (which remain unchanged) is shown below.

```
#include <stdio.h>
#include "readline.h"

#define NAME_LEN 25
#define FILE_NAME "parts.dat"

struct part {
  int number;
  char name[NAME_LEN+1];
  int on_hand;
};

typedef struct part Part;
```

```
int find_part(int number, Part* p);
void insert(void);
void search(void);
void update(void);
void print(void);

/*************************************************************
 * main: Prompts the user to enter an operation code,       *
 *       then calls a function to perform the requested     *
 *       action. Repeats until the user enters the          *
 *       command 'q'. Prints an error message if the user   *
 *       enters an illegal code.                            *
 *************************************************************/
main()
{
  char code;

  for (;;) {
    printf("Enter operation code: ");
    printf("(Insert, Search, Update, Print, or Quit): ");
    scanf(" %c", &code);
    while (getchar() != '\n')    /* skips to end of line */
      ;
    switch (code) {
      case 'i': case 'I': insert(); break;
      case 's': case 'S': search(); break;
      case 'u': case 'U': update(); break;
      case 'p': case 'P': print(); break;
      case 'q': case 'Q': return 0;
      default:  printf("Illegal code\n");
    }
  }
  printf("\n");
  return 0;
}

/*************************************************************
 * find_part: Looks up a part number in the inventory       *
 *            file. If the part is found, stores the part   *
 *            in p, and returns the part's file position.   *
 *            If the part is not found, returns 0.          *
 *************************************************************/
int find_part(int number, Part* p)
{
  FILE *fp;
  long int file_position;

  if ((fp = fopen(FILE_NAME, "rb")) == NULL)
    return 0;
  while (fread(p, sizeof(*p), 1, fp) != 0)
    if (p->number == number) {
      file_position = ftell(fp);
      fclose(fp);
      return file_position;
    }
  fclose(fp);
  return 0;
}
```

```
/************************************************************
 * insert: Prompts the user for information about a new     *
 *         part and then inserts the part into the          *
 *         database. Prints an error message and returns    *
 *         prematurely if the part already exists.          *
 ************************************************************/
void insert(void)
{
  FILE *fp;
  Part p;
  int number;

  printf("Enter part number: ");
  scanf("%d", &number);
  if (find_part(number, &p) > 0) {
    printf("Part %d already exists.\n", p.number);
    return;
  }
  p.number = number;
  printf("Enter part name: ");
  read_line(p.name, NAME_LEN);
  printf("Enter quantity on hand: ");
  scanf("%d", &p.on_hand);
  if ((fp = fopen(FILE_NAME, "ab")) == NULL) {
    printf("Can't open file !\n");
    exit(1);
  }
  fwrite(&p, sizeof(p), 1, fp);
  fclose(fp);
}

/************************************************************
 * search: Prompts the user to enter a part number, then    *
 *         looks up the part in the database. If the part   *
 *         exists, prints the name and quantity on hand;    *
 *         if not, prints an error message.                 *
 ************************************************************/
void search(void)
{
  Part p;
  int number;

  printf("Enter part number: ");
  scanf("%d", &number);
  if (find_part(number, &p) > 0) {
    printf("Part name: %s\n", p.name);
    printf("Quantity on hand: %d\n", p.on_hand);
  } else
    printf("Part not found.\n");
}

/************************************************************
 * update: Prompts the user to enter a part number.         *
 *         Prints an error message if the part doesn't      *
 *         exist; otherwise, prompts the user to enter       *
 *         change in quantity on hand and updates the        *
 *         database.                                         *
 ************************************************************/
```

```
  void update(void)
  {
    FILE *fp;
    long   file_position;
    Part p;
    int number, change;

    printf("Enter part number: ");
    scanf("%d", &number);
    if ((file_position = find_part(number, &p)) > 0) {
      printf("Enter change in quantity on hand: ");
      scanf("%d", &change);
      p.on_hand += change;
      if ((fp = fopen(FILE_NAME, "rb+")) == NULL) {
        printf("Can't open file !\n");
        exit(1);
      }
      fseek(fp, file_position - sizeof(p), SEEK_SET);
      fwrite(&p, sizeof(p), 1, fp);
      fclose(fp);
    } else
      printf("Part not found.\n");
  }

  /***********************************************************
   * print: Prints a listing of all parts in the database,   *
   *        showing the part number, part name, and          *
   *        quantity on hand. Parts are printed in the       *
   *        order in which they were entered into the        *
   *        database.                                        *
   ***********************************************************/
  void print(void)
  {
    FILE *fp;
    Part p;

    if ((fp = fopen(FILE_NAME, "rb")) == NULL) {
      printf("Can't open file !\n");
      return;
    }
    printf("Part Number    Part Name    "
           "Quantity on Hand\n");
    while (fread(&p, sizeof(p), 1, fp) != 0)
      printf("%7d      %-25s%11d\n", p.number,
             p.name, p.on_hand);
    fclose(fp);
  }
```

22.3   Programming Exercises

1. If you wish to add data to a text file, but also want to leave the existing data undisturbed, which `fopen` mode string should you use?

2. Write a small program that returns the size of a file in bytes.

3. If you wish to input a hexadecimal number, what conversion specifier should you use with `scanf`? Is there any other step you should take besides specifying this conversion specifier?

4. Consider the following structure:

    ```
    struct example {
        int field1;
        float field2;
        char field3;
    };
    ```

    Write a program that will save an array of these structures in binary form in a file.

5. Write a function that will load into an array a file of `structs` as described in Exercise 4.

6. Complete the implementation of the bank simulation program in Solved Exercise 1. Add a function that will locate a specific account in the file.

7. Write a program that will merge the contents of two files and produce its output in a third file. The names of the three files are specified on the command line. The first file contains odd numbers in ascending order, one per line; the second one even numbers, also in ascending order, also one per line. The output should be in the same format as in the input files.

8. Consider the output file in Exercise 7. Write a function whose declaration is

    ```
    int get_num(FILE *fp, int pos);
    ```

    This function should return the number in position `pos` in the file pointed by `fp`.

9. Describe the output of the following call to `printf`.

    ```
    printf("%-+#5X", 12345);
    ```

10. Modify the bank simulation program so accounts include the name of the owner.

11. Modify the parts database program (Solved Exercise 2) to allow deletions.

12. Modify the parts database program to obtain the filename from the command line.

13. Write a small program that reads a line from the user and prints the numeric value of each of the characters typed. For example, if the user enters HELLO WORLD!, the program should print 7269767679 877982766833. The space shouldn't be printed as a numeric value.

14. Write a program that takes two file names as command-line parameters and compares the files. The program should report the line number of the first byte in which the files differ.

15. Under what circumstances is it necessary to flush the file buffer?

16. Write a program that concatenates two files on a line-by-line basis. A program like this was used to create the side-by-side C and C++ comparison in Section 19.2.1.

17. Write a program that will print the last n lines of each of the files specified as its command-line arguments. The value of n should also be specified on the command line.

18. Write a program that appends the contents of one file to the end of another.

19. Write a program that allows the user to examine any specified line in a file. First construct an index table, in which the nth entry holds the starting position of line n in the file. Then allow the user to request a given line, and use `fseek` to obtain it from the file.

20. Write a program that extracts and prints certain lines from its input file. The lines to be printed are those specified on the command line as single numbers or as a range of numbers. For example, extract 10-30 62 76 file will keep lines 10 through 30, line 62, and line 76 from file.

21. Rewrite the bank simulation program so that the bank data is stored in the file in binary form.

23 Library Support for Numbers and Character Data

23.1 Chapter Summary

In this chapter five headers are described: `<float.h>`, `<limits.h>`, `<math.h>`, `<ctype.h>`, and `<string.h>`.

`<float.h>` provides no types or functions. It provides macros defining various ranges for floating types. `FLT_ROUNDS` specifies the rounding mode for floating addition (for which there are five alternatives), and `FLT_RADIX` specifies the base in which the exponent is stored (at least 2). The remaining macros come in groups of three, prefixed with `FLT_`, `DBL_`, or `LDBL_` to indicate `float`, `double`, or `long double`. These are useful almost exclusively to specialists in numerical analysis.

- `FLT_MANT_DIG`, `DBL_MANT_DIG`, and `LDBL_MANT_DIG`, the number of significant digits, usually in base 2.
- `FLT_DIG`, `DBL_DIG`, and `LDBL_DIG`, the number of base-10 significant digits.
- `FLT_MIN_EXP`, `DBL_MIN_EXP`, and `LDBL_MIN_EXP`, the smallest exponent in base `FLT_RADIX`.
- `FLT_MIN_10_EXP`, `DBL_MIN_10_EXP`, and `LDBL_MIN_10_EXP`, the smallest exponent in base 10.
- `FLT_MAX_EXP`, `DBL_MAX_EXP`, and `LDBL_MAX_EXP`, the largest exponent in base `FLT_RADIX`.
- `FLT_MAX_10_EXP`, `DBL_MAX_10_EXP`, and `LDBL_MAX_10_EXP`, the largest exponent in base 10.
- `FLT_MAX`, `DBL_MAX`, and `LDBL_MAX`, the largest number representable.
- `FLT_MIN`, `DBL_MIN`, and `LDBL_MIN`, the smallest positive number representable.
- `FLT_EPSILON`, `DBL_EPSILON`, and `LDBL_EPSILON`, the smallest representable difference between two numbers.

The `<limits.h>` header provides macros that describe the characteristics of integers and characters.

- `CHAR_BIT`, the number of bits per character (at least 8).
- `SCHAR_MIN` and `SCHAR_MAX`, the smallest and largest signed character, and `UCHAR_MAX`, the largest unsigned character.
- `CHAR_MIN` and `CHAR_MAX`, the smallest and largest character.
- `MB_LEN_MAX`, the largest number of bytes in a multibyte character.
- `SHRT_MIN` and `SHRT_MAX`, the smallest and largest short integer, and `USHRT_MAX`, the largest unsigned short integer.
- `INT_MIN` and `INT_MAX`, the smallest and largest integer, and `UINT_MAX`, the largest unsigned integer.
- `LONG_MIN` and `LONG_MAX`, the smallest and largest long integer, and `ULONG_MAX`, the largest unsigned long integer.

These are useful to determine whether numbers are large enough in our particular implementation, to choose between, say, `int` and `long int`.

The `<math.h>` header contains a number of prototypes of functions commonly used in mathematics. These functions handle errors by storing an error code in a variable named `errno`, such as `EDOM` (domain error) and `ERANGE` (range error). The following trigonometric and hyperbolic functions are provided: `acos`, `asin`, `atan`, `atan2`, `cos`, `sin`, `tan`, `cosh`, `sinh`, and `tanh`. All take one `double` argument (except `atan2`, which takes two `double` arguments) and return `double`.

The exponential and logarithmic functions are:

- `exp(x)`: calculates *e* raised to the power of x.
- `log(x)`: calculates the logarithm base *e* of x.
- `log10(x)`: calculates the logarithm base 10 of x.
- `modf(x, &i)`: returns the fractional part of x and stores the integral part of x in i.
- `frexp(x, &n)`: returns *f* and changes n so that x equals $f * 2^n$.
- `ldexp(x, n)`: calculates $x * 2^n$.

The power functions are `pow(x, y)`, which calculates x^y, and `sqrt(x)`, which calculates the square root of x. The last four functions in `<math.h>` are:

- `ceil(x)`: nearest integer greater or equal to x.
- `floor(x)`: nearest integer less or equal to x.
- `fabs(x)`: absolute value of x).
- `fmod(x, y)`: remainder after dividing x by y.

The `<ctype.h>` header contains prototypes for the following functions for testing and mapping characters:

`isalnum(c)`	is c alphanumeric?
`isalpha(c)`	is c alphabetic?
`iscntrl(c)`	is c a control character?
`isdigit(c)`	is c a decimal digit?
`isgraph(c)`	is c a non-space printing character?
`islower(c)`	is c a lower-case letter?
`isprint(c)`	is c a printing character including space?
`ispunct(c)`	is c a punctuation character?
`isspace(c)`	is c a white-space character?
`isupper(c)`	is c an upper-case letter?
`isxdigit(c)`	is c a hexadecimal digit?
`tolower(c)`	if c is a letter, returns its lower-case version. Otherwise returns c.
`toupper(c)`	if c is a letter, returns its upper-case version. Otherwise returns c.

The `<string.h>` header includes prototypes of functions for manipulating strings.

- `memcpy(s1, s2, n)` and `memmove(s1, s2, n)`. These copy n bytes from s2 to s1; memcpy doesn't necessarily work if the memory areas overlap, but memmove does.
- `strcpy(s1, s2)` and `strncpy(s1, s2, n)`. These copy the string in s2 into s1, although strncpy copies at most n characters.
- `strcat(s1, s2)` and `strncat(s1, s2, n)`. Both functions append string s2 at the end of s1; strncat will append at most n characters.
- `memcmp(s1, s2, n)`, `strcmp(s1, s2)`, and `strncmp(s1, s2, n)`. These all compare character arrays s1 and s2 and return a negative, zero, or positive value, depending whether s1 is less than, equal to, or greater than s2. The usual lexicographical order is used. memcmp compares at most n characters, whether they are null or not. strcmp stops when it reaches a null character. strncmp stops when it reaches a null character, or after processing n characters. The strcoll function compares strings but depends on the current locale. The `strxfrm(s1, s2, n)` function transforms string s2, storing the result in s1. The transformation eliminates the "locale-specific" need for strcoll: if t1 and t2 are obtained from s1 and s2 using strxfrm, then t1 and t2 can be compared using strcmp, and the result will be the same as if we had used strcoll to compare the original strings s1 and s2.

`<string.h>` provides prototypes for a number of search functions. `strchr(s, c)` returns a pointer to the first occurrence of character c in string s. `memchr(s, c, n)` is similar, but stops searching after n characters. `strrchr(s, c)` is also similar, but searches the string backwards from the null character at the end of s. `strpbrk(s1, s2)` searches s1 for the first occurrence of *any* character in string s2. strspn(s1, s2) searches s1, and returns the integer position of the first character *not* in s2. strcspn is similar, but returns the integer position of the first character that *is* in s2. strstr(s1, s2) searches s1, and returns a pointer to the first occurrence of string s2. The last and most complex function is strtok(s1, s2), which scans and delimits a token in s1. The token consists of a sequence of characters that are not in s2. strtok places a null character in s1, just after the last character in the token, and returns a pointer to the first character in the token. Subsequent calls to strtok can use NULL as the first argument, and the function will continue scanning from where it left off after the previous call. Finally, memset(s, c, n) stores n copies of character c in memory block s, and strlen(s) returns the length of string s.

23.2 Solved Exercises

23.2.1 Solved Exercise 1: A Text Formatter (Revisited)

In Chapter 15 of the main text (page 313), a simple text formatting program is presented. The program reads in text, recognizing and appending words to the current line (using strcat), until one more word would make the line exceed the desired length. Then the line is printed with justification, with enough spaces evenly interspersed among the words in the line so that every line has exactly the same length. The heart of the program is the function write_line, which we reproduce here.

```
void write_line(void)
{
  int extra_spaces, spaces_to_insert, i, j;

  extra_spaces = MAX_LINE_LEN - line_len;
  for (i = 0; i < line_len; i++) {
    if (line[i] != ' ')
      putchar(line[i]);
    else {
      spaces_to_insert = extra_spaces / (num_words - 1);
      for (j = 1; j <= spaces_to_insert + 1; j++)
        putchar(' ');
      extra_spaces -= spaces_to_insert;
      num_words--;
    }
  }
  putchar('\n');
}
```

To print a justified line, this function prints the characters in line one by one. At the end of each word (i.e., at each space character), additional spaces are printed if necessary. The function calculates the total number of extra spaces needed, and calculates the appropriate number of spaces to be printed after each word by dividing the number of remaining necessary spaces by the number of remaining words.

Suppose we wish to modify this function, so that instead of merely printing the contents of line with additional spaces, we actually modify line by *inserting* spaces into the appropriate locations, and printing line with a single call to puts when we're done. In real life, a text formatter might need the justified string, to subject it to additional formatting modifications, which might perhaps even include justifying the line again later.

Let's write a new write_line function, which uses string library functions to justify the line in place, and then print it. We first obtain the pointer (end) to the end of the string. For this, we use a string idiom from Chapter 13. The number of extra spaces required is the difference between the pointer to the end of the line array, and the pointer to the end of the string. Then, instead of processing each character in the string, we'll jump from one space to the next, locating each space using strchr, and quitting when that function returns NULL. For each space (pointed to by p) in the string, we calculate the number of spaces to insert, and then move end - p + 1 characters (i.e., all the remaining characters, including the NULL at the end of the string) from p to p + spaces_to_insert. The void created by moving those characters must be filled with spaces. We do that with another call to memmove. We then move p to the next nonspace position, update end (which points to the end of the string), update the number of spaces still needed (extra_spaces), and update the number of remaining words. After justifying the string, a single puts prints it. Below is the new function.

```
void write_line(void)
{
   int extra_spaces, spaces_to_insert;
   char *p, *end;
   char spaces[6] = "      ";

   end = line;
   while (*end)
     end++;
   p = line;
   extra_spaces = &line[MAX_LINE_LEN] - end;
   while ((p=strchr(p, ' ')) != NULL) {
     spaces_to_insert = extra_spaces / (num_words - 1);
     memmove(p + spaces_to_insert, p, end - p + 1);
     memmove(p + 1, spaces, spaces_to_insert);
     p = p + spaces_to_insert + 1;
     end += spaces_to_insert;
     extra_spaces -= spaces_to_insert;
     num_words--;
   }
   puts(line);
}
```

Happily, these changes require require no additional change elsewhere in the program. Good design pays off once again. You are encouraged to plug in the new function and verify that the program works just as before.

23.2.2   Solved Exercise 2: A Tokenizer Program

Below is a program that decomposes its input text into tokens, an activity that is know as ***tokenizing***. The tokens extracted by the program are merely words, or sequences of characters that do not include certain delimiting characters. Thus we will use the terms "word" and "token" interchangeably. The program reads from standard input and can therefore be given a file via command-line redirection. We first read the input into a long string, terminate it with '\0', and then use strtok to delimit the words on successive calls. The delimiters are stored in the string

```
delims[]=" `~!@#$%^&*()_+|-=\\\"\t\n;:',./<>?".
```

The first call to strtok returns p, a pointer to the beginning of the first word. Then, as long as p is not null, we print our current token and call strtok(NULL, delims) to delimit the next token.

```
/******************************************************/
/*                                                    */
/* This program reads a string from the input and prints   */
/* the words in it, each on a separate line. The program   */
/* uses the strtok function to delimit words.         */
/*                                                    */
/******************************************************/

#include <stdio.h>
#include <string.h>

#define MAXLENGTH 1000

main()
{
   char string[MAXLENGTH+1];
   char delims[] = " `~!@#$%^&*()_+|-=\\\"\t\n;:',./<>?";
```

```
    int c, i = 0;
    char *p;

    while ((c = getchar()) != EOF)
      if (i < MAXLENGTH)
        string[i++] = c;

    string[i] = ' ';

    p = strtok(string, delims);
    while (p) {
      puts(p);
      p = strtok(NULL, delims);
    }
}
```

We took the first seven lines of the above file and used it as input to this program. Below is the output.

```
        This
        program
        reads
        a
        string
        from
        the
        input
        and
        prints
        the
        words
        in
        it
        each
        on
        a
        separate
        line
        The
        program
        uses
        the
        strtok
        function
        to
        delimit
        words
```

23.3   Programming Exercises

1.   Write a program that receives as command-line arguments the name of a file and one string. The program should list all the words in the file that are anagrams of the string.

2.   Write a program that receives as command-line arguments a file name and two strings a and b, and which replaces every occurrence of a in the file with b.

3.   Write a program that receives as a command-line argument the name of a file, then changes every upper-case letter in that file to its corresponding lower-case version, and vice versa.

4.   Write a program that receives as a command-line argument the name of a file, then counts the number of characters of each type that is identifiable using the standard library character-testing functions. Have your program prepare a report on the number and percentage of each type of character.

5. Write a program that prints a complete report showing the values of the constants provided by the `<float.h>` and `<limits.h>` headers.

6. Write an overflow-detection function `int multiply(int a, int b)`, which will detect whether multiplying the two integer numbers a and b would cause an overflow error.

7. Write a program that reads text from standard input and prints copy-edited text to standard output. The copy-editing task is simple: after each period, we wish to ensure that there is exactly one space, and if the next character after the space is a letter, it should be an upper-case letter. Your program should remove unnecessary spaces after a period and capitalize the next character after that, if it is a letter.

8. Extend the program in the previous exercise so that all words in the sentence are in lower-case letters.

9. Rewrite the simple text formatter that appears in Chapter 15, starting on page 313, using the `strtok` function to delimit words.

10. Write a program that reads in words from standard input, sorts them in alphabetical order, and prints the sorted words to the standard output. Use the string library functions to compare the words.

11. Extend the plotting program of Chapter 9 so that it will plot any of the functions in the `<math.h>` library header.

12. Write a censorship program that takes as command-line arguments a file and a four-letter word, locates every occurrence of that four-letter word in that file, and replaces the middle two letters of that word with asterisks. For example, `sort` becomes `s**t` (now, now, take your mind out of the gutter!).

24   Error Handling

24.1   Chapter Summary

In real life, programs need to be bulletproof.[1] One of the more difficult tasks in programming is making a program capable of surviving almost any input that is thrown at it, intentionally or otherwise. A good quality program handles all errors gracefully, instead of merely crashing. C is not one of the best languages when it comes to error detection and handling, but it does have a few good features.

The <assert.h> header provides the assert macro, which takes an integer expression and evaluates it. The intent is that under normal circumstances the expression (called an *assertion*) should evaluate to a nonzero value, or "true." If not, assert terminates the program's execution and prints a descriptive message, providing the expression (in source form) that failed, the name of the source file, and the line number. assert is useful for programs to monitor their own progress and behavior, but it does reduce the program's efficiency. For example, the call assert(i >= 1) ensures that the value of i is at least 1 at the point in time in which assert is invoked. The assert function can be disabled by defining the macro NDEBUG prior to including the <assert.h> header.

The <errno.h> header provides several facilities for error handling. The <errno.h> header declares the errno variable, which is used and set by various functions (mostly those in <math.h>) in the standard library. To detect an error, we first set errno to zero, call the function, and then examine errno to see if it was changed by the function call. The library functions typically change errno to one of two values: EDOM and ERANGE, both of which are macros defined in <errno.h>. EDOM is a *domain* error: the value passed in was inappropriate for that function. ERANGE is a *range* error: the return value is too large to be represented as a double.

The perror function takes a string (an error message), and constructs and prints a complete error message consisting of the user-supplied error message, a colon, a space, and an additional error message determined by the value of errno. To obtain the latter error message, we use the strerror function, which takes an error code and returns the error message determined by the value of errno.

The <signal.h> header provides facilities for handling exceptional conditions known as *signals*. These are special conditions that arise, sometimes due to errors, other times due to events external to the program, such as termination of the program by the user. When they occur, the signal is said to be *raised*. The <signal.h> header has a number of macros that represent certain known signals: SIGABRT (abnormal program termination), SIGFPE (arithmetic error), SIGILL (illegal instruction), SIGINT (program interrupt), SIGSEGV (invalid storage access), and SIGTERM (termination request). These are not necessarily raised automatically, since the conditions vary from one computer system to another.

The signal function is used to install a signal-handling function. Its arguments are an integer code for the signal and a pointer to the handler function. The handler function is invoked when the signal is raised and takes the signal code as an argument. It is expected to perform some useful action, and then either terminate execution by calling exit, or return, generally (but not always) returning to the point where the signal was raised. Returning from a handler for the SIGABRT signal is futile: the program will abort execution anyway. Returning from a handler for the SIGFPE is unwise: the result is undefined. There are two predefined signal handlers: SIG_DFL (default), which handles the signal in an implementation-defined manner (usually terminating execution), and SIG_IGN (ignore), which ignores the signal raised. A third macro, SIG_ERR, is not a signal handler but a pointer to an integer value, which is returned by signal if the given handler cannot be installed.

signal returns a pointer to the previous handler function, which can be stored in a variable if we wish, so that the old handler can be reinstalled later. Handlers must be reinstalled after each time the signal is raised. One way to accomplish this is to have the handler install itself (or some other handler) as part of its duties. Most signals are raised automatically, as when a program is interrupted by its user.

---

1 Some say "idiot-proof."

Still, sometimes we wish to raise a signal ourselves within a program. For this we have the `raise` function, whose argument is the signal code for the signal to be raised.

The `<setjmp.h>` header provides a mechanism for jumping from one function to any other active function within a program. The `goto` statement won't do, because it can only jump to a label within the same function. Invoking `setjmp(env)` marks the place in the program where it is called, stores the current environment in `env`, and returns zero. Later, whenever `longjmp(env, n)` is called, the program returns to the place where `setjmp` was called, and this time the value returned by `setjmp` is `n`.

24.2   Solved Exercises

24.2.1   Solved Exercise 1: Efficient String Search

Consider the problem of searching through a file of words looking for a given word. We'll assume one word per line. Normally, we would search sequentially through the file for the given string. But now we will process the file beforehand, creating a *hash table* that will allow our search for a given string to be more efficient. The hash table will allow us to search through only a small portion of the file, rather than searching through all of it. We do this by mathematically mapping each string to an integer in a convenient range (typically 0 through a certain maximum) via a hash function.

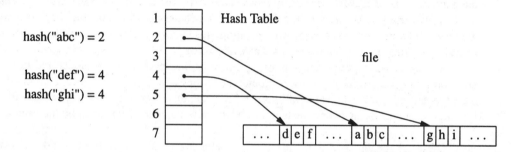

We will store the file position of each string in a table called the *hash table*. In the example shown above, string `"abc"` hashes to bucket 2, and both strings `"def"` and `"ghi"` hash to bucket 4. At the respective locations in the hash table, we store the file positions of those strings. Often two or more strings will have the same hash value. In our case, `"def"` and `"ghi"` hash to the same value of 4. In these cases, called hash collisions, we move on sequentially to the next available slot in the hash table.

When searching for a string, say `"ghi"`, we need not process all strings that precede it. Instead we search only through the portion of the table that begins at the hash value for `"ghi"`. On average, this should mean many fewer string comparisons.

Typically, the hash function tears the string to shreds,[2] character by character, and performs some arithmetic operation on the characters to yield a number.

We begin by writing the header file for the abstract data type (ADT) `Table`. A hash table is an array of buckets. Conceptually, each bucket is a starting point to search for strings. Each bucket contains the file position of the string in question. There are five operations available on hash tables: `initialize`, `hash`, `insert`, `retrieve`, and `print`.

```
/***************************************/
/*  table.h   -- ADT Hash Table      */
/***************************************/

#ifndef TABLE_H
#define TABLE_H
```

---

2 As in shredded potatoes, called (not coincidentally) hash browns.

```
#define MAXBUCKET 256  /* Max number of buckets */
#define MAXLINE   100  /* Max number of chars per line */
#define EMPTYBUCKET -1

typedef long Table[MAXBUCKET];

void initialize(Table tab);
void insert(FILE* fptr, Table tab, const char *str, long position);
void retrieve(FILE* fptr, const Table tab, const char *str);
void print(FILE* fptr, const Table tab);

#endif
```

Now, we implement the ADT table, by implementing the five operations. The hash function performs an exclusive-or operation on all the characters in the string. Then, to ensure a number within the required range, we apply the remainder operator.

The insert function is the heart of the matter. Hashing yields an initial value for index. If location index is not already taken, then we place the file position of the string in location index, and we're done. If location index is taken, we attempt to match the file position at index with the file position of the string we're inserting. If there's a match, the string is already in the table, and we're done. If not, it's time to search sequentially through the buckets beginning at index, using the file pointers to access the actual strings from the file and comparing them to the one at hand. If we encounter the string, the function returns. If not, we place the new string in the first unoccupied bucket.

The retrieve function is similar. After obtaining a hash index, we check the file position at index. If it's unused, we report that the string wasn't found. Otherwise, we search through the file positions starting at index, and report whether the string was found or not. Here's the table.c file.

```
/****************************************/
/*  Implementation of ADT Hash Table */
/****************************************/

#include <stdlib.h>
#include <stdio.h>
#include <string.h>
#include <assert.h>
#include <errno.h>
#include "table.h"

static int hash(const char* str);

void initialize(Table tab)
{
  int i;

  for (i = 0; i < MAXBUCKET; i++)
    tab[i] = EMPTYBUCKET;
}

int hash(const char *str)
{
  int res;

  for (res=0; *str != '\n'; str++)
    res ^= (unsigned char) *str;
  return res % MAXBUCKET;
}
```

```
void insert(FILE* fptr, Table tab, const char *str, long position)
{
  char str2[MAXLINE+1];
  int index;

  assert((index = hash(str)) >= 0);
  if (tab[index] == EMPTYBUCKET) {
    tab[index] = position;
    return;
  }
  do {
    errno = 0;
    if (fseek(fptr, tab[index], SEEK_SET)) {
      printf("File error 1, program quits.\n");
      exit(1);
    }
    fgets(str2, MAXLINE, fptr);
    if (strcmp(str, str2) == 0) return;
    index = (index + 1) % MAXBUCKET;
    assert(index >= 0);
  } while (index != EMPTYBUCKET);
  tab[index] = position;
}

void retrieve(FILE* fptr, const Table tab, const char *str)
{
  char str2[MAXLINE+1];
  int index, comparisons = 0, found;

  assert((index = hash(str)) >= 0);
  do {
    if (tab[index] == EMPTYBUCKET) {
      found = 0;
      break;
    }
    errno = 0;
    if (fseek(fptr, tab[index], SEEK_SET)) {
      printf("File error 2, program quits.\n");
      exit(1);
    }
    fgets(str2, MAXLINE, fptr);
    comparisons++;
    if ((found = (strcmp(str, str2) == 0))) break;
    index = (index + 1) % MAXBUCKET;
  } while (index != EMPTYBUCKET);
  if (found)
    printf(" String found. ");
  else
    printf(" String not found. ");
  printf("Needed %d comparison(s).\n", comparisons);
}

void print(FILE* fptr, const Table tab)
{
  int i;
  char str[MAXLINE+1];

  printf("\nHash Table:\n");
  printf("Index  FPOS  String\n");
  printf("-----------------------------\n");
  for (i = 0; i < MAXBUCKET; i++) {
    printf("%4d %6ld: ", i, tab[i]);
    if (tab[i] == EMPTYBUCKET)
```

```
          printf("<EMPTY BUCKET>\n");
     else {
          fseek(fptr, tab[i], SEEK_SET);
          fgets(str, MAXLINE, fptr);
          printf("%s", str);
     }
   }
}
```

The code has been interspersed with error checks, although more could be added (see the Exercises). Some assertions are unnecessary as the program stands now (such as checking that the hash function doesn't return a negative value), but they safeguard us against future errors. We've used a simple numbering scheme to identify the errors, which in general is a good idea. The main program is rather simple: we open the file and insert every string in the hash table. Note that we save the file position each time, since `insert` modifies it. We then repeatedly prompt the user for strings and retrieve them from the table. Here's the main program:

```
/**********************************************************/
/* This program stores the position of each string in    */
/* the input file, in a hash table. Efficient retrieval   */
/* of strings can then be performed. The program deals    */
/* with some of the error conditions that may arise,      */
/* using the <errno.h> and <assert.h> libraries.          */
/**********************************************************/

#include <stdio.h>
#include <stdlib.h>
#include <assert.h>
#include <errno.h>
#include "table.h"


main(int argc, char *argv[])
{
   FILE *fptr;
   Table tab;
   char str[MAXLINE+1];
   long position, new_position;

   initialize(tab);
   if (argc < 2) {
     printf("Program requires name of data file.\n");
     exit(1);
   }
   errno = 0;
   if ((fptr = fopen(argv[1], "r")) == NULL) {
     printf("File error 3: Cannot open file %s.\n", argv[1]);
     exit(1);
   }
   new_position = 0;
   printf("Reading strings from file '%s' ...\n", argv[1]);
   while (1) {
     position = new_position;
     fseek(fptr, position, SEEK_SET);
     if (fgets(str, MAXLINE, fptr) == NULL) break;
     new_position = ftell(fptr);
     insert(fptr, tab, str, position);
   }
#ifndef NDEBUG
   print(fptr, tab);
#endif
   while(1) {
     printf("Please enter a string: ");
```

```
        if (fgets(str, MAXLINE, stdin) == NULL) break;
        if (str[0] == '\n') break;
        retrieve(fptr, tab, str);
    }
    fclose(fptr);
    return 0;
}
```

24.2.2   Solved Exercise 2: An Interruptible File Printer

Let's write a program that repeatedly requests the user for the name of a file and displays the contents of that file, but can be interrupted at (almost) any time during the process. When interrupted, the program stops processing the current file and asks the user to enter another file name. While in between files, that is, while waiting for the user to enter the file name, and while opening and closing the file, the program is not interruptible.

We'll implement this using signals and the longjmp facility. The program is shown below. The print_file function is simple enough: it copies input characters to the output. The main function first marks the beginning of the program for a future longjmp, and then repeatedly reads a file name, opens that file, and prints its contents. Interruptions are ignored while the file name is being read, and while the file is being opened. While printing the file, an interruption is handled by the handler function, which prints a message, closes the file, and jumps to the beginning of the program.

```
#include <stdio.h>
#include <signal.h>
#include <setjmp.h>
#include <string.h>

#define NAME_SIZE 128

jmp_buf env;
FILE *fptr;
void handler(int sig);
void print_file(void);

main()
{
    char name[NAME_SIZE+1], *p;

    setjmp(env);
    while(1) {
        signal(SIGINT, SIG_IGN);
        printf("File: ");
        fgets(name, NAME_SIZE, stdin);
        if ((p = strchr(name, '\n')) != NULL)
            *p = '\0';
        if (name[0] == '\0') break;
        if ((fptr = fopen(name, "r")) != NULL) {
            signal(SIGINT, handler);
            print_file();
        }
        else
            fprintf(stderr, "Can't open file!\n");
    }
    return 0;
}
```

```
void handler(int sig)
{
  fprintf(stderr, "program interrupted !\n");
  fprintf(stderr, "Closing file.\n");
  fclose(fptr);
  longjmp(env, 1);
}

void print_file(void)
{
  int c;

  while ((c = getc(fptr)) != EOF)
    putchar(c);
}
```

24.3 Programming Exercises

1. Modify the indentation program in Chapter 13 to handle errors. Specifically, guard against errors in `strcpy` and `strcat`, and check that the command line argument is an integer.

2. Modify the sets program in Chapter 15 to guard against errors such as out-of-range array indices. Also, allow the program to be interrupted while it is waiting for input, and have the program issue an appropriate error message.

3. The sets program in Chapter 17 is rich in opportunities for errors. Add a handler for the `SIGSEGV` signal, which will usually be raised if a pointer with an undefined value is used.

4. The hash table program is not completely bulletproof. For example, when inserting a new string, what happens if the table is already full? Make any necessary changes.

5. Modify the hash table program so that hash collisions overflow into a linked list instead of the next available bucket. First, modify the `bucket` structure, so the `next` field is a *pointer* to a `struct bucket`, rather than an integer index. Then, when a hash value lands in an occupied bucket, traverse the linked list of `bucket` structures, and if necessary, add the new string to the end of the list. Make your changes error-proof, especially against errors in using pointers.

6. Modify the hash table program so that after building the hash table, the program will take query strings from a file instead of querying the user. Have your program produce statistics on the average number of comparisons.

7. Change some of the error handling in the hash table program. Examine the value returned by `fopen`, raise a signal (instead of printing a message and quitting), and implement a handler for it.

8. Implement a signal and a handler that will determine if the hash table program has been invoked without a command-line parameter, instead of merely printing a message and exiting. Although this is not the way you would normally handle things, it's good practice.

9. Make the hash table program as bulletproof as you can. This would include guarding against array subscripts that are out of range and against all file access errors (not just when calling `fseek` or `fopen`). It's possible to go too far in this, so exercise good judgment.

10. Make the interruptible file printer program bulletproof.

11. Write a handler for the `SIGINT` signal that asks the user to interrupt a second time in order to really quit, or to press the `Enter` key to continue. On UNIX systems, `Ctrl-C` (pressing the C key while holding down the `Ctrl` key) interrupts a program. On DOS systems, `Ctrl-D` usually does the trick.

12. Write a handler for the `SIGINT` signal that prompts the user for verification, asking "Do you really want to quit?", reads a single character `y` or `n` answer, and acts accordingly.

25 International Features

25.1 Chapter Summary

In the 1980s, the experts who developed the C Standard recognized that many features of the C language were specific to the United States. The C Standard provides the `<locale.h>` header, which allows the programmer to tailor a program's behavior to a particular *locale* (a country, region, or even a culture). Issues affected by different locales include the formatting of numerical values (whether the decimal point is displayed as a period or as a comma), the formatting of monetary values (especially the currency symbol), the character set (Asian countries have much larger character sets), and the appearance of date and time values.

The "current locale" can be changed at run-time by choosing from an implementation-defined set of available locales. These vary from compiler to compiler; the C standard defines the `"C"` locale, which specifies a locale consistent with the original, U.S.-only definition of the C language. When we change locales, we change various features of the run-time library. To change locales, we use the function

```
char *setlocale(int category, const char *locale);
```

There are five predefined locale categories that can be changed, as illustrated in the following table:

Category Name	Behavior affected
LC_COLLATE	The `strcoll` and `strxfrm` functions in `<string.h>`.
LC_CTYPE	The character handling functions in `<ctype.h>` and the multibyte functions in `<stdlib.h>`.
LC_MONETARY	The monetary information returned by `localeconv`.
LC_NUMERIC	The decimal point character used to read and print `float`s, and the `atof` and `strtod` functions in `<stdlib.h>`. Also the nonmonetary information returned by `localeconv`.
LC_TIME	The `strftime` function in `<time.h>`.

The C Standard defines only two values for the second argument to `setlocale`: `"C"` and `""`. At the beginning of the execution of any program, a call of the form `setlocale(LC_ALL, "C")` takes place. After the program's execution has begun, you can change to the *native locale* with the call `setlocale(LC_ALL, "")`, allowing the program to adapt to the native (i.e., local) environment. The C Standard says nothing about the native locale: it is implementation-defined. Some implementations provide other locales, with names like `"Spain"`. Implementations of the C language can also provide additional locale categories, provided they begin with `LC_`. The `setlocale` function (if it succeeds) returns a pointer to a string associated with the category in the new locale. If it doesn't succeed, it returns the null pointer. The `setlocale` function can also be used to inquire about the current locale by sending it the null pointer as the second argument. If the first argument is `LC_ALL`, then the string returned gives us the settings for all categories. This string can be saved for later use.

The information provided by `setlocale` does not come in a useful form. To convert it we use the `localeconv` function, which returns a pointer to a structure of type `struct lconv`. This structure contains detailed information about the current locale. The table below summarizes the members of this structure.

Name	Description
decimal_point	decimal-point character
thousands_sep	"thousands" separator character
grouping	size of digit groups to be separated
int_curr_symbol	international currency symbol, e.g., "ITL." for Italy
currency_symbol	local currency symbol
mon_decimal_point	monetary decimal-point character
mon_thousands_sep	monetary "thousands" separator character
mon_grouping	monetary size of digit groups
positive_sign	string indicating nonnegative value
negative_sign	string indicating negative value
int_frac_digits	number of fractional digits (international format)
frac_digits	number of fractional digits (local format)
p_cs_precedes	indicates whether currency_symbol precedes or succeeds nonnegative value
p_sep_by_space	indicates whether currency_symbol is separated by a space from nonnegative value
p_sign_posn	position of positive_sign, relative to currency_symbol and value, for nonnegative value (five options available; see the main text, page 555)
n_cs_precedes	same as p_cs_precedes, for negative values
n_sep_by_space	same as p_sep_by_space, for negative values
n_sign_posn	same as p_sign_posn, for negative values

Many, many variations can be obtained with the above values. Keep in mind that the C standard library provides no facilities for carrying out the actual formatting of monetary values. Someone must write a C program to do that.

The C language allows compilers to provide an *extended* character set for those locales in which the ASCII character set is inadequate. The extended character set can be encoded in two ways. One way uses *multibyte* characters, in which one or more bytes represent the extended character. The number of bytes per extended character varies. The other way to encode an extended character set is using *wide characters*. Each extended character is encoded in an integer of type wchar_t, which is implementation-defined. A string of such characters is an array of type wchar_t[]. A wide character, or a string of wide characters, can be expressed using a C character constant or string literal if prefixed by the letter L. The maximum number of bytes that can be used to form a multibyte character is given by MB_CUR_MAX, which is not a constant expression because it can change from locale to locale. The mbtowc and wctomb functions convert multibyte characters to wide characters and vice versa. Similarly, the mbstowcs and wcstombs functions convert strings of multibyte characters into strings of wide characters, and vice versa.

Finally, a *trigraph sequence* is a three-character code that can be used as an alternate way to express certain ASCII characters that are already reserved in the C language for specific purposes. Those characters are #, [, \,], ^, {, |, }, and ~. In some locales, these characters are not available in the local variant of the ASCII code. The trigraphs required by the C Standard are:

Trigraph Sequence	??=	??(	??/	??)	??'	??<	??!	??>	??-
ASCII Character	#	[	\	]	^	{			}	~

25.2   Solved Exercises

25.2.1   Solved Exercise 1: Printing Locale Information

The following program asks the user for the name of a locale and switches to that locale, if possible. It then uses `localeconv` to obtain the various locale-specific values in the `lconv` structure, and prints them. A word of warning: the values stored in strings `grouping` and `mon_grouping` are integers stored in character form. When printed as part of a string, it's possible for them to appear as control characters on your screen display, producing unexpected results (see Exercise 6).

```c
#include <locale.h>
#include <stdio.h>
#include <stdlib.h>
#include <limits.h>
#include <string.h>

#define MAX_NAME 100

void printstring(const char *title, const char *str);
void printchar(const char *title, char c);

main()
{
  struct lconv *p;
  char name[MAX_NAME+1];
  char *temp;

  printf("Please enter name of locale: ");
  fgets(name, MAX_NAME, stdin);
  if ((temp = strchr(name, '\n')) != NULL)
      *temp = '\0';
  printf("LOCALE is \"%s\"\n", name);
  temp = setlocale(LC_ALL, name);
  if (temp == NULL) {
    printf("That locale is not available.\n");
    exit(1);
  }
  p = localeconv();
  printstring("decimal_point     ", p->decimal_point);
  printstring("thousands_sep     ", p->thousands_sep);
  printstring("grouping          ", p->grouping);
  printstring("int_curr_symbol   ", p->int_curr_symbol);
  printstring("currency_symbol   ", p->currency_symbol);
  printstring("mon_decimal_point", p->mon_decimal_point);
  printstring("mon_thousands_sep", p->mon_thousands_sep);
  printstring("mon_grouping      ", p->mon_grouping);
  printstring("positive_sign     ", p->positive_sign);
  printstring("negative_sign     ", p->negative_sign);

  printchar("int_frac_digits  ", p->int_frac_digits);
  printchar("frac_digits      ", p->frac_digits);
  printchar("p_cs_precedes    ", p->p_cs_precedes);
  printchar("p_sep_by_space   ", p->p_sep_by_space);
  printchar("p_sign_posn      ", p->p_sign_posn);
  printchar("n_cs_precedes    ", p->n_cs_precedes);
  printchar("n_sep_by_space   ", p->n_sep_by_space);
  printchar("n_sign_posn      ", p->n_sign_posn);
  return 0;
}
```

```
void printstring(const char *title, const char *str)
{
  printf("%s: \"%s\"\n", title, str);
}

void printchar(const char *title, char c)
{
  printf("%s: ", title);
  if (c == CHAR_MAX)
    printf("UNAVAILABLE\n");
  else
    printf("%d\n", c);
}
```

25.3   Programming Exercises

1. Find out the number of bytes occupied by a variable of type `wchar_t` on your system.

2. Write a program that reads the text of a C program from standard input and prints that same file to standard output, having replaced each occurrence of an ASCII character that corresponds to a trigraph, with that trigraph.

3. Write a program that reads the text of a C program from standard input, recognizes trigraph sequences, and prints that same file to standard output, having replaced each trigraph with the corresponding ASCII character.

4. Determine the values of `MB_LEN_MAX` and `MB_CUR_MAX` in your system.

5. Write a function that takes as arguments a `float` and a string (the name of the locale), then prints the corresponding monetary value in accordance with the values in that locale's `lconv` structure.

6. Modify the locale information printing program to print `grouping` and `mon_grouping` safely. Each character in these strings is an integer stored in character form, and if printed as such, could appear as a control character on the display. Instead of printing characters, extract each corresponding integer and print it.

26 Miscellaneous Library Functions

26.1 Chapter Summary

There are three remaining headers in the C library: `<stdarg.h>` (a facility for defining functions with a variable number of arguments), `<stdlib.h>` (general utility functions), and `<time.h>` (functions for manipulating dates and times).

26.1.1 Variable Argument Lists

The `<stdarg.h>` header defines the `va_list` type and three macros, which can be thought of as functions having the following prototypes:

```
void va_start(va_list ap, parameterN);
type va_arg(va_list ap, type);
void va_end(va_list ap);
```

To use these macros, we first declare a variable of type `va_list`. Then we call `va_start`, giving it the name of our `va_list` variable (say, ap), and the name of the last *named* parameter, or the one after which the variable list begins. Then successive calls to `va_arg` fetch the actual parameters. These three macros can be used to process any number of arguments, and you do not need to know how many there will be.

The following three functions are provided in `<stdio.h>`, but are invariably used inside a function with a variable argument list.

```
int vfprintf(FILE *stream, const char *format, va_list arg);
int vprintf(const char *format, va_list arg);
int vsprintf(char *s, const char *format, va_list arg);
```

These three functions behave in the same way as `fprintf`, `printf`, and `sprintf`, except that instead of taking a variable number of arguments, they take an argument of type `va_list`. This argument, `arg`, is declared in the function in which we are working, allowing the function to take a variable number of arguments, wrap them in the variable `arg`, and pass them all at once to the printing function.

Calling a function with a variable argument list is quite an error-prone feature in an already error-prone language. There is no typechecking whatsoever of the arguments. Default argument promotions take place, so attempting to process `char` or `float` arguments is futile. You must rely on the actual data provided in the function call to determine when to stop processing arguments. It is easy to move beyond the last argument, wreaking havoc with the program.

26.1.2 General Utilities

A number of utility functions are available in the `<stdlib.h>` header, and they fall into seven groups: string conversion functions, pseudo-random sequence generation functions, memory management functions, functions for communicating with the environment, sorting and searching functions, integer arithmetic functions, and multibyte character and string functions.

There are both old and new string conversion functions. The old ones (from the original C definition), are `atof`, `atoi`, and `atol`. They convert a string to a `double`, `int`, or `long int` value. They skip white-space characters at the beginning of the string and perform the conversion on an "as-can" basis—they stop at the first character that can't be part of the number. The new functions (added by the C Standard) are `strtod`, `strtol`, and `strtoul`, which convert a string to `double`, `long int`, and `unsigned long int` respectively. All three take as their first argument the string to be converted. The new functions indicate where the conversion stopped by modifying the second argument, which is of type `char **`. Thus it's possible to tell whether the conversion consumed the entire string. `strtol` and `strtoul` have a third argument: the base of the number being converted (between 2 and

36). The new functions handle errors better than the old ones, and although the old functions remain in the library for compatibility reasons, the new functions are recommended for new programs.

There are two pseudo-random sequence generation functions, `rand` and `srand`. `rand` returns an integer between 0 and `RAND_MAX` (a macro provided in `<stdlib.h>`). The numbers returned by `rand` are not truly random: they are generated from an initial number called the ***seed***. The `srand` function is used to supply the seed for `rand`. A good way to seed the random generator is to use the `time` function.

The `exit` function is used to terminate program execution and return a value to the operating system. Two macros are provided as exit values: `EXIT_FAILURE` and `EXIT_SUCCESS`. The `atexit` function allows us to register a function, to be called upon program termination. Typically, such a function might print a message, flush file buffers, close files, or perform other housekeeping chores. Several functions can be so registered; the most recently registered one is called first. The `abort` function is used to terminate program execution immediately, without even calling functions registered with `atexit`. On some systems, this can leave unfinished business: unflushed file buffers, unclosed streams, and temporary files that were not deleted. Operating systems typically provide an ***environment***, consisting of strings that describe some of the goings-on that surround the program. For example, the `PATH` variable typically describes the directories in which to search for a given executable file. The `getenv` function takes a pointer to a string that is understood by the execution environment, and returns a pointer to another string, the "value" of that argument. The `system` function allows the program to execute operating system commands. Its argument is a pointer to a string, the operating system command we wish to execute.

The `bsearch` function is used to carry out binary search on a sorted array for a particular value. Its first argument is `const void *key`, a pointer to the key value for which to search. The second argument is `const void *base`, a pointer to the array itself. The third argument is `size_t nmemb`, the number of elements in the array. The fourth argument is `size_t size`, the size (in bytes) of each array element. The fifth argument is `int (*compar)(const void *, const void *)`, a pointer to the comparison function. `compar` takes pointers to the key and an array element, and must return a negative, zero, or positive value, depending (respectively) on whether the key is smaller than, equal to, or greater than the array element. `bsearch` returns a pointer to an array element that matches the key; it returns `NULL` if there's no match.

The `qsort` function is used to sort an array of values. Its four arguments are the same as the last four for `bsearch`: the array to be sorted, the number of elements in the array, the size of each array element, and the comparison function.

There are four integer arithmetic functions in `<stdlib.h>`. `abs` and `labs` return the absolute value for integers and long integers. `div` and `ldiv` perform integral division on integers and long integers, storing the quotient and remainder in a structure.

26.1.3   The `<time.h>` header

The `<time.h>` header provides three types, each used to store a time in a different way: `clock_t` (time measured in "ticks"), `time_t` (time and date, compactly encoded), and `struct tm` (a broken-down time structure). The members of the `tm` structure are seconds after the minute (`tm_sec`), minutes after the hour (`tm_min`), hours since midnight (`tm_hour`), day of the month (`tm_mday`), months since January (`tm_mon`), years since 1900 (`tm_year`), days since Sunday (`tm_wday`), days since January 1 (`tm_yday`), and a Daylight Savings Time flag (`tm_isdst`).

The `clock` function returns the number of ticks since the beginning of the program's execution. This value can be converted to seconds by dividing it by `CLOCKS_PER_SEC`. It's best to call `clock` twice, once at the beginning of `main`, and again later, and to use the difference between the two values. This will exclude from the calculation the start-up time of the program.

The `time` function returns the current calendar time, which can be stored in a variable of type `time_t`. The `difftime` function returns the difference between two times, measured in seconds.

The `mktime` function converts a broken-down time (a `struct tm`) into a calendar time, which it returns. `mktime` also brings values in the structure into their proper ranges, adjusting others as necessary. For example, if `tm_mon` exceeds 11, it is reduced to the proper range, and `tm_year` is adjusted accordingly. This feature is useful for performing arithmetic on dates and times, e.g., for answering the question, "What day of the week was March 21, 1937?" or "If I have exactly 17 days from today to repay the local loan shark, on what date should I expect an unpleasant visit?"

The time conversion functions can convert calendar times to broken-down times and to character strings suitable for output. `gmtime` and `localtime` both convert a calendar time to a broken-down time; `gmtime` uses UTC (Coordinated Universal Time, formerly known as Greenwich Mean Time), while `localtime` produces a local time. The `asctime` function takes a broken-down time and produces a string of the form `Thu Feb 27 11:49:17 1997` (the day I wrote this!). The `ctime` function is similar: it takes a calendar time and returns a string describing a local time. The `strftime` function is a much more elaborate mechanism for converting a broken-down time into a string; using a format string, you can specify the format of the string to be produced, in a manner similar to printing functions such as `sprintf`. A number of conversion specifications are available (see the main text). Occasionally, even the formatting capabilities of `strftime` are not enough; in those cases we can always extract the information from the broken-down time structure, and print it ourselves using `printf`.

26.2   Solved Exercises

26.2.1   Solved Exercise 1: Sorting Random Numbers

Let's develop a program that uses some of the library functions described in this chapter. We wish to sort a collection of randomly generated numbers using the `qsort` function. To compare the numbers, we have a `compare` function. To print them (before and after sorting), we have a `print_array` function. We'll report both the processor time taken by the program, and the elapsed time, which includes time spent waiting for the user to enter data. These statistics will be reported as the program ends, in a function named `report_timing`, which is registered via the `atexit` function.

We'll prompt the user for the number of values to be generated, and for the largest such value. To read these two numbers, instead of the usual `scanf` calls, we'll read a string using `fgets` and use the `strtol` conversion function. Immediately after the conversion, we call `check_endptr`, to ensure that the entire string was consumed in the conversion (by checking that `endptr` points to a null character). If not, we use the `abort` function to terminate execution without calling the `report_timing` function.

Throughout the program, we want to be able to print information that's useful for debugging. The `debug` function takes two strings (the name of the function and the format string), and a variable number of additional arguments. `debug` prints the function name, and then passes its format string and its variable argument list to `vprintf`. Thus the call `debug("f", "i = %d", i)` prints a message such as this: `DEBUGGING f: i = 3`. The program is sprinkled with calls to the `debug` function. The program does some things in an unnatural way, for the sake of demonstrating as many library functions as possible.

Here's the complete program:

```
#include <stdio.h>
#include <stdlib.h>
#include <stdarg.h>
#include <time.h>
#include <string.h>

#define MAX_STR_LEN 30
#define CONVERSION_BASE 10
#define NUMS_PER_LINE 10
#define DEBUG

clock_t before, after;
time_t start_time;
```

```
int compare(const void *a, const void *b);
void print_array(int a[], int array_size);
void debug(const char *fname, const char *format, ...);
void check_endptr(const char *endptr);
void report_timing(void);

main()
{
  int i, *a, array_size, max_value;
  char s[MAX_STR_LEN+1];
  char *endptr, *p;

  atexit(report_timing);
  start_time = time(NULL);
  printf("How many random values to sort? ");
  fgets(s, MAX_STR_LEN, stdin);
  if ((p = strchr(s, '\n')) != NULL)
      *p = '\0';
  array_size = strtol(s, &endptr, CONVERSION_BASE);
  check_endptr(endptr);
#ifdef DEBUG
    debug("main", "array_size is %d\n", array_size);
#endif
  a = malloc(sizeof(int) * array_size);

  printf("Largest random value? ");
  fgets(s, MAX_STR_LEN, stdin);
  if ((p = strchr(s, '\n')) != NULL)
      *p = '\0';
  max_value = strtol(s, &endptr, CONVERSION_BASE);
  check_endptr(endptr);
#ifdef DEBUG
    debug("main", "max_value is %d\n", max_value);
#endif
  srand((unsigned)time(NULL));
  for (i = 0; i < array_size; i++) {
    a[i] = rand() % (max_value + 1);
  }
  print_array(a, array_size);
#ifdef DEBUG
    debug("main", "begin sorting ...\n");
#endif
  before = clock();
  qsort(a, array_size, sizeof(a[0]), compare);
  after = clock();
#ifdef DEBUG
    debug("main", "end sorting ...\n");
#endif
  print_array(a, array_size);
  return 0;
}

int compare(const void *a, const void *b)
{
  int na = *(int *)a;
  int nb = *(int *)b;

  if (na < nb) return -1;
  if (na == nb)
    return 0;
  else
    return 1;
}
```

```
void print_array(int a[], int array_size)
{
  int i;

  #ifdef DEBUG
    debug("print_array", "begin printing ...\n");
  #endif
  for (i = 0; i < array_size; i++) {
    if (i % NUMS_PER_LINE == 0)
      printf("\n");
    printf("%4d ", a[i]);
  }
  printf("\n");
  #ifdef DEBUG
    debug("print_array", "end printing ...\n");
  #endif
}

void debug(const char *fname, const char *format, ...)
{
  va_list args;

  printf("DEBUGGING %s: ", fname);
  va_start(args, format);
  vprintf(format, args);
  va_end(args);
}

void check_endptr(const char *endptr)
{
  if (*endptr != '\0') {
    debug("main", "input error: bad character is '%c'\n", *endptr);
    abort();
  }
}

void report_timing(void)
{
  clock_t elapsed;
  time_t t;

  elapsed = after - before;
  printf("Processor time = %6.2f ticks = %.2f seconds\n",
         (double)elapsed, (double)elapsed / CLOCKS_PER_SEC);
  t = time(NULL);
  printf("Elapsed time = %.2f seconds.\n", difftime(t, start_time));
  printf("Program ends: %s", ctime(&t));
}
```

Some sample output of this program is shown below.

```
How many random values to sort? 30
DEBUGGING main: array_size is 30
Largest random value? 100
DEBUGGING main: max_value is 100
DEBUGGING print_array: begin printing ...

  61    8   68    1   17   83   87   40   86   28
   7   41   15   99   20   67   66   43    9   35
  34   63   80   45   46   46   27   22   15   21
DEBUGGING print_array: end printing ...
DEBUGGING main: begin sorting ...
DEBUGGING main: end sorting ...
DEBUGGING print_array: begin printing ...
```

```
   1    7    8    9   15   15   17   20   21   22
  27   28   34   35   40   41   43   45   46   46
  61   63   66   67   68   80   83   86   87   99
DEBUGGING print_array: end printing ...
Processor time =    0.00 ticks = 0.00 seconds
Elapsed time = 2.00 seconds.
Program ends: Thu Feb 27 11:05:12 1997
```

26.3   Programming Exercises

1. Modify the max_int(int n, ...) function (main text, page 564) so that n doesn't represent the number of values in the variable argument list, but instead the value of the last argument. For example, the call max_int(-1, 3, 67, 2, 14, -1) uses −1 as the sentinel value to indicate the end of the variable argument list. What happens with a call such as max_int(-1, 2, 3, -1, 4, 3)?

2. Write a max_min(int* min, int* max, int n, ...) function that calculates the largest and smallest values in the variable argument list, storing them in the locations pointed to by min and max, respectively. n is the sentinel value. For the sake of practice, calculate max and min by traversing the list twice.

3. Change the sorting program so that it prints the random numbers as they are generated, and so that the program prints every pair of numbers that are compared.

4. Extend the sorting program so that after sorting the numbers, the program repeatedly prompts the user for a number and searches through the sorted array for that number. Use the bsearch function to do the searching. Calculate and report the time required to do the searching. Is this amount of time significant?

5. Modify the sorting program so that it prints the total number of comparisons necessary to sort the numbers.

6. Modify the sorting program to offer the user a choice of the times to be measured. The user might choose to measure printing times, the time spent sorting, and/or the time spent waiting for input.

7. Modify the sorting program so that after sorting the numbers, the program sorts them again, this time in reverse order. Have your program report the time it takes to sort the number in each case. Do you see a difference in qsort's performance?

8. Write a function read_double, which reads a string from stdin, converts the input string to a double using strtod, and returns that value. The function call should abort if the conversion produces an error (i.e., if a value is stored in errno), or if the entire string is not consumed in the conversion process.

9. Write a function named get_input, which prompts for and reads input. getinput, however, has a simplified control string (at least in comparison to, say, scanf), in which s stands for string, f stands for float, and i stands for int. The arguments following the control string are prompt-address pairs. For example,

```
getinput("sfi", "Name ? ", name,
         "Salary ? ", &salary, "Age ? ", &age);
```

10. There are many algorithms for generating pseudo-random numbers. One criterion for the quality of an algorithm is *uniformity*, or how evenly distributed the numbers are in a given range. Write a program that evaluates this criterion for your rand function. Generate, say, ten thousand random numbers, each between 0 and 99. Count how many numbers that fall into each of ten categories: 0 through 9, 10 through 19, 20 through 29, etc. Calculate the percentage each such figure represents of the total and print out these percentages. The closer these figures are to 10% apiece, the more uniform your scaled random numbers are. However, this depends heavily on the method used to

scale the numbers obtained from rand to the range 0 to 99. The standard way of scaling the numbers is to calculate (rand() % 100). A better way is suggested in Exercise 8 of the main text (page 585), by working on the high-order bits of the result yielded by rand rather than the low-order bits. Implement both scaling methods and compare the resulting distributions.

11. Many operating systems allow the environment to contain user-defined strings, not just the predefined ones such as the UNIX or DOS path string. Choose some program you've implemented earlier and change the way in which the user communicates with the program. Instead of specifying a string on the command line, have the user store that information in an environment string. Your program should access it from there.

12. Write a program that allows the user to interactively display the contents of the current directory. Use the system function to create a file containing the list of files in the current directory. The necessary command is either ls (under UNIX) or dir (under DOS). Both can be instructed to redirect their output to the file of our choice. Then open that file and display the list of files.

13. Write a program that prompts the user for a month and a year and prints a nicely formatted calendar for that month. *Hint:* use the mktime function to find out the day of the week of the first day of the month and year specified by the user. Then print the calendar for that month, in a manner similar to that suggested in Chapter 6, Exercise 8 (page 107) of the main text.

14. Write a function that takes three integer arguments—the day, the month, and the year—and returns a string ("Sunday", "Monday", etc.) indicating the day of the week of that date. Be careful not to return a pointer to a local string: you'll need to use malloc to allocate memory for the string and then return its address.

15. Write a countdown-to-the-millennium program that accesses the current date and calculates the number of days until January 1, 2001. If the current date is later than January 1, 2001 (who knows, you might be running this program a few years from now!), calculate the number of days *since* the beginning of the millennium.

16. Write a function that takes a number representing a choice of format and returns a string containing the current date, in one of four formats, exemplified below.

```
Letter: "March 3, 1997"
Notepad: "Mon, Mar 3, '97"
Memo: "3/3/97"
Old-fashioned: "the third day of March, in the year
        nineteen hundred and ninety-seven"
```

You may restrict the years to the range 1900 to 2099.